本著作为湖南省普通高等学校教学改革研究项目"基于中华文化传承的大学英语期望教育研究"（HNJG–2021–0339）成果

U0107613

雅思口语
主题模块解析及运用

丁蕙　　廖永清　　冯芬玲 ⊙ 编著

Analysis and Application of
Thematic Modules in IELTS Speaking

中南大学出版社
www.csupress.com.cn
·长沙·

图书在版编目（CIP）数据

雅思口语主题模块解析及运用／丁蕙，廖永清，
冯芬玲编著. —长沙：中南大学出版社，2024.4
ISBN 978-7-5487-5779-5

Ⅰ. ①雅… Ⅱ. ①丁… ②廖… ③冯… Ⅲ. ①
IELTS－口语－自学参考资料 Ⅳ. ①H319.9

中国国家版本馆 CIP 数据核字（2024）第 072486 号

雅思口语主题模块解析及运用
YASI KOUYU ZHUTI MOKUAI JIEXI JI YUNYONG

丁　蕙　廖永清　冯芬玲　编著

□出 版 人	林绵优
□责任编辑	谢金伶
□责任印制	唐　曦
□出版发行	中南大学出版社
	社址：长沙市麓山南路　　　　邮编：410083
	发行科电话：0731-88876770　　传真：0731-88710482
□印　　装	广东虎彩云印刷有限公司

□开　　本	787 mm×1092 mm 1/16	□印张 16	□字数 504 千字
□版　　次	2024 年 4 月第 1 版	□印次 2024 年 4 月第 1 次印刷	
□书　　号	ISBN 978-7-5487-5779-5		
□定　　价	49.00 元		

编委会

编　著　丁　蕙　廖永清　冯芬玲

参编人员　李静茹　谭　玥　李卓雅

夏一洋　陈　洽　陈珂米

戴怡宁　赵　琪　石　灵

前言
Foreword

大多数考生在雅思口语考试中最大的困惑莫过于不知道该说什么，回答问题内容空洞，言之无物，或者虽有想法，但不知如何表达，口语表述用词简单、语法单一、逻辑混乱、中式英语倾向严重。究其原因是考生在语言层面缺乏丰富的词汇与句式、必要的时态与语态变化，在逻辑层面缺乏条理性与框架性、严密论证与谋篇布局的能力，这又严重影响了口语表达的流利性、准确性及内容的充实性。

针对以上问题，本书以"主题"为线索，将语言模块与框架模块融为一体，将模块输入与模块输出融为一体，力图突破考生在口语表达上的语言与逻辑障碍，实现口语输出内容充实、用词地道、逻辑清晰。框架模块提供答题的思路与逻辑，针对雅思口语 Part 1、Part 2 和 Part 3 的答题要求，提出 SE、PDF 和 ORDER 框架。语言模块提供语言素材，将主题词、主题语块与句型、语法、主题情境密切结合。语言模块与框架模块通过真题实例，密切融合并贯穿全书。

本书第一章为雅思口语考试简介，第二到第四章分别为雅思口语 Part 1、Part 2 及 Part 3 的模块解析及运用。模块解析以主题为线索，通过实例论证，深入解析并密切融合语言模块与框架模块。模块运用则基于模块解析，提供雅思口语真题的答案范例。模块解析与运用让学生在输入大量语言素材的同时，掌握答题思路与框架，并开展大量真题练习，实现输入与输出的互相促进，实现语言与信息的密切结合，解决学生说什么和怎么说的问题。

本书具有以下几个特色：

1. 系统全面的主题网络

本书不仅密切融合语言模块与框架模块，也注重主题之间的关联、整合与拆分，形成兼具全面性、丰富性与完整性的系统化主题网络，帮助考生实现不同主题、不同题型之间的融会贯通。

2. 贯穿始终的主题线索

全书分主题进行编排，从每个章节的模块解析与运用，到真题整合及附录中的主题谚语，均以主题为线索，把输入与输出聚焦于特定的主题，不仅有助于考生把语言输入及时运用于相应主题的语言输出，从而起到巩固强化、活学活用的效果，也有助于考生系统性、针对性地提升自己的语言储备与素材积累，提升口语输出的语言复杂性及丰富性。

3. 源于生活的主题素材

雅思口语 Part 2 的题目要求讲述考生的个人生活或过往经历。我们针对 Part 2 的真题，采访了 80 多位在校大学生，将收集到的事例按主题进行编排、改写与调整。主题素材符合考生的年龄特点与生活背景，具有较大的推广性与实用性。

4. 授之以渔的主题探索

与大部分仅提供参考答案的雅思口语教材不同，本教材提出主题模块答题法，先教授方法再进行真题演练。从 Part 1 到 Part 3，题型各不相同，难度逐步增加，但都以主题模块为依据，以主题为线索，结合框架模块与语言模块，循序渐进，开展主题探索。

本书中涉及的事例大部分来源于大学生的真实生活，在此，对提供素材的学生表示衷心感谢！他们是中南大学应用物理 T2101 班、材料科学与工程 T2101 班、冶金科学与工程 T2101 班的同学们。中南大学外国语学院研究生张正媛、胡雪娟、王蓉丽、陈雨凡在资料收集与整理、书稿修订与校对方面做了大量细致的工作，在此一并表示感谢。

鉴于我们的专业水平及编写时间有限，本书难免出现纰漏与错误，不足之处，敬请读者朋友批评指正，以便我们改进工作，进一步提高图书质量。

著者

2024 年 1 月 15 日

目录 *Contents*

附　录　　　　　　　　　　　　　　　　　　　　　　　　　　　　　　　　189

第一章 雅思口语考试简介

第一节 雅思口语考试流程

一、Part 1：简短交流（4~5 分钟）

考官向考生进行自我介绍，询问考生的姓名、职业（或专业）等基本信息并就考生熟悉的话题进行询问，内容涉及日常性的观点和信息、常见的生活经历或情形等。此部分如同雅思口语考试的热身对话，问题比较简单，回答不需要太长但也不能太短，通常每个问题回答 1~3 句话。

此部分旨在考查考生对日常性的观点和信息、常见的生活经历或情形进行交流的能力。

二、Part 2：话题陈述（3~4 分钟）

考生针对某个话题进行 2 分钟陈述。话题及话题陈述的要点均显示在一张答题任务卡上，考官给考生答题任务卡及纸笔，考生有 1 分钟的准备时间，并允许做笔记。1 分钟之后，考生应就此话题进行 2 分钟的陈述，若超过时间，考官会打断考生，并就考生的陈述提 1~2 个问题。

此部分旨在考查考生在没有任何其他提示的情况下，就一个特定的话题进行较长时间陈述的能力，考查考生是否能恰当地运用语言，是否能连贯地组织自己的观点。

三、Part 3：话题讨论（4~5 分钟）

考官针对考生 Part 2 的陈述，提出 4~5 个讨论题，题目通常从易到难，不仅有现象类的题目，更有通过现象探析本质的抽象类题目。

此部分旨在考查考生表达和论证观点的能力、探讨和深入思考问题的能力。

第二节　雅思口语评分标准

雅思口语考试分为 0 分到 9 分共 10 个等级,并从四个方面进行评分。

一、流利度及连贯性

流利度是指语速和语言连续性。连贯性是指句子之间以及句子内部的逻辑顺序,比如:讨论、叙述和论证的阶段层次递进以及连接手段(包含连词、代词和过渡词)的使用。

二、词汇资源

考查学生使用词汇的广度和准确性,以及使用其他词汇解释他们所不知道的词汇的能力。

三、语法结构

考查考生语法结构的多样性和准确性,包括句子的长度和复杂度,使用从句的能力以及句子结构的多样性,尤其是在一定的语言量中语法错误的数量以及语法错误对沟通理解的影响程度。

四、语音语调

考查考生语音语调的准确性与纯正性,比如连读、爆破、语气与语调等。

具体评分标准如表 1-1。

表 1-1　雅思口语评分表

得分	流利度与连贯性	词汇资源	语法结构	语音语调
9	说话时极少有重复或自我更正,偶尔的停顿也是由于在思考内容,而非搜寻合适的词汇和语法。发言连贯,上下文流畅,联系自然而充分;全面而得体地围绕话题展开内容	词汇使用丰富,运用灵活自如,表达意思准确。准确熟练地运用习语及俗语	全程自然得体地运用多样化的语法结构。虽然偶尔会犯一些英语为母语者也会犯的口误	语音标准纯正。准确运用各种语音特征,能表达微妙的差异。理解起来非常轻松
8	说话时很少有重复或自我更正,偶尔的停顿也多是对内容而不是词汇的思考。连贯得体地围绕话题进行交流	能自然灵活地使用多样化的词汇准确表达思想,允许偶尔用词不准确现象。能按要求有效准确地转述语言	灵活使用多种结构,大部分语句无误,极偶尔情况下出现错误或个别简单错误	表达过程中始终准确运用丰富多样的发音特点,能表达微妙的差异。表达易于听者理解,母语口音对听者的影响较小

续表1-1

得分	流利度与连贯性	词汇资源	语法结构	语音语调
7	能充分展开且不会有刻意思考的痕迹，没有语言上的不连贯，能较灵活地使用连接词或信号词。偶尔出现因语言困难导致的重复或自我更正	能灵活使用丰富的词汇讨论多种话题，能使用一些常见的词汇及习语。对语体及词汇搭配有所认识，但偶尔词语选择不够恰当。能有效进行转述	较灵活地使用多种复杂的语法结构，虽然反复出现一些语法错误，但整体来看，语句错误较少	表现出6分水平中的所有积极表现，也表现出8分水平中的部分积极表现
6	表现出充分交流的意愿，但有时由于偶尔重复，自我纠正或犹豫而缺乏连贯性。能使用一系列连接词及语篇标记，但无法保持一贯恰当	有足以详尽讨论各种话题的词汇量，虽然有时使用不当但意义表达清晰。基本上能成功进行转述	能使用简单或复杂的句型，但灵活性有限。使用复杂结构时经常出现错误，但极少造成理解困难	使用有限的发音特点，但掌握程度不一。发音常有错误，导致理解困难
5	通常能保持语流，但需通过重复、自我纠正或降低语速来维持表达。过度使用某些连接词及语篇标记。能用简单的语言进行流利的表达，但在进行更为复杂的交流时则表达不畅	能讨论熟悉和不熟悉的话题，但词汇使用的灵活性有限。尝试进行转述，有时成功，有时失败	能使用基本句型，且具有合理的准确性。使用有限的复杂句结构，但通常会出错且造成部分理解困难	表现出4分水平中所有的积极表现，也表现出6分水平中部分积极表现
4	回答问题有明显的停顿，且语速有时缓慢，出现频繁重复及自我纠正。能连接简单的句子，但重复使用简单的连接词，有时缺乏连贯性	能谈论熟悉的话题，但对不熟悉的话题仅能表达基本意思，且经常用词不当。很少尝试转述	能使用基本句型并正确使用一些简单句式，但极少使用从句。常出现错误并造成误解	使用有限的发音特点，尝试多种发音特点，但频繁出现偏差。经常出现发音错误，造成理解困难
3	表达过程中有长时间停顿。连接简单句的能力有限。仅能简单作答，且无法表达基本意思	能使用简单词汇表达个人信息。讨论不熟悉的话题时词汇匮乏	尝试使用基本句型，但准确度有限，或依赖先背诵的几句话。除预先背诵的内容外，错误很多	表现出2分水平中的部分表现，以及4分水平中的部分积极表现
2	出现长时间停顿，几乎无法进行交流	仅能说出零散的单词或预先背诵的几句话	不能使用基本句型	表达通常无法理解
1	无法交流，语言无法评估			
0	缺席考试			

第二章　Part 1 模块解析及运用

第一节　Part 1 框架模块 SE

Part 1 是雅思口语考试三个部分中最容易的一部分。考试在考官与考生的互相介绍与问候中正式开始，双方就一些简要的问题进行一问一答的交流，其对话方式类似于拉家常，考生在此阶段应尽量放松心情，缓解紧张情绪，越把考试看成跟朋友的谈天说地，语言表达会越流畅自然，考试成绩也会越理想。

考场上的从容淡定离不开考前的充分准备，雅思考试题库庞大，现场问题无法预测，如何在没有临场准备的情况下，能够对答如流地回答每一个问题呢？以框架模块来回答每一个问题不失为一个有效的方式，它能让我们拿到题目之后，知道怎么说、说什么。

Part 1 的回答不需要太长，可以按照 SE 模式展开，其中 S 代表"statement"，E 代表"explain"。

S：观点意见，可以是一个短语，也可以是一个短句或长句。

E：解释拓展，举例子和说明原因是常见的两种方式。举例的方式很多，如在时间、地点、人物、事件、感受等多个要素中任选一两个要素开展举例论证。

比如以下问题：

How do you feel about advertisements？

Statement：Well, I think advertisement is quite a nuisance, particularly the cold calls.

Explain：It really gets on my nerves when I pick up the phone but only to find it is advertisement from someone I don't know（例子：事件）. The cold call not only ***brings me*** interruption but also anxiety from the awareness that my personal information is somehow leaked（原因）.

一、观点意见（statement）

Part 1 中大部分问题是一般疑问句，需要用"yes"或"no"来明确表述观点态度，但在观点句中，尽量对观点进行拓展，而不只是简单的"yes"或"no"。

比如：

① ***Do you like music***？

Yes, definitely! I am a big fan of music.

② *Do you collect things*？

Yes, I have collected stamps for ages.

③ *Do you often feel bored*？

No, not at all. I hardly ever feel bored.

④ *Do you like swimming in the sea or in the pool*？

I have never swum in the sea but I assume it would be much more challenging to swim in the sea than in the pool.

Part 1 的观点句可以多种方式展开，以下列出了几种常见方法，但自由流畅的口语交流可以随心所欲，针对主题自由发挥，不应固化为有限的几种回答模式。以下方法仅是抛砖引玉，启发思路。

1. 概括法

先概括整体情况再针对具体问题给出答案。这样做的目的一方面是通过由总到分的结构使条理清晰，另一方面为后面的回答赢得一定的思考时间。

① *Why do people collect things*？

Well, people collect stuffs for multiple purposes.

② *What is your daily routine*？

My daily routine may seem to be rather boring and monotonous to many people.

2. 定位法

开头先把自己定位为某一类跟主题相关的人，展示主题词汇并进入主题。

① *Where do you usually meet your friends*？

As a sports enthusiast, I usually meet my friends in the gym or on the playground, where we work out together.

② *Do you enjoy cooking*？

Yes, I am a No. 1 chef in my family. I absolutely enjoy cooking.

③ *What outdoor activities do you most like to do*？

Well, I am a nature enthusiast and I love outdoor activities, particularly hiking on the mountain.

运用于定位的主题词汇有如下几种。

（1）人物定位：people、person、sporty person、sport enthusiast、nature enthusiast、sun worshipper、shopaholic、workaholic、travel butt、computer butt、nerd、foodie、a big fan of。

（2）地点定位：food destination、cosmopolitan city、landmark icon、tourist/shopping mecca、mecca for the foodies/tourists/shopaholics。

3. 简约法

直截了当，开门见山，简短明确。

① *How often do you drink water*？

All the time！

② *Do you often go to the picnics*？

Less than I'd like to.

4. 引言法

用谚语或引语表达观点，是比较有说服力又能展示语言能力的答题方法。此方法可以用于雅思口语考试的任何部分，既可用于阐述观点也可用于论证观点。

What is the importance of learning history？

As we say, history is the mirror through which we reflect and draw lessons.

二、解释拓展（explain）

阐述观点后，接下来可以用一两句话进行解释，拓展答案。此部分应围绕观点句，对观点展开论证。考生说出自己的观点并不困难，难的是提出观点之后，该如何去论证。对观点的论证可以从时间、地点、人物、事件、感受、原因、结果、内容等多方面展开。

① *Is eating snacks healthy*？

Statement：No, not at all.

Explain：Snacks usually consist of many additives as well as much fat and sweet（原因），therefore, they are high in calories but low in nutrition（结果）. Over eating of snacks tends to leave you overweight with various health problems（结果）.

② *Do you often listen to music*？

Statement：Yes, I listen to music all the time.

Explain：My first thing in the morning（时间）is to turn on the Bluetooth speaker and play my favorite song in the playlist to welcome my brand new day（事件），which makes me fresh and energetic（感受）. I also enjoy the catchy melodies from my earphones on my way to and from school（地点）. I'm really into all kinds of music, including pop, rock and roll, country music, etc（内容）. Music gives me tremendous pleasure as well as great relaxation（感受）.

需要指出的是，回答 Part 1 的问题不宜过长，从时间、地点、人物、事件、感受、内容等诸多方面中，任意选一到两个方面阐述即可。

第二节　Part 1 语言模块

雅思口语中常用到的语言模块包括喜好模块、频率模块、感受模块、记忆模块、现在完成时模块、让步模块及两分模块。其中，前三个模块在 Part 1 中运用最为频繁，分别用于回答有关喜好、频率及感受方面的问题。

（1）喜好类的问题，比如：

Do you like …

Do you prefer …

What is your favorite …

（2）频率类的问题，比如：

Do you often …

How often do you …

（3）感受类的问题，比如：

Do you think … is useful/important/beneficial?

How do you feel …

以上三类问题是 Part 1 中的常见话题，这三类问题本质上密切相关，喜欢的事情往往做得比较频繁，给人积极感受，反之亦然。因此，考生可以准备一些表达喜欢、频率与感受的语言模块，并把这三个模块整合起来，灵活运用于以上三类问题的回答中。

除了以上三个模块，记忆模块、让步模块及两分模块都在雅思口语考试中广泛应用。我们将在语言模块学习的基础上，进行大量相关练习，把语言模块运用于 Part 1 的答题中。

一、喜好模块

关于喜好的问题，在 statement 中可以用一句话表达观点，说明自己喜欢或者不喜欢什么。关于喜好的问题在考试中比重非常大。Part 1 的题目中，会被多次问到对不同主题的喜好，如果考生每次都用 like、be interested in 等常见词汇答题，会出现语言重复、词汇简单的问题。为此，背诵并灵活运用表达喜好的主题模块，对 Part 1 的答题会非常有帮助。

1. 表达喜欢

I'm very interested in literature.

I am really into hiking.

I am a big fan of movies/music/reading.

I'm a big photographer/shopper/reader/movie watcher/tea drinker …

I really enjoy/like watching TV, travelling …

I prefer cooking at home.

2. 表达不喜欢

I can't stand jogging.

I hate jogging.

I am not really interested in literature.

I am not really into jogging.

I am not a big fan of music.

以上模块用不同的语言表达不同程度的喜好，大部分表达可通用，但有些表达方式的使用略有差异，比如，be interested in something 常用于表达喜欢某学科与教育方向的内容，而 be into something、be a fan of something 则多用于表达某项娱乐活动的爱好。

在回答喜好类题目时，statement 部分，先回答 yes 或 no，随后用喜好模块写一句完整的观点句；explain 部分，从时间、地点、人物、内容、事件、感受、原因等多个角度中，选择一两个方面说明喜好的原因或者程度。

真题范例

① **Do you like sports?**

Statement：Yes, definitely. **I'm a huge fan of** sports, which has been an indispensable part of my daily routine over the years.

Explain：There is a long list of the sports that I like, from cardio exercise to strength training, jogging, swimming, rope skipping, boxing, to name just a few（内容）. Doing sports keeps me fit and helps me stay in shape（感受）.

本例的 statement 部分用一个长句表达观点，explain 部分则说明了哪些 sports，以及 doing sports 的感受。

② **Is there any food you dislike?**

Statement：Well, **I hate fish.** I've stayed away from fish for many years.

Explain：I had some traumatic experience of eating fish. I was seriously choked by a fish bone when I was a child. I ended up taking that damn fish bone out in the hospital（原因）. I've never liked fish ever since.

③ **Do you like cooking?**

Statement：Definitely yes. **I'm a cooking enthusiast.**

Explain：I learned cooking simply by following those how-to videos or watching my mom cooking（如何学）. My friends who have tasted what I cooked often shower me with compliments（评价）, but I can't stand washing up after the meal, which makes my hands greasy（感受）.

本例中的 explain 部分通过阐述如何学会做菜（how）以及别人对"我"做的饭菜的评价（what）来进行拓展，同时用了"不喜欢"模块中的一个句式"I can't stand ..."，既符合题意也再次展示了语言技能。

④ **Do you prefer listening to recorded music or going to concerts?**

Statement：Well, **my preference goes to** recorded music, which I can listen anytime anywhere.

Explain：I listen to music on my way to and from school（地点）, on my bed（地点）before I go to sleep（时间）or in the living room（时间）when I hang out with my family（人物、事件）.

在本例中，statement 给出了观点并用一个从句 which I can listen anytime anywhere 说明原因。explain 部分，则对随时随地听音乐进行举例，与主题句中的 anytime anywhere 相呼应。

⑤ **Is there anything you dislike about your current home?**

Statement：Yes, **I really can't stand** climbing the stairs.

Explain：The apartment I currently live in is not equipped with a lift, and what makes things worse is that I live on the top floor, that is, the sixth floor. Climbing the stairs really makes me go nuts, especially after a hectic working day.

在本例中，explain 部分进行了背景介绍，即原因。

二、频率模块

频率问题也是 Part 1 的常见题目，在回答此类题目时，statement 部分宜直截了当，不需对整体进行概括，也不必刻意使用长句、复杂句。针对"How often"的问题，考生应开门见山用一个频率副词作答，随后也可用一个句子强调频率的高低。在 explain 部分，可从时间、地点、原因、内容、背景等方面任选一两个方面进行拓展延伸。常见的表达频率的词组：always/all the time; whenever I have time; on a regular/daily/weekly/monthly/yearly basis; once/twice/three times/several times a day/week/month; not that much（或 not do sth. very much）; every now and then; less than I'd like; once in a while; once in a blue moon; never/hardly ever 等。例句：

I read books whenever I have time.

I call my family on a weekly basis.

I go to cinema once or twice a year.

I follow the news all the time.

I watch TV after dinner quite often.

I hardly ever drink tea.

I don't listen to music that much.

I go hiking less than I'd like.

I eat out every now and then.

I go hiking once in a while.

I hardly ever go swimming at the weekend.

真题范例

① *How often do you use Wechat*?

Statement：Well, I am on Wechat *all the time*.

Explain：I can't go a day without Wechat. I actually check it *every now and then*（频率），texting, making voice or video calls, making digital payments, browsing and posting Wechat moments etc（内容）. It makes my life more convenient and colourful（感受）.

② *How often do you drink water*?

Statement：*All the time.*

Explain：When I wake up in the morning（时间）I drink a glass of water because it keeps me hydrated（原因）. During the day（时间）, especially at work（地点）, I drink a lot of water as well. I'm not a big fan of fizzy drinks like Coke or Pepsi, so sometimes even if I go to a restaurant I will just drink water（地点）.

此例中，对 all the time 的解释，通过时间、地点论证举例，说明频繁做某事。从时间、地点的角度进行论证解释是对喜好及频率题论证的常见方式。

③ *How often do you use a computer*?

Statement：*All the time*! I can't go a day without using computer, which is essential in my professional and personal life.

Explain：I do all my work and study on the computer（内容）. I have entertainment and socialization on the computer, reading the news, doing the shopping, sending emails, watching movies, etc（内容）.

④ *How often do you take a taxi*？

Statement：*Not that much*. Maybe just *once or twice a month.*

Explain：I *usually* take subways, buses or ride bikes to get around, as they are more economical and environmental-friendly（原因）. I will take a taxi though if I am in a hurry or if there are too many transfers by public transportation（原因）.

⑤ *How often do you spend time with teenagers*？

Statement：Well, *less than I'd like.*

Explain：People around me are basically peers of my age or elders like teachers or parents（背景）. I do have two teenager cousins but it's a shame that I can't meet them frequently since we live quite far apart. I can only meet them during the Spring Festival when I visit my hometown（原因）.

⑥ *How often do you travel by boat*？

Statement：Well, traveling by boat is *once in a blue moon* experience for me.

Explain：The last time I traveled by boat was 7 years ago when I had the cruise travel along the Three Gorges with my family, and that was the only time I traveled by boat（事件）.

⑦ *How often do you upgrade your computer*？

Statement：Well, *less than I need to*, I guess.

Explain：I have very poor proficiency in computers. I should say I am just a little bit better than those who are computer illiterate. I simply don't know how to upgrade my computer（原因）. Whenever anything goes wrong with my computer or when it runs really slowly, I will just bring it to the technician who will fix everything for me（事件）.

⑧ *How often do you buy new clothes*？

Statement：*Less than I'd like*.

Explain：*I'm really into* fashion and therefore I am a shopaholic in clothes. However, you know those fancy clothes usually cost an arm and a leg（原因）. So I try to refrain myself in purchasing too many clothes. I just buy a few clothes at the end-of-season sales during the summer and the winter（时间）.

⑨ *How often did you eat foreign food when you were young*？

Statement：*Not that much*, actually.

Explain：When I was a kid, there were not so many restaurants serving foreign food（原因）. My first experience of tasting the foreign cuisine can be traced back 10 years ago when I ate hamburgers and French fries in KFC with my friends（时间、地点、人物）.

⑩ *Do you often listen to music*？

Statement：Yes, I listen to music *all the time*.

Explain：My first thing in the morning（时间）is to turn on the Bluetooth speaker and play my favorite song on the playlist to welcome my brand new day, which makes me fresh and energetic（感受）. I also enjoy the catchy melodies from my earphones on my way to and from school（地点）. I'm really into all kinds of music, including pop, rock and roll, country music, etc（内容）.

⑪ **Are you late very often**?

Statement：No, **hardly ever**. I am very reliable and punctual.

Explain：If I have an appointment with others, I will definitely get well-prepared at least one hour ahead of time and then hit the road on time（事件）. I just can't stand making people wait for me. Being late is a sign of disrespect（原因）.

三、感受模块

在喜好与频率的话题中经常需要提及感受，用以说明原因"为什么喜欢或不喜欢""为什么常做或不常做某事"。对感受的描述在雅思口语考试的三个部分中均频频出现，因此有必要学习一些表达感受的词汇，以提高表达的多样性及准确性。

喜怒哀乐都是人的情感，表达情感的词汇很多，词性也很多，名称、动词、形容词都可用于表达情感。情感词汇可以与几个简单动词(make、keep、give、help)组合成感受模块。

Swimming makes me healthy（形容词）.

Swimming keeps me healthy/in shape（形容词/介词）.

Swimming gives me pleasure（名词）.

Swimming helps me stay in shape（动词）.

基于以上句型，可以衍生出很多情感的表达方式。在前面的喜好及频率模块的例子中，我们也用到了很多类似的句子。

Doing sports keeps me fit and helps me stay in shape.

Listening to music in the morning makes me fresh and energetic.

Music gives me tremendous pleasure as well as great relaxation.

I can't stand washing up after the meal, which makes my hands greasy.

真题范例

① **What things are boring to you**?

Statement：Actually quite a lot of things are pains in my neck.

Explain：To name just a few, getting stuck in traffic during rush hour, waiting in a long line, listening to a tediously long speech given by a politician, and the list can go on and on. **Those things give me a headache and make me frustrated.**

② **Would you like to go on a long boat trip**?

Statement：Yes, I've been looking forward to a long boat trip since I had my first cruise along the Three Gorges 7 years ago.

Explain：Boat trip is appealing to me because **it gives me** opportunities to appreciate the stunning views of the nature：the blue sky, the white cloud and the roaring birds. Being emerged in nature **helps me** purify my mind and stay relaxed. A long boat trip is certainly a very good relaxation to let my hair down.

③ *Do you think breakfast is important*?

Statement：Yes, definitely. It *gives me* energy for the start of the day.

Explain：I actually feel a bit sleepy and sluggish if I don't eat breakfast. I eat very nutritious breakfast that consists of egg, milk, bread, fruit and veggie, so that I get the balanced nutrients of protein, carbohydrate and fat.

④ *Do you like meeting new people*?

Statement：Yes, definitely. *I am really into* meeting new people.

Explain：I am sociable and extroverted in nature. I've made tons of new friends over the years at various parties or social clubs. Meeting new people *helps me* expand my social sphere and widen my horizon.

⑤ *Did you have a favorite teacher at school*?

Statement：Yes. *I am a huge fan of* my English teacher back in middle school.

Explain：She is very hilarious. She has a knack for cracking up students and her classes were very engaging, which *made us* very attentive and interested. She brought us tons of laughter and cultivated our interest in English.

⑥ *Is it necessary to take a nap every day*?

Statement：Yes, I think taking a nap in the afternoon really makes differences.

Explain：Afternoon napping *helps us* recharge our batteries after half-day exhausting work. It *makes us* refreshed and energetic. Napping also *gives us* more sleep, which is especially important for people like me who don't sleep well at night.

⑦ *What outdoor activities do you most like to do*?

Statement：Well, *I am a nature enthusiast* and *I love* basically all the outdoor activities, particularly hiking on the mountain.

Explain：Right behind our campus is Yuelu Mountain where my friends and I climb several times a month. It's a great exercise to *help me* stay in shape and recharge my battery.

四、记忆模块

Part 1 的很多题目涉及考生对自己过往经历的回顾，Part 2 的大部分题目要求描述考生过往的经历。考生在描述过去事件时，往往会从头到尾用一般过去时以流水账的方式讲自己的故事，不能有效体现语法和词汇的多样性，语言不够精炼。运用记忆模块有助于克服这类问题。最常用的记忆模块素材是 remember doing sth. 或者 remember (that)，used to do something, would do sth.，以及 when … when … 双重条件句。这几种表达方式可以串联起来运用，把动名词、宾语从句、不定式、过去将来时及双重条件句运用于对过去事情的描述，既体现了语法的多样性，也使语言表达更为精炼充实。

1. I remember doing sth.

意思是"我记得我做了某事"。动作主语即 remember 的主语。

I remember hanging out in the mall with my friends.

I remember travelling with my family.

I remember hanging out in the mall with my friends.

I remember dancing in the square.

I remember doing laundry by the river.

I remember planting trees on the mountain with my parents.

2. I remember (that) …

意思是"我记得某某……"。可用于描述动作也可以描述状态。后面的从句中有自己的主语。

I remember my father taught me to plant trees.

I remember my aunt sent me a pair of sneakers as my birthday gift.

I remember my teacher cheered me up when I failed in the examination.

I remember I invited my friends for dinner when I won a prize in a contest.

I remember that my English teacher was very hilarious.

3. I used to do sth.

表示过去常做某事，但现在不再做某事。此表达方式也可以与表示频率的词连用。

I used to work in the gardens with my father.

I used to do morning exercise with my buddies.

I used to tell bedtime stories to my nephew.

I used to work really hard for the entrance examination.

I used to get plenty of compliments for my good work.

I used to work in the gardens all day long on weekends.

I used to visit my grandparents once or twice a year.

I used to argue with my parents all the time.

I used to check my phone every hour.

4. I would do sth.

表示过去总是做某事，过去习惯于做某事。它往往可以跟过去时间的 every 连用，如 every day、every month、every hour 等。

Every weekday I would do morning exercise.

Every night my sister would help me with my study.

Every special day my family and I would eat out.

Every Spring Festival we would decorate our houses.

Every summer I would go swimming in the river.

Every winter I would spend most of the time indoors.

Every day after school my friends and I would do assignment together.

used to do sth. 表示的是在过去某段时间经常做的事情，因此通常有一个明确的过去时间。但是当有 every 等频率词出现的时候，used to do sth. 与 would do sth. 可以交替使用。

I would skip rope every day after school.

或者：I used to skip rope every day after school.

I would check my phone every hour.

或者：I used to check my phone every hour.

5. when ... when ...

用 when ... when ... 引入双重条件句，即在一个句子中运用两个条件句。在描述过去的句子中，我们经常会用一个主句加一个表达过去的时间状语从句，而主句中有时还包含一个描述过去的短语，比如：

During my childhood when I visited my hometown, I would hike up the mountain with my childhood friends.

During my childhood when I hiked up the mountain, I would collect the mushrooms along the way.

During my childhood when I collected some mushrooms on the mountain, I would cook them over the open fire.

如果我们把 During my childhood 替换为 When I was in primary school 或者 When I was a kid 或者 When I was growing up，就有了以下双重条件句：

When I was in primary school, when I visited my hometown, I would hike up the mountain with my childhood friends.

When I was a kid, when I hiked up the mountain, I would collect the mushrooms along the way.

When I was growing up, when I collected some mushrooms on the mountain, I would cook them over the open fire.

我们可以把以上记忆模块结合起来去描述过去的事情，体现语法和语言的多样性。比如：

I used to ride my bike in the park with my friends. I remember that it was green and had a small basket on the front. My dad would put it in the back of our car and drive it into the countryside.

I used to spend quality time with my parents on holiday. I remember cooking delicious dishes and chitchatting with them. We would savor big meals while binge watching wonderful TV shows.

I used to have a doll. I remember it could blink and giggle. I would carry it with me wherever I go.

I used to have a dog named Huanhuan. I remember it was cute, smart and cuddly. I would walk it twice a day both in the mornings and in the evenings.

I used to enjoy every day at university. I remember having a hectic day, registering, settling down in my dormitory, meeting new friends and exploring the campus on my first day at university. I would snap a picture whenever I came to a crossing, just in case I would forget my way back.

When I was a child, every day when school was over, I would climb the mountain with my classmates. I remember collecting the mushrooms and cooking them over the open fire, but today you can see many kids tend to become couch potatoes, spending huge amount of time staring onto the screen. The sedentary lifestyle is not at all healthy compared with life decades ago.

真题范例

① *Did you get bored much when you were younger?*

Statement: Hardly ever.

Explain: I used to have a lot on my plate when I was in middle school. I remember getting up early, attending classes, doing assignments, preparing for quizzes on weekdays. During the weekends my whole family would have various family events, hiking, picnicking, watching movies, etc. Boredom simply never bothered me, even smart phones were not prevalent at that time.

② *Were there any foods you disliked when you were younger?*

Statement: Oh, yes.

Explain: I used to hate fish because once I was seriously choked by a fish bone in my childhood. I remember trying out every method to get it down, swallowing water, vinegar, rice, but nothing helped. I ended up taking that damn fish bone out in the hospital. I took me quit a few years to walk out of the trauma and to start eating fish and loving it again.

③ *What did you like to do with your friends when you were growing up?*

Statement: Well, I was born and raised in the countryside and so I used to immerse myself in the nature and do a lot of outdoor activities with my childhood friends.

Explain: I remember that we went hiking and had picnics, that we collected wild berries and mushrooms on the mountains and caught fish and shrimps in the river. We simply wouldn't miss a chance to explore the nature.

④ *Did you like reading when you were younger?*

Statement: Yes, I used to be a bookworm.

Explain: I couldn't go a day without reading. I remember every day after school I would just stay in my room hour after hour reading whatever interested me, magazines, novels, biographies, etc. It's a shame that I am so tied up with my work currently that I don't read as much as I used to.

⑤ *What was your favorite sport when you were young?*

Statement: Well, when I was a child I used to be crazy about many sports, particularly rope skipping.

Explain: I remember every day after school I would skip rope either by myself or with my friends on the playground. Rope skipping used to give me tremendous pleasure as well as enjoyable socialization with my peers.

⑥ *Did you try new activities when you were younger?*

Statement：Well, I am rather curious and adventurous in nature. I used to try tons of new activities when I was little.

Explain：When I was in elementary school I would register in some clubs or training classes almost every summer. I remember learning painting, swimming, rock climbing, and even snorkeling, my life was thereby very colourful and fulfilled.

⑦ *What did you do during wintertime when you were a child*?

Statement：Well, when I was a child I used to stay indoors where it was warm and cozy.

Explain：I have always hated cold weather throughout my life, but interestingly, I love snow. I remember building snowmen and having snowball fighting with my buddies during my childhood.

⑧ *What was your favorite animals when you were a child*?

Statement：Well, my favorite animals were birds, fish and frogs.

Explain：Because those were animals that I used to catch when I was a kid. I remember that my friends and I caught squirrels in the winter and we caught fish throughout the year. I remember that we once dissected a frog we caught. That was our first biological lesson from nature. I really enjoyed this experiential way of learning.

记忆模块不但可回答关于过去的问题，也可用于讨论今昔对比的话题，或者通过今昔对比，讨论当下的情况，比如：

① *Do you feel life today is not as healthy as it used to be*?

Statement：Yes, absolutely.

Explain：When I was a child, every day when school was over, I would climb the mountain with my classmates. I remember collecting the mushrooms and cooking them over the open fire, but today you can see many kids tend to become couch potatoes, spending huge amount of time staring onto the screen. The sedentary lifestyle is not at all healthy compared with life decades ago.

② *Do you like outdoor activities*?

Statement：Yes, I am a nature enthusiast.

Explain：I am a big fan of outdoor activities like fishing, hiking, picnicking. Particularly I am really into hiking. When I was a child, every time I visited my hometown, I would hike up the mountain with my childhood friends. I remember collecting the mushrooms and cooking them over the open fire. So hiking has been my hobby over the years.

五、现在完成时模块

现在完成时在雅思口语考试中非常重要，比如在 Part 1、Part 3 中有部分题目以现在完成时提问，这时就需要用现在完成时来回答。有些不是以现在完成时提问的问题，有时也可以用现在完成时进行回答。这样做的好处：首先，体现语法的多样性。语法的多样性在雅思口语考试中占了 25% 的分值，因此要得高分的考生，尽量要用多种时态。其次，现在完成时能够在有限的时间内，表达更多的内容，考生只需要说出做过什么事情、有过什么经历，而不需说出具体的时间、地点等诸多细节，答题更加简明扼要。这点在 Part 1 答题中尤其重要，因为 Part 1 的每道题只有 30 秒左右的答题时间。

1. 常用的时间短语

在现在完成时的句子中，可以添加常用的时间短语，既可以把场景切换到过去的某个时间段，也可以增加句子的长度与复杂性。

用于现在完成时模块的时间短语主要有 since 时间短语和 for 时间短语。

（1）since（过去某个时间以来）：

since I was a child

since I was little

since I was at school/at university

since I came to this city

since last year/since 2019

（2）for（过去的一段时间）：

for a couple hours/days

for two weeks

for several years

for decades/ages

for as long as I can remember

（3）其他用于现在完成时模块的时间短语：

over the years

throughout my life

比如：

I've been to many different cities in my country over the years.

I've bought lots of different smartphones from different companies in my life.

I've given lots of expensive gifts to my girlfriend for the last three years.

I've seen lots of famous landmarks all over the country since I was at school.

I've taken the IELTS test twice before.

I've eaten at lots of up-scale restaurants in my life.

I've flown on a couple of long-distance flights since I was a kid.

I've been robbed before, unfortunately.

I've been a big fan of music since I was a child.

I've swum for as long as I can remember.

I've been really into photography for decades.

I've been a huge fan of music throughout my life.

2. 拓展思路

回答现在完成时问题，可以是肯定回答也可以是否定回答，但不管肯定或否定，都应该对答案进行拓展，如果是肯定回答，可从原因、地点、人物等方面进行拓展。比如：

Have you ever visited an art gallery？

Yes, I have. I've visited quite a few art galleries in my life. My father is a big fan of painting and when I lived with my parents, if we traveled to a new place, we would visit the local art galleries. I've visited the art galleries in Shanghai, Beijing, San Francisco and a few others in some other cities since I was a kid.

此例中把现在完成时模块与多个模块结合起来运用，用了喜好模块 My father is a big fan of painting，用了记忆模块的双重条件句 when I lived with my parents, if we traveled to a new place, we would visit the local art galleries。

如果是对现在完成时问题进行否定回答，则可以说我没做过某事，但我希望将来能做，如果那样，就太棒了，由此充实答案内容，并能借此机会运用虚拟语气。比如：

Have you ever been abroad?

No, I've never been abroad but I've been looking forward to travelling abroad. New Zealand has been on top of my travel list since I watched the movie "The Lord of the Rings" which was filmed in New Zealand. It would be amazing to visit those stunningly beautiful places in person.

除了肯定与否定的回答，我们也可以进行混合式回答，既包含肯定的回答，也包含否定的回答。比如：

Have you visited any foreign countries?

I have been to lots of different countries in Europe. I've been to Spain, France, Germany, Belgium and Serbia. I haven't been to Italy, but I would love to visit it one day.

真题范例

① ***Have you ever lost your way?***

Statement: Yes, I have, I've got lost for countless times in my life.

Explain: I have poor direction and what makes things worse is that I am not good at reading maps. Although I can use Baidu map on my phone, I've encountered quite a few situations over the years when I had to ask my way when the GPS on my phone gave some silly routes.

② ***Have you been to a new place recently?***

Statement: Yes, I have. I've been to quite a couple of interesting places lately.

Explain: I've dined with my friends in a newly opened restaurant on top of Yuelu Mountain close to my home and I've also taken a business trip to Hangzhou, which, strictly speaking, is not a new place to me, but I've explored the outskirts of the city a bit and seen some new parts of the city, including the village which is famous for Longjing Tea.

③ ***What kind of places have you visited in your life?***

Statement: Well, personally I'm a traveling enthusiast. I've been to many different places, ranging from the metropolitan cities like Shanghai and Hong Kong to some remote villages in mountainous areas.

Explain: All of theses are haunting memories for me since taking a trip really helps me get away from it all. But I haven't travelled abroad. I would like to take trips to foreign countries one day.

六、让步模块

让步模块是指含有让步从句的复合句，表达"虽然……但是……"。让步模块把两个互相对立、相反的主题，以让步的关系连接在一起。让步模块的运用有利于提高句式的多样性，也有利于把复杂的、矛盾的两个想法或事实用一句话表达出来，让语言尽可能精练、内容尽可能完整。

需要注意的是，although 和 but 不能同时出现在一个句子中，这跟中文的习惯不同。

Although travelling makes me refreshed, but it costs me a pretty penny. （×）

Although travelling makes me refreshed, it costs me a pretty penny. （√）

Travelling makes me refreshed, but it costs me a pretty penny. （√）

1. 包含"虽然"的句子

表达"虽然"的词有 though、although、even though。这三个词意义差不多，很多情况下可以通用，但就转折语气而言，though 最弱，even though 最强。

Although the restaurant looks small outside, it is actually very big inside.

Even though I was on a diet, I couldn't resist the temptation of the delicious dessert at the party.

Even though he is in his 80s, he spared no efforts to lend a hand to people in need.

He always tries to hold his ground, even though he is wrong.

I spend a lot of time looking at my phone, even though I know it makes my eyes tired.

Although this recipe looks long, it is actually very quick to prepare.

2. 包含"但是"的句子

表达"但是"的词有 but、however、that said。这三个词也仅有语气上的区别，however 语气最强且多用于书面语，that said 语气最弱且通常用于口语中。

The train is expensive and crowded, but it's the best way to get around in my city.

He is a wealthy business man, but he leads very frugal life.

I prefer reading ebooks on my tablet. That said, I do enjoy the feeling of turning the pages when I read a physical book.

I don't think colours have a very big influence on people. That said, my office is painted blue and white and it definitely helps me relax and concentrate on my work.

More often than not, I feel like staying at home and enjoying the tranquility when I'm on vacation. That said, I'm still interested in outdoor activities, which helps me breathe in some fresh air.

I love public gardens, because it's a bustling place. That said, sometimes I would prefer to spend time in a personal one, which protects my privacy and gives me peace.

真题范例

① *Do you prefer hot or cold weather*?

Statement：I prefer hot weather,

Explain：even though the scorching weather makes me sweat and keeps me tired and sluggish, I can do tons of fun things in hot weather：Wearing beautiful dresses, eating ice cream, swimming or camping.

② *What's your favorite animals*?

Statement：Well, basically I love all the animals,

Explain：whom I regard as our siblings in mother nature. That said, I am particularly take a liking to some small animals with smooth and silky fur, like cats, dogs, rabbits, and so on. I enjoy developing intimacy with those cute furry friends.

③ *Do you like to sit in the front or back when travelling by car*?

Statement：Personally I enjoy sitting in the front.

Statement：Because front seat has better views than back seats. That said, I don't often sit in the front. In my culture we are supposed to reserve the front seat to people older in age or higher in social status.

④ *Do you remember your first mobile phone*?

Statement：Yes. I remember very clearly that I got my first mobile phone on my 10th birthday.

Explain：It was a pink flip phone. Looking back it was indeed a very basic phone merely for texting and making calls. That said, I was on top of the world upon receiving it, as few of my friends owned a phone at that time.

七、两分模块

两分模块是指依情况而定(It depends …)，分两种不同的情况回答问题。两分模块一方面能让考生更全面、完整、真实地回答问题，另一方面能让答案结构清晰、条理清楚。观点句概括了从哪两个方面来讲，解释部分即从这两方面展示，结构非常清晰，用词也很精练。除此之外，两分模块也展示了语法、词汇的多样性。需要注意的是，两分模块用的条件句都是真实条件句，而不是虚拟条件句，条件句的时态用一般现在时或一般将来时。

两分模块的观点句有如下两种模式。

1. It depends on sb. /sth.

比如：It depends on the time/my schedule/the weather/the person 等。

It depends on the person. If it's someone very special to me, I will …, if it's someone not close to me, I will …

It depends on the website. If I read a news story on a website I've never heard of, I will…, but if it is posted on some reliable and authoritative link, I will …

It depends on the season. If it is in spring and autumn, I will …, if it is in summer and winter, I will …

It depends on my bank account. If I have money, I will …, but if I am strapped on cash, I will …

It depends on the age of the people. The young generation …, but for elders …

2. It depends on 疑问词+从句

比如：It depends on where I want to go/whom I send the gifts to/what style it is 等。

It depends on whom I travel with. If I am to travel with my family or friends, I will …, if I am to travel with strangers then I …

It depends on what I am up to. If I am to attend some special events …, I will …, if I am to spend a usual day …, I will …

It depends on how much it costs. If it is too expensive, I will …, if it is not that costly, I will …

真题范例

① *How often do you buy gifts for people*？

Statement：Well, it depends on the person.

Explain：If it's someone very special to me, like one of my parents or siblings, then I will buy gifts for them pretty often. I will bring them souvenirs when I get back from a long trip. I will send them gifts on special festivals or holidays, but if it's someone not very close or special to me, I may rarely send them gifts.

② *Do you think the Internet is a good place to get news*？

Statement：Well, it depends on the website.

Explain：If I read a news story on a website I've never heard of, I will doubt the truth of the story, but if it is posted on some reliable and authoritative link like "China Daily", I will just trust it. Actually I've kept track of the news from "China Daily" over the years.

③ *Do you like going to the park*？

Statement：It depends on the season.

Explain：If it is in spring and autumn, I will definitely enjoy visiting the parks as the weather is pleasant and the parks are stunningly beautiful. If it is in summer and winter, I will prefer staying at home as it is scorching in summer and freezing in winter in my city.

④ *Do you like shopping*？

Statement：It depends on my bank account.

Explain：If I have money, I will be a shopaholic, but if I am strapped on cash, I will have to refrain myself in shopping. Generally speaking, I think I am really into shopping and so long as I have money, I will shop and shop, online or off-line.

⑤ *Do you stay up late or go to bed early*？

Statement：It depends on my work.

Explain：When I am up to my ears in my work, I will have to burn the midnight oil, but when I am not so fully occupied, particularly during the weekends or holidays, I will go to bed early. Generally speaking, I try not to stay up late. I believe early rising makes a man healthy.

⑥ *Do people like eating foreign food in your country*?

Statement：It depends on the age of the people.

Explain：The young generation seem to be really into foreign food. Take myself as an example, I've tasted several different kinds of exotic food, like sushi from Japan, kimchi from Korea, taco from Mexico, to name just a few, but for elders like my parents, they can't stand foreign food. They've got used to eating traditional Chinese cuisines.

⑦ *Would you prefer to stay in a resort or in a small apartment while on holiday*?

Statement：It depends on my bank account.

Explain：If I have money, I will stay in a resort, admiring the breathtaking sceneries while enjoying the good facilities in the resort, but if I am strapped on cash, I will and have to squeeze in a small apartment.

⑧ *How much time do you spend doing outdoor activities*?

Statement：Well, it depends on the time of the year.

Explain：If it is during the semesters, I will be up to my neck in my study, maybe I can only spare a couple hours each week for outdoor activities, but if it is during the summer and winter holidays, I will definitely hang out with my family or friends on daily basis, participating in tons of outdoor activities like picnicking, hiking, boating, etc., which can really let my hair down and help me build a closely-knit relationship with my loved ones.

⑨ *Do you prefer to travel by plan or by train*?

Statement：It depends on how far away the destination is.

Explain：If my travel is to cover a long distance like thousands of kilometers, I will opt to fly, which will be quicker and less exhausting, but if it is a short distance of a few hundred kilometers, I will take the train.

⑩ *Do you like to travel alone or with others*?

Statement：It depends on whom I travel with.

Explain：If I am to travel with my family or friends, I will enjoy the company and strengthen the bond with them during the trip, but if I am to travel with strangers as in a package tour, then I would rather choose to travel by myself. I just feel awkward to be around people I don't know.

⑪ *Do you like wearing jewellery*?

Statement：Well, it depends on what I am up to.

Explain：If I am to attend some special events, such as a party, a wedding or a ceremony, I will certainly put on my face as well as the best accessories like earrings and necklace, which can certainly enhance my appearance, making me more presentable, but if I am to spend a usual day at home or at work, I will dress more casually and there will be no need to wear jewellery.

⑫ *Do you prefer buying brand name clothes*?

Statement：It depends on how much it costs.

Explain：If it is too expensive, I won't buy, but if it is not that costly, I mean if it is affordable to me, I will consider buying. Overall, I am fond of brand-name clothes, which are usually more reliable and fashionable, so if I can afford, I will buy.

　　我们介绍了回答雅思口语 Part 1 的常用语言模块, 这些模块也可用于 Part 2 和 Part 3 的问题中。需要指出的是, 模块之间存在内部的关联性和相通性, 比如, 喜欢的事情往往就有更高的发生频率及相应的积极感受等。因此, 喜好模块、频率模块、感受模块及记忆模块等不同模块可以在口语答题中巧妙地结合起来。比如:

① *Did you get bored much when you were younger*?

No, not at all. I hardly ever got bored when I was younger (频率). I was born and raised in the countryside. Whenever I had time I would explore the nature with my friends. I remember climbing the mountain, collecting mushrooms, fishing, picnicking, etc. Immersing myself in nature used to make my life so colourful and fulfilled (记忆、感受).

② *Did you have a favorite teacher at school*?

Yes, I am a fan of my English teacher in middle school (喜好). She was very hilarious and humorous, which made her class very appealing (感受). I remember looking forward to her classes every day. She made me so much interested in English (感受) that I would take every opportunity to speak English. I used to be showered with tons of compliments for my oral English (记忆).

③ *What TV shows did you like as a child*?

Well, personally I've been quite interested in TV programs, ever since I was a little kid (喜好), sitcom, cartoon, drama series, etc. I still remember immersing myself in my favorite shows such as "Home with Kids" "Pleasant Goat and Big Big Wolf" "Tom and Jerry", to name just a few. Every time I finished my homework, I would definitely spend the rest of the day binge-watching them (频率、记忆).

④ *What did you like to do with your friends when you were younger*?

Well, I am a huge fan of all kinds of movies, including action movies, sci-fi movies, comedies, and thrillers (情感). My friends and I used to appreciate blockbusters in the cinema almost every weekend (频率). I remember eating popcorn and drinking soda while admiring the fantastic audio-visual effect with them, which really helped us blow off some steam at our leisure (记忆、情感).

第三节　**Part 1 真题实训**

一、兴趣爱好类

1. Music

① *Do you often listen to music*?

Yes, I listen to music all the time. My first thing in the morning is to turn on the Bluetooth speaker and play my favorite song in the playlist to welcome my brand new day, which makes me fresh and energetic. I also enjoy the catchy melodies from my earphone on my way to and from school.

② *What kinds of music do you often listen? Why?*

Well, it depends on what I am up to. If I am working out in the gym, I would listen to hip-hop or rock, which can help me keep up with the fast rhythm. If I am dining or reading, I would opt to some light music such as classic music or folk music, which creates some soothing or romantic atmosphere.

③ *Have you ever learned to play any musical instrument?*

Yes, I have played the piano for as long as I can remember. I used to take piano lessons during the weekends when I was in elementary school. I remember playing the piano in special events as weddings, birthdays, festivals, etc. I would be showered with compliments every time when I played.

2. Reading

① *Do you often read books?*

Yes, I read books all the time. I simply can't go a day without reading. I will read on my phone when I queue up or when I take a ride on public transportation. I will read on my laptop or read the physical books in the library, dormitory or in the classroom. I read various genres of books, fiction, non-fiction, novels, drama, poetry, to name just a few.

② *Are your reading habits now different than before?*

Sure. I used to be utilitarian when choosing what to read, that is, I used to read only those books related to my work or study: text books and reference books, to be exact. That said, now I'm really into the literary books: fiction, novels, poetry, etc. Those books open the realm of literature for me and give me inspiration and enlightenment about life.

③ *Which do you prefer: reading books or watching movies?*

Well, it depends on the purpose of reading. If I read for entertainment and relaxation after a hectic working day, I will opt to watch movies, which is more entertaining and interesting, but if I read for understanding or learning, I will turn to books, that way, I have time for detailed reading and critical thinking.

④ *Did you like reading when you were younger?*

Yes, I used to be a bookworm. I couldn't go a day without reading. I remember every day after school I would just stay in my room hour after hour reading whatever interested me: magazines, novels, biographies, etc. It's a shame that I am so tied up with my work currently that I don't read as much as I used to.

3. Weather

① *Do you prefer hot or cold weather?*

Well, that's a hard question because I hate both, I prefer mild weather. That said, if I have to choose, I think I prefer hot weather, even though the scorching weather makes me sweat and keeps me tired and sluggish, I can do tons of fun things in hot weather: wearing beautiful dresses, eating ice cream, swimming or camping.

② *Has the weather in your country changed much in the past few years*?

Yes, to a large extent. Just like in most part of the world the temperature in my country has been rising greatly over the years, due to the global warming. In my hometown we used to have heavy snows in winter and the temperature in summer used to be no more than 38 degrees centigrade, but now it hasn't snowed for two straight years and it is unbearably hot this summer. It is reported that the last July was the hottest month on record with 14 days reaching 41 degrees centigrade.

③ *What is the weather usually like in your country*?

Well, it varies from area to area. In the south of the country we have distinctive four seasons whereas in the north, people have to undergo the cold and long winter, which starts in November and lasts all the way into April or even May. We do have some places that feature pleasant weather all the year round, like Kunming, which is also known as "spring city".

④ *Do you prefer sunny or rainy days*?

Definitely sunny days! I am a sun worshipper. If I open the curtain in the morning and the sun shines on me, that will instantly give me a boost. Basking in the sun during winter days is so cozy and comfy! I don't like rainy days because it brings me down. What makes things worse is that I hate bringing umbrella when I go out, so it is highly likely that I will be caught in the rain if it rains. I was drenched from head to toe the other day when the heaven suddenly broke up.

4. Collecting

① *Do you collect things*?

Yes, I have collected stamps for ages and therefore I have thousands of stamps from all over the world covering a wide range of topics as animals, sceneries, celebrities and so on. I categorize the stamps in different themes and make explorations of each theme. Stamp collection gives me tremendous pleasure as well as profound knowledge in various disciplines.

② *Why do people collect things*?

Well, people collect stuffs for multiple purposes. Some people obsessively collect antiques with the expectation to make a fortune when they sell them in many years. Other people tend to collect things that have special meanings to them, which helps them recall their memory and keep them connected with their loved ones or their ancestors.

③ *Where can people get their collections*?

It depends on what kind of stuff they collect. If they collect the stuff like antiques or artifacts, they may access them through the antique shops, flea markets or on-line stores. If they collect the personal and sensational items that have special meanings to them, they just obtain them from their family or friends.

5. Swimming

① *Do you like swimming*?

Yes, I am really into swimming. I learned to swim 6 years ago, which was back in 2018 when I was studying in senior middle school. Ever since then I have swum in pools, rivers, lakes and even reservoirs. Swimming helps me stay in shape and gives me good health.

② *Do you like swimming in the sea or in the pool*?

I have never swum in the sea but I assume it would be much more captivating to swim in the sea than in the pool. I am a nature enthusiast. Swimming in the sea would give me the open-air experience: listening to the tide, watching the birds, taking in the fresh air. Nothing would be more fascinating than totally immersing myself in nature.

③ *Is swimming popular in your country*?

Yes, definitely swimming is rather popular in my country, particularly in recent years when swimming skills are mandatory to the kids in many elementary schools, which gives rise to the booming of swimming clubs and training classes. In addition, with the increase of people's disposable income, people are more concerned than ever about their health and entertainment. Swimming, as a low-impact sport, suits everybody: young or old, male or female.

6. History

① *Do you like learning history*?

Well, not until I entered university, I used to hate history back in my middle school. Memorizing all the figures and facts for the sake of examination really drove me up to the wall. It's interesting that somehow my passion for history has been woken up since I went to university. I have learned history from every possible sources: books, TV programs, movies, lectures, etc.

② *What is the importance of learning history*?

As we say, history is the mirror through which we reflect and draw lessons. For example, we learn from history why our country was so prosperous in Tang dynasty and how it fell in Late Qing dynasty. Learning history and analyzing the causes for success and failures help us accumulate knowledge and wisdom.

③ *Do you think it is possible to learn history from TV programs/films*?

Yes, I think it is possible but not the best way to learn history from TV programs or films, which reveals history in a vivid and lively way that can impress the viewers with the gripping plot and visual effect. However, the history portrayed in the movies are often adapted to such extent that they are not at all trustworthy or reliable. I think documentary is a better resource for tracking history.

7. colours

① *What's your favorite colour*?

I love green and blue the best, not only because I look good in those colours but also because they are the dominant colours of nature. Green is the colour of mountain and blue of the sky and sea.

② *Do you prefer dark colours or bright colours*?

I go for bright colours because they enhance my mood. Bright colours are usually associated with positive emotions and qualities, for example, white is the symbol of purity, red the symbol of passion whereas black is associated with gloom, monotony or even death.

③ *Do any colour have a special meaning in your culture*?

Yes, the colour red means a lot to Chinese. It is considered to be an auspicious colour that wards off evil and brings in good luck. Therefore, red is the dominant colour in some special occasions such as wedding and spring festival, you will see people wearing red clothes and houses decorated with red lanterns and red couplets, and you will also see people exchanging red envelopes with money inside as gifts.

④ *What colours are the walls in your home*?

All the walls in my home are white. I believe beauty is in simplicity and the white colour makes the wall look clean and spotless. Apart from that, I personally have a strong fascination with the colour white. When I am surrounded by this colour, I feel a deep sense of calmness. And also white walls are easy to match the colours of the furniture or curtains.

8. Advertisements

① *How do you feel about advertisements*?

Well, I think advertisements is quite a nuisance, particularly the cold calls. It really gets on my nerves when I pick up the phone but only to find it is advertisement from someone I don't know. The cold call not only **brings me** interruption but also anxiety from the awareness that my personal information is somehow leaked.

② *Where can you see advertisements*?

Well, in this commercial world we are bombarded with advertisements anywhere anytime. We can see them on TV, on the Internet, on the billboards and on social media. They have really penetrated into every aspect of our lives.

③ *Do you like advertisement on TV or on magazine*?

Well, I like neither, but if I have to choose between the two, I would say I prefer advertisement on magazine, cause I can turn over that page and I don't have to read it if don't want to. Whereas the advertisement on TV just pops up anywhere anytime. It brings much distraction and simply ruins the fun when you are watching some fascinating TV programs.

9. Cinema

① *Do you prefer watching movies at home or at the cinema*?

Well, I prefer watching movies at home, cause I am kind of a couch potato with laid-back lifestyle. In my spare time, for example, during the evening after a hectic day at work, I enjoy lying on the couch, munching on some snacks and putting my feet high. It's just comfy and relaxing.

② *Did you usually go to the cinema when you were a child*?

Yes, I used to go to the cinema with my buddies now and then. Going to the cinema was an important pastime to me. When I was in the elementary school every time when there was a blockbuster I would invite my friends to watch movies in the cinema. I remember eating the popcorn, drinking the pepsi at the cinema and discussing about the plot and characters with my friends on the way back home.

③ *Do you often go to the cinema with your friends*?

Well, these days I don't go to the cinema that much. I've been more used to watching movies at home by myself or with my family. That said, I do go to the cinema with my friends occasionally for some special events, such as birthday celebrations or friends reunions. Going to the cinema is not only an entertainment but also some social to catch up with friends.

10. Websites

① *What kind of websites do you usually use*?

Well, I have quite a couple of favorite links that I visit pretty often, but the one that I use most frequently is Baidu. Just like Google, it is an Internet search engine which gives me resource in every domain: information in history, literature, entertainment, medicine, you name it. Even though the information provided are not always reliable or authoritative, it has good reference value.

② *Are there any changes about the website you usually use*?

Well, to tell the truth, so far I haven't noticed any obvious changes on the websites I often visit, be it Baidu, Taobao or Bilibili. There might have been some changes but I am too careless to find out. Another reason might be related with the selective attention, I mean, my attention might be more focused on the content rather than on the websites.

③ *What is your favorite website*?

My favorite website is definitely Taobao, one of the most popular on-line shopping links. I am a huge fan of Taobao, which is a mecca for shopaholics like me. On Taobao you can find whatever you want: furniture, clothes, accessories, food, even services from tutors, designers, etc. , but what makes it so appealing is the low price, good delivery service and the 7-day unconditional refunding policy.

④ *What kinds of websites are popular in your country*?

Well, I think the most popular websites today should be the short video platforms like Tiktok or Bilibili. The attraction of short-form social videos lies in their "snackable" nature. Short videos suit our fast-pace lifestyle, brief attention spans, and the need to consume content quickly and easily. You can watch them on the mobile phone anywhere anytime, very handy, entertaining and efficient.

二、地点环境类

1. Meeting places

① *Where do you usually meet your friends*?

As a sports enthusiast, I usually meet my friends in the gym or on the playground, where we work out together. I often start my day with jogging on the playground where I exercise and socialize.

② *Do you think there are some places suitable for meeting others*?

Well, the suitable meeting places vary from person to person. As I said, sports lovers like me would choose gyms or playgrounds as our meeting places, campers will go for camping sites and fishers will probably meet by the water, while shopaholics will regard shopping malls as their favorite meeting places.

③ *Have the meeting places changed now compared with the past*?

Yes, definitely, more venues for socialization are available today due to the ever-richer resources of entertainments such as cafeterias, bars and clubs. I remember that people used to meet each other in the more traditional meeting places like parks, cinemas and teahouses years ago.

2. Street markets

① *What do street markets sell*?

Well, basically street markets in China sell everything: clothes, foods, artefacts, furniture, electrical appliances, etc., but you may not find all these in one street market, as each market usually deals with certain commodities, with the farm products as the most common merchandises.

② *Do you prefer to go shopping in the shopping mall or the street market*?

It depends on what is my priority when making purchases. If my priority is quality, say, to buy some fancy and chic clothes, then I will opt to the shopping mall. If I am more concerned about the price, then I will shop in the street market, where I often buy some casual and inexpensive clothes.

③ *When was the last time you went to a street market*?

The last time I went to the street market was a couple of weeks ago when I was taking a three-day trip to the scenic spot named Fenghuang. When I was there every evening my friends and I would buy some fruits and snacks in the street market. I remember shopping in the market, then walking along the river while eating the food we had just bought.

④ *Are there many street markets in China*?

Yes, street markets are very important shopping places for Chinese. This is partly because the percentage of our population with private cars are pretty low. The street markets are usually scattered in the residential areas where people can just walk to buy groceries and life necessities.

3. New places

① *Have you been to a new place recently*?

Yes, I've just been to a fabulous restaurant on the top of Yuelu Mountain. My high-school classmate Amy who visited my city last weekend wanted to climb the Yuelu Mountain, a local scenic spot, but I couldn't do that due to my knee problem. Amy then found this restaurant online which offered to pick up its customers from the parking lot at the foot of the mountain. We had a good meal and good views at this restaurant.

② *What's the difference between this place and other places of the same kind*?

Compared with the other restaurants, the most arresting feature of this restaurant is the stunningly beautiful scenery you can see from your dining table. Located just steps away from the observation deck on top of the mountain, every outdoor table in the restaurant provides the diners with an amazing view of the city.

③ *Do you feel nervous when you travel to new places*?

Well, it depends. If I travel to places where there are friends or family out there guiding me around, then I will be at ease and at home, but if I travel to a new place alone without any local people helping me out, I will feel butterflies in my stomach to face all the uncertainties and adventures lying ahead.

4. Old buildings

① *Have you ever seen some old buildings in your city*?

Well, my city Changsha is rich in history and culture and therefore is filled with historical architectures. I have seen tons of ancient buildings in my city, particularly along the Taiping Street. At the starting point of the street is a majestic stone gate with delicate inscriptions. On both sides of the street stand the very exquisite wooden buildings with traditional overhanging tile roofs.

② *Do you think we should keep old buildings in cities*?

Well, we don't have to keep all the old buildings but we do have to maintain those buildings that have some special values, be it aesthetic value, cultural or historical value. Old buildings not only help us connected with the history, give us a sense of pride but also make the city attractive and unique, thereby boost economy by developing the tourist industry.

③ *Do you prefer living in an old building or a modern house*?

Well, I definitely prefer to live in a modern house. Compared with the old buildings the floor plans of modern houses are more open and spacious, the interior design is more trendy and the appliances and facilities are more advanced. So I think modern houses can better cater to my lifestyle and better serve my various needs of entertainment, relaxation, dining, etc.

5. Public parks or gardens

① *What do you usually do when you go to a park or a garden*?

Well, I've done tons of activities in parks. I used to do some strenuous exercise like running and rock climbing before I had my knee injury. Currently I visit the parks on the daily basis, doing Taiji, boating, jogging, taking photos, etc.

② *How have parks changed today compared to the time when you were a child*?

Wow, great changes have taken place in the parks over the years. The parks used to be smaller with limited facilities, I remember when I was little every time when I visited the Yuehu Park, the greatest park in my city, I didn't have too many choices except boating or playing in the amusement park, whereas the kids today can have fun in the expanded parks with rich amenities, from recreation centers to barbecue areas, from swimming pools to adventure courses, from hiking trails to various exhibitions.

③ *Would you prefer to go to a personal garden or public garden*?

It depends on what I am up to in the garden. If I am to go jogging and admire the scenery then I will opt to a public garden which is larger with more sceneries but if I am to do some reading or work on my laptop, as I often do in the garden, I will go to a personal garden, which is more peaceful and quiet that helps me to concentrate.

三、生活经历类

1. Time management

① *Do you make plans every day*?

Yes, making daily plans is essential in my life. I have a calendar which I jot down my daily plans on the previous day, detailing the tasks as well as the time frame for each task. Making plans helps me better organize my time and allows me to accomplish the tasks in time.

② *Is it easy to manage time*?

Well, for me, it's not difficult to manage my time as I am a well-organized person and I hate procrastination. I try to accomplish tasks well ahead of time, so should anything happens, say, if I feel under the weather or have some urgent tasks coming up, I could still keep my schedule.

③ *Do you think it's useful to plan your time*?

Yes, definitely, planning my time is of vital importance to me. As we say, the busiest person finds the most time. I am a busy person, I am always up to my neck in my work and study. Scheduling helps me find time to finish each task. I know I can't afford to idle away my time and I have to carefully schedule my time to make every minute count.

④ *Do you like being busy*?

Yes, I am used to being busy and I enjoy my tight schedule. Apart from attending classes and doing assignments, I participate in tons of social or leisure activities during my spare time. I try to squeeze as many tasks as possible in each day because I don't want to waste my precious time. Keeping myself busy makes my life fulfilled and gives me a sense of satisfaction.

2. Getting lost

① *Have you ever lost your way*?

Well, I lose my way all the time. I was born with a poor sense of direction, which I believe is a genetic thing. My father has the same problem. I have lost my way for countless times when visiting new places, shopping in big malls or hanging around my city. The poor direction has been a pain in my neck throughout my life.

② *How can you find your way when you are lost*?

I usually rely on GPS on my phone when I get lost. As I said I have very poor direction and fortunately I live in this modern world when smart phones are all the rage and the GPS on the phone is just our trustworthy guide showing us the direction anywhere anytime.

③ *Have you ever helped someone who got lost*?

Yes, I have given directions for many times to strangers in my city over the years. And the occasion that was most impressive to me was 3 years ago when I was studying in high school. I ran into an American couple in my neighborhood who couldn't find their way to the railway station. As I was going in the same direction, I took them there and we ended up becoming penpals. We've written each other over the years.

④ *Would you use a map when you get lost*?

Well, probably not. I am not good at studying maps and thanks to the fast growing technology, I can easily find my way through GPS on the phone, then why do I bother with the map reading. I mean I don't have to read the maps, I just follow the direction given by the app.

3. Primary school

① *What did you like to do most when you were in primary school*?

I remember learning to play badminton in PE class in primary school. Then I became such a big fan of it that I would play badminton with my buddies/besties for at least an hour every day after school. Playing badminton gave me relaxation, entertainment as well as socialization.

② *How did you go to your primary school*?

Well, I used to walk to school as I lived very close by. If my memory serves me right, the school was just around 500 meters from where I lived. I remember just walking straight, taking a left and the school was right there.

③ *How did you like your primary school*?

Well, my primary school left me ponds of favorite memories. The campus was stunningly beautiful with a couple of gorgeous gardens, a crystal clear lake and lots of exquisite pavilions. The school was a closely-knit community. The teachers and students were loving and caring.

4. Daily routine

① *What is your daily routine?*

My daily routine may seem to be rather boring and monotonous to many people. I've been pretty tied up with my work and study, so I basically spend the whole day working on my computer either at school or at home, except for doing some physical exercise at around 6 AM and 7 PM respectively.

② *Have you ever changed your routine?*

My routine is pretty fixed and stable with little changes except during the finals, when I'm up in my ears with my preparation for the exams and I have to cancel my daily exercise and get fully devoted in my study.

③ *Which part of your routine do you like best?*

I usually start my day with jogging along the Xiang River across the street from where I live. That is the best part of my day. Jogging makes me energized and fully awake in the morning when I am sluggish and it also helps me stay in shape. And in good days I can even admire the sun rising over the mountain on the other side of the river.

5. Dreams

① *Do you often remember your dreams?*

Not always, sometimes I remember pretty well a comprehensible event in my dream like a family trip to some places of interest, but most of the time I merely remember some broken fragments of the dreams, for example I repeatedly dreamed of the scenario that I slid down the stairs very fast, so fast that I almost flew. I have no clue though regarding the explanation or interpretation of that dream.

② *Are you interested in others' dreams?*

No, not at all. I am not interested even in my own dreams, why do I bother with dreams of others? Though it is said that dreams is associated with the dreamer's sub-consciousness or hidden desires, I have no idea about dream interpretation and dreams don't make any sense to me. So I have little interest in discussing dreams, either my own dreams or others' dreams.

③ *Do you want to make your dreams come true?*

Well, that depends, I wish I could realize all my beautiful dreams, like travelling all over the world with my loved ones, but I definitely don't want to turn my nightmares into reality, like getting COVID-19 positive.

6. Feel bored

① *Do you often feel bored?*

No, not at all. I hardly ever feel bored. I've been up to my neck in my study over the years. My life has been too fulfilled to be boring. When I do take some time off, I have a long list of things to keep life fun: hiking, swimming, reading, shopping, etc. I just make every minute count.

② *What kind of things would make you feel bored*?

Well, I think the household chores are boring and monotonous to me, such as sweeping, vacuuming, doing laundry, so I usually listen to music or English when I do the housework.

③ *What would you do if you feel bored*?

As I said, doing household chores is boring and time consuming, but it doesn't require much attention or concentration, therefore there is always space for speculation or meditation. I can allow my mind to roam freely while I do housework or I can listen to music to relax myself.

7. Sitting down

① *Where is your favorite place to sit*?

Well, I have a bean-bag chair and I think that's where I love to sit in because it's really large and comfortable. And you know with its soft and squishy materials inside, it can mold itself into the body shape of whoever sitting in it. It helps me quiet my mind and relax my body, sometimes it even helps alleviate my neck and shoulder pain.

② *Do you always sit down for a long time*?

Yeah, I guess so. I have to sit in front of the computer for at least 5 hours a day. And I know this kind of sedentary lifestyle is quite unhealthy but I have so many assignments to do on a computer since I'm still a student at present. So, there is not much I can do about it.

③ *Do you feel sleepy while sitting down*?

Sometimes, like if I sit down right after having a big meal, I tend to get really drowsy or sluggish. I guess because my body works very hard to digest the big meal, which makes me feel exhausted, but a cup of tea or coffee will just keep me awake.

④ *When you were a kid do you usually sit on the floor*?

The memory is too far to recall, maybe I have to ask my mom about that. But as far as I can see, children basically like to sit on the floor so that they can play games like lego, building towers and stuff like that. On the floor there is more space to spread out and play around. Moreover, it seems a safer choice to sit on the floor than on a couch where a little kid is way likely to fall off.

四、特品物件类

1. Mirrors

① *Do you like looking at yourself in the mirror*?

Well, yes. I look into the mirror many times a day to make sure that I am presentable: my face is clean, my clothes are spotless and my hair is tidy. I carry a small foldable mirror in my handbag, so it's pretty handy to check my appearance and fix my makeup anytime throughout the day.

② *Have you ever bought mirrors*?

Yes, I have bought tons of mirrors in my life, ranging from the foldable mirror in my handbag to the wall mirror in the bath room, the free-standing mirror in the living room, and the furniture mirror on the closet.

③ *Would you use mirrors to decorate your room*?

Well, probably. Last week a mosaic mirror with a Victorian frame in an antique shop really caught my eyes. It was just an exquisite work of art. Maybe one day when I save up enough money I will buy that mirror and hang it on the living room wall. It will definitely add aesthetic value to my home.

2. Watches

① *Do you wear a watch*?

Well, I used to wear a smart watch three years ago but then I lost it during a business trip. So currently my smart phone takes over the tasks that used to be performed by the watch, checking the time, setting calendar reminders, monitoring my sleep and checking my steps, etc.

② *Have you ever got a watch as a gift*?

Yes, the smart watch I've just mentioned is a birthday gift which I got 5 years ago from my uncle. It is a Huawei Smartwatch, which was quite a rage at that time. My uncle spent an arm and a leg on it but unfortunately I lost it 2 years later.

③ *Why do some people wear expensive watches*?

Well, people wear expensive watches for multiple reasons. To start with, they may genuinely appreciate a high quality timeless watch that can last for ages. Further more, they may regard watches as important accessories. And a luxurious watch not only elevates their looks but also enhances their personal dignity, self-esteem and social status.

3. Emails

① *Do you often send emails*?

Well, not that often. I may send a couple of emails a month to my foreign friends because we use different social networks. Here in China we connect with people on Wechat, but my foreign friends use Instagram. So I stay in touch with my foreign friends through emails.

② *Is sending emails popular in China*?

Not as much as it used to be. When I was in high school every day when I got up I would check my email because that was how I kept up with my friends and family, but today we are all on the Wechat all the time. Wechat has made interpersonal communication a lot easier by texting, sending voice messages or making video or voice calls.

③ *Do you think sending emails will be more or less popular in the future*?

I reckon that emails will be less popular in the future. As I've just mentioned, the social networks like Wechat or Instagram are more appealing in keeping touch with people. Emails are definitely losing their popularity, even though they won't completely die out, for example, people may send important official documents through email.

4. photos

① *Do you like to take photographs*?

Yes, I'm a total photography enthusiast. I love taking photos of everything, people around me, natural views as well as exquisite artefacts. Every time when I take photos for my friends or family, they always shower me with compliments, which gives me a great sense of accomplishment.

② *Do you ever take photos of yourself*?

Yes, I've taken lots of selfies ever since I bought a selfie stick a couple of years ago. When I visit some scenic spots I will take a selfie with the gorgeous scenery as the background. When I am in two minds whether I should buy some clothes I try on, I will take a couple of selfies and send them to my friends for suggestions.

③ *What is your favorite family photo*?

My favorite family photo is the one taken last spring festival at my grandma's 90th birthday party. All the family members scattered all over the country returned home and got together to celebrate grandma's 90th birthday. All together 38 members from the extended family were there on this photo with grandma sitting right in the middle, smiling heartily.

④ *Do you want to improve your picture-taking skills*?

Yes. I'd love to but not now. Currently I've been up to my neck in my work and study, and I don't think I can spare the time studying about photography. That said, I will probably enhance my photo-taking skills in near future. I may sign up for some training classes, or work part time in some photo studios during the coming summer holiday.

5. Memory

① *Why do some people have good memory while others just don't*?

Well, the reasons for the disparity about people's memory retention are manifold. Even though genes definitely play a role, some people are born with good memories while others are not. I reckon people's diet and nutrition as well as memorization training also make the differences.

② *Why do more people rely on cellphones to memorize things*?

Because the cellphones do a good job in helping us memorizing things and reminding us of the tasks we have to deal with. The cellphones today usually come with some very good apps, such as note taking or event reminder, which are just like our faithful assistants that help us organize and remember things and tasks.

③ *Are you good at memorizing things*?

Well, it depends on what those things are. I have a very good memory in language. When I was in elementary I used to recite all the texts in English and Chinese textbooks. I remember I could even recite some paragraphs on my maths textbooks. That said, I am not good at memorizing people's names or faces.

④ *Have you ever forgotten something that was important*?

Yes, recently I have forgotten to return an expensive dress I bought on Taobao. It was a pink dress that looked stylish and cost me an arm and a leg. However, I just looked plump and awkward in it, so I decided to return it under the 7-day unconditional return policy. Two weeks had passed when I saw the dress in my wardrobe last week.

6. Evening time

① *Do you like morning or evening*?

I like morning better. Morning is the best time of my day. In the morning I jog along the river while admiring the breathtaking views along the way, which helps fresh my mind and boost my mood, and I am happy and ready to welcome a brand new day.

② *What do you usually do in the evening*?

In the evening I usually study in the classroom or in the library, except on Friday evening when I take some time off and have some entertainment with my buddies, watching a movie, playing computer games or working out in the gym.

③ *Are there any differences between what you do in the evening now and what you did in the past*?

Well, honesty speaking, no. I spend evenings pretty much the same as I used to in the past. I've been up to my neck in my study for as long as I can remember and as a result my evenings have been dedicated to studying. That said, I wish I wouldn't be so busy and would have more spare time in the future.

7. Shoes

① *Do you like shoes*?

I've been really into shoes for as long as I can remember. I have tons of shoes with different styles, colours and materials, each matches with different clothes in my wardrobe. Shoes play an important role in making me presentable.

② *Do you ever buy shoes online*?

Yes, I have once bought a pair of black leather shoes on Taobao and that was the only time I bought shoes online. They simply didn't fit me and with each step I took, my feet hurt a little more. I ended up returning it.

③ *Do you prefer comfortable shoes, or good-looking fashionable shoes*?

It depends on where I am going. If I am to attend some formal and special occasions, be it a wedding or a birthday party, I will prefer fancy fashionable shoes, but if I am to spend a usual day at home or in my office, I will go for comfortable shoes.

④ *What kind of shoes do you like most*

I am obsessed with the pointed high-heeled shoes. Altogether I have three pairs of those shoes with different colours: white, black and blue. The pointed high-heeled shoes are always a good match with any kind of formal clothes, dresses or trousers. They really help to enhance the overall appearance.

8. Pets and animals

① *Did you have any pets when you were a child*?

Yes, I used to have a ginger little dog named Huanhuan when I was in elementary school. Every day when I got home Huanhuan would jump at me and follow me closely just like my shadow. I remember snuggling in my bed while holding Huanhuan in my arms to keep each other warm in those freezing winter nights when we had no heating.

② *Do you like to see animals in the zoo*?

Yes, I am a huge fan of animals and I have visited tons of zoos in different cities in my life. Even though currently due to my tight schedule, I don't visit the zoo as often as I'd like to, I enjoy watching videos about the animal world, which is quite a fascinating unknown world to me.

③ *What's your favorite animals*?

Well, basically I love all the animals, whom I regard as our siblings in mother nature. That said, I particularly take a liking to some small animals with smooth and silky fur, like cats, dogs, rabbits, and so on. I enjoy developing intimacy with those cute furry friends.

④ *What is the most popular animal in China*?

Surely, panda is the most popular animal in China, cause it is our national animal as well as our mascot. They are just like Chinese embassadors, travelling and making friends all over the world, which helps strengthen our international relationship.

9. Computers

① *In what condition would you use a computer*?

I am a computer butt. The computer has become an essential part of my life. I use it in my work, searching for information, doing assignment and attending online conferences. I use it in my personal life, chatting, shopping, playing games, watching movies, etc.

② *When was the first time you used a computer*?

The first time when I used a computer was around 10 years ago when I was studying in elementary school. My father bought a computer which cost him an arm and a leg. As my parents didn't want me to get addicted to computer, I was allowed to use it for no more than 30 minutes daily. I spent most my computer time playing games.

③ *What would your life be like without computers*?

Well, life without computers would be quite a disaster, a nightmare. To start with, I would be completely cut out with the world. Losing virtual contact with all my friends and family would drive me crazy. In addition, all my data is stored in my computer, without which I wouldn't be able to continue with my work.

④ *In what conditions would it be difficult for you to use computers*?

Well, I am on my computer all the time and I don't think there are too many occasions under which I can't use computers but there are some exceptions, though, for example, I wouldn't be able to use computers if there was no access to Internet or if I took a ride on some bumpy road.

10. Cars

① *Do you like to travel by car*?

It depends on how far away the destination is. If my travel is to cover a long distance like thousands of kilometers, I would like to travel by plane, which will be quicker and less exhausting, but if it is a short distance of a few hundred kilometers, I will take the car.

② *What is the farthest place you traveled to by car*?

The farthest car trip I have ever taken was the one to Fenghuang, a scenic spot 500 kilometers away from where I lived. My friend Tom and his wife Susan took turns to drive. Unfortunately we were caught by a sudden downpour and we ended up getting to the hotel at late evening.

③ *Do you like to sit in the front or back when travelling by car*?

Well, personally I enjoy sitting in the front cause front seat has better views than back seats. That said, I don't often sit in the front. In my culture we are supposed to reserve the front seat to people older in age or higher in social status.

11. Mobile phones

① *Do you remember your first mobile phone*?

Yes. I remember very clearly that I got my first mobile phone on my 10th birthday. It was a pink flip phone. Looking back it was indeed a very basic phone merely for texting and making calls. That said, I was on top of the world upon receiving it, as few of my friends owned a mobile phone at that time.

② *Do you often use your mobile phone for texting or making phone calls*?

Well, I text my friends or family numerous times a day but I haven't made a call to anybody recently. I even don't remember when I made my last call. I've always felt reluctant to call people for fear that they might be in the middle of something and a phone call would distract them. I prefer to send them messages.

③ *How has your mobile phone changed your life*?

Wow, my mobile phone has transformed my life incredibly. I am tightly glued to my phone. I use my phone to make electronic payment, to monitor my sleep and exercise, to stay in touch with my loved ones, to take photos and have entertainments. Every thing is rolled into this small gadget.

④ *Will you buy a new mobile phone in the future*?

Yes, although I don't know when exactly, I am bound to replace the current phone. Cause the gadgets like phones or laptops update incredibly fast, which means the current ones will be obsolete soon. Even though my phone functions well, the future phone will definitely work more brilliantly.

12. Talents

① *Do you have a talent, or something you are good at*?

Well, I reckon my communication skill and presentation skill are well above average. I have won tons of prizes and awards in debates and speech contests in my life. All of my friends think I am articulate and eloquent.

② *Do you think your talent can be useful for your future work*?

Yes, even though I am not one hundred percent sure about my future job, it is highly likely that I will seek a teaching position. On this position I can well display and further exploit my communication and presentation skills through my lectures as well as through the interactions with students.

③ *Do you think people in your family have the same talents*?

Yes. We have a long line of educators in my family: my parents, uncles and aunts, who are all dauntingly articulate. Actually it is my parents that have nurtured my communication skills. I remember they used to encourage me to participate in debates and speech contests. Every time when I took part in those contests when I was little, they would bend over backward to help me, giving me instructions, feedback and constant support.

第三章　**Part 2 模块解析及运用**

第一节　**Part 2 框架模块 PDF**

一、**Part 2 题型分析**

Part 2 要求考生讲述自己的过往经历，描述曾经经历过的人、事、物等。此部分准备时间为 1 分钟，讲述时间为 2 分钟。1 分钟的现场准备时间非常有限，临时准备故事素材，会让考生陷入困境，不知道该讲哪个故事，或者考生并没有相关的生活经历。因此，话题准备对 Part 2 非常重要。Part 2 的考场表现与素材准备的充分程度直接相关。

在 Part 2 的回答中，考生通常会遇到以下几类常见问题：

（1）心情紧张，脑袋空白，不知道说什么好；

（2）1 分钟的准备时间不知如何有效利用，思绪较乱；

（3）讲述不流利，自我重复较多，或不知如何表达；

（4）由于讲述不流利，或太啰嗦，抓不住重点，2 分钟过去了还没讲到点子上。

为了解决以上问题，考前可把故事素材用一定的框架模块进行组织。

雅思口语题库中 Part 2 的考题多达三四百道，不可能逐一准备。但对附录中 Part 2 题库进行分析，你会发现这几百道题目并不是杂乱无章、无序可循的，而是分为人物、地点、事件、物品四大类。这些类别之间以及类别内部的题目之间密切关联，甚至很多题目大同小异，完全可以用同一个故事来回答。有些题目虽然表面看上去没有很多关联，但考生可以把自己的人生经历进行改编，把两个或多个貌似不相关的题目进行牵线搭桥，使用同一个故事讲述尽可能多的题目。雅思口语考试是允许考生编故事的，考生不一定要讲自己的真实故事，考官并不在乎考生的故事是否真实、情节是否曲折（当然，曲折的情节更能吸引考官的注意力）。雅思口语考试的目的在于借助故事描述与问题讨论来考查考生的语言水平和逻辑思维能力。讲故事仅仅是一个背景和媒介，故事本身是否真实并不重要。当然，考生也不应完全抛弃自己的生活经历，凭空编造故事。相反，考生如果诉说自己经历过的真人真事，讲起来会更亲切、更流畅、更自然。一个比较好的方法是把自己的亲身经历或所闻所见进行改编，使它最大限度地适用于更多的题目。通常来说，雅思口语考试 Part 2 的当季题目有 50 多道，如果进行故事改编、整合与串联，准备十多个话题的素材就可套用于当季 Part 2 的所有考题。

二、Part 2 PDF 模块简介

Part 2 的问题, 可以按照 PDF 的框架模块回答, P 代表 past, D 代表 description, F 代表 future, 分别运用于 Part 2 答题中的开头、主体与结尾部分。

1. P: past, 用于开头部分, 笼统描述过去的经历

比如: Describe a person who likes to talk a lot.

开头用两句话笼统地描述过去: 我过去曾经碰到过很多(或者很少)很健谈的人, 而最健谈的则是某某。我是在做什么的时候认识他的。

I have met many people who talks a lot and the most talkative person is my friend Paul. I came across/got to know Paul when I was studying in university/was jogging on the campus.

开头这么说的好处是什么呢? 首先, 开头两句话用了现在完成时、定语从句、一般过去时以及过去进行时, 很好地体现了语法和句式的多样性。其次, 这样的开头经过大量的练习, 考生拿到题目就可脱口而出。说出准确流利、语言优美、句式多样的开头, 不但解决了开头难的问题, 也避免了"背答案"的嫌疑。因为这不是死记硬背套答案, 而是学会方法和思路, 自己组织语言。此外, 这样的开头简练, 入题快, 两句话之后就可以讲下面的主体部分。开头两句话大概二三十秒。

2. D: description, 用于主体部分, 对事件进行细节描述

主体部分需根据具体的故事进行有针对性的细节描述。在这部分考生可以将题目所给的小问题作为提示, 逐个回答, 也可以按照自己的思路, 以时间、地点、人物、事件、背景等为线索逐一展开。由于开头及结尾加起来将近一分钟, 主体部分只要讲一分钟左右即可。这就大大减少了考生的实际准备内容量, 减少了回答难度。如果故事比较复杂, 一分钟讲不完, 可以讲一分半钟, 结尾可以不讲或只用简短的一句话结尾。

3. F: future, 用于结尾部分, 表达遗憾或展望未来

还是刚才这个题目: Describe a person who likes to talk a lot.

结尾部分在展望未来之前可以加一个让步: 虽然他是个话痨, 但是我很喜欢他。遗憾的是, 我没有留下他的联系方式。我希望能够再次碰到他。如果我们再次重逢的话, 他一定会跟我讲很多有趣的话题, 我们可以尽情畅聊。

Even though he is a chatter box, I like him very much. I regret I didn't get his contacting information. I wish I could meet him again and should we meet again, he would certainly bring up tons of interesting topics for us to have nice and long talks.

这样的结尾方式有两个突出的好处。第一, 句式时态和语态的多样性。Part 1 中我们学过的让步从句, 在这里再次使用, 另外, 这里特意加了一句"遗憾的是, 我没有留下他的联系方式", 这样说是为了方便后面使用虚拟语气。茫茫人海, 如果没有联系方式, 很有可能将来不能重逢, 因此用虚拟语气表达对未来的愿望。第二, 结尾的长度非常灵活, 可以多说也可以少说。以上的回答中, 可以将任何一句话作为结尾, 甚至没有结尾也是可以

的。因此，学会说一个比较长的结尾，将会给你的 Part 2 的回答备下不时之需，如果内容讲完了，时间不到，可以用结尾补上。

PDF 答题框架可以让考生在面对任何题目时，都可以用不同的时态、句式和语态进行答题，一方面体现了语言的多样性，另一方面因为有固定的答题思路和模式，可以极大地缓解考试压力，同时让答案结构清晰、条理清楚。

总之，Part 2 答题以故事素材为线索，串联框架模块与语言模块。从故事中学习如何套用题目，从故事中学习如何运用框架模块与语言模块。PDF 用于不同的题目，产出各不相同的 Part 2 答案，但在这些答案中，却可以找到很多相通、相似的表达与句式。尤其是开头、结尾的描述，把一些常用语言模块稍加变动调整，便能灵活运用于不同的题目。另外，由于故事的基本素材来源于生活，因此 Part 2 的主体模块大部分是描述考生所熟悉的日常生活的，比如排队、交通阻塞、美食、户外活动等。建议考生把那些跟生活关联密切的主体模块进行背诵，并在相应的生活情境中进行使用，使背诵的内容最终内化为自己的语言积累。

第二节　Part 2 开头模块

很多考生拿到题目，往往不知道从哪里入手，如何开头。Part 2 的题目是讲述考生自己的故事。故事的开头可以先介绍背景。不管题目问哪方面的问题，需要讲述哪些故事，背景的介绍都可以从笼统到具体，并在描述中展示词汇与语法的多样性。具体地说，开头模块可以用两个句子导入主题：第一个句子用现在完成时进行笼统描述；第二个句子用现在进行时进行细节描述。

一、现在完成时模块

用现在完成时进行笼统描述，根据题目进行词汇替换：**I have done/been … + 时间状语（笼统+替换）… and/but …（点题+替换）**。

其中，时间状语：since I was a child/I graduated from university/became an adult …；for a while now/for ages/for a long time/ for as long as I can remember …；in my life/over the years/throughout my childhood，等等。

这部分在对题目所指向的事件或人物进行笼统描述的基础上，进行点题，说明将要说的人或事。该模块表达两个层面的内容：

（1）自从什么时候，类似的事情或人物（替换题目中的修饰语）"我"经历过很多或很少。

（2）其中最……（替换修饰语）的是某事或某人。

此模块对题目中的修饰语进行两处同义替换，给考生提供了展示词汇多样性的机会，但对同一个修饰语进行两次同义替换，存在一定难度。考生也可以前半句用题目中的原词进行表述，后半句则用一些套话进行点题，比如"印象最深刻的是……""我想说的是……"。

比如：

① Describe a person who likes to talk a lot.

I have met lots of *chatty* people throughout my life and the most *talkative* person is my friend Amy.

开头先笼统说明：在我的人生中，有很多话痨。随后进行点题：但是最健谈的是我的朋友 Amy。chatty 与 talkative 替代题目中的修饰语 who likes to talk a lot。

② Describe a popular/well-known person in your country.

I've been a fan of lots of celebrities in my country over the years, and the one that impressed me most at this moment is Ailing Gu.

③ Describe a city you would recommend as a nice place to live in (not your hometown).

I've been to tons of interesting cities since I became an adult, and the city that I strongly recommend people to live in is definitely Changsha, the capital of Hunan.

④ Describe a photo you took that you are proud of.

I've taken tons of awesome pictures since I entered university, but the one that I've taken the most pride in is a photo of my father admiring the sunset on top of the Yuelu Mountain.

二、过去进行时模块

用过去进行时进行细节描述，说明伴随动作，对主题词进行关联：I ... （主题词）when I was doing ...

开头模块 P 的第一句话针对题目进行笼统描述并点题说明所要描述的人或事。第二句话则针对该事或人用过去进行时描述一个相关的伴随动作。比如：我是在上高中的时候做这件事的，我是在跑步的时候认识这个人的，我是在参加朋友聚会的时候知道这个地方的，等等。

I came across this book when I was studying in the library.

I learned to play basketball when I was studying in high school.

I found this place when I was having a picnic with my family three years ago.

I lost the phone when I was taking a trip from Shanghai to Hangzhou.

三、开头模块完整形式

开头模块把两个句子结合起来，用现在完成时模块进行笼统描述，用过去进行时模块进行特定细节的描述。比如：

① Describe a person who likes to talk a lot.

I have met lots of *chatty* people throughout my life and the most *talkative* person is my friend Amy. I got to know her when I was attending our mutual friend Tom's birthday party about 3 years ago.

② Describe a popular/well-known person in your country.

I've been a fan of lots of celebrities in my country over the years, and the one that impressed me most at this moment is Ailing Gu. I got to know her when I was watching the Olympic Games two years ago/when I was browsing the news online.

③ *Describe a city you would recommend as a nice place to live in* (*not your hometown*).

I've been to tons of interesting cities since I became an adult, and the city that I strongly recommend people to live in is definitely Changsha, the capital of Hunan. I first visited Changsha when I was studying in high school.

④ *Describe a photo you took that you are proud of.*

I've taken tons of awesome pictures since I entered university, but the one that I've taken the most pride in is a photo of my father admiring the sunset on top of the Yuelu Mountain. I took this photo when my father and I were dining on a restaurant.

四、真题演练(现在完成时模块+过去进行时模块)

1. 人物类话题

① *Describe a person who likes to talk a lot.*

I have met lots of chatty people throughout my life and the most talkative person is my friend Amy. I got to know Amy when I was attending our mutual friend Tom's birthday party about 3 years ago.

② *Describe a friend you like to talk with.*

I have always enjoyed talking with my besties since I was a little kid and Amy is my special friend with whom I will talk about every thing under the sun. I got to know Amy when I was attending my friend Tom's birthday party about 3 years ago.

③ *Describe a person you know who loves to grow vegetables/fruits.*

I've been around many farmers and gardeners in my life and I think my father is the greatest green finger I have ever known. My father learned gardening when he was studying in elementary school, so he is a very experienced gardener.

④ *Describe a popular/well-known person in your country.*

I've been a fan of lots of celebrities in my country over the years, and the one that impressed me most at this moment is Ailing Gu. I got to know her when I was watching the Olympic Games last year/when I was browsing the news online.

⑤ *Describe a person you know who is from a different culture.*

I've made lots of foreign friends since I entered university and the one that has made far reaching influence on me is my oral English teacher Rebecca. I learned a lot from her when I was attending her classes or the extracurricular activities she held.

⑥ *Describe a person who is fashionable.*

I've been around many stylish people in my life over the years and my fashion icon is my friend Amy. I got to know her when I was attending my friend Tom's birthday party.

⑦ *Describe a person who you follow on social media.*

I've been a huge fan of many Internet influenzers and I have followed closely Liulaolao on her Douyin, the Chinese social media platform. I got to know her when I was browsing the short videos online.

⑧ *Describe a teenager you know.*

I've been around many teenagers over the years, but one teen that has left my indelible imprint is named Amy. I got to know her when I was attending my friend Tom's birthday party.

2. 地点类话题

① *Describe a popular place for sports(e. g. a stadium).*

I've been exercising in various spots in my life and one of the most popular places for working out in my city is the hiking trail on Yuelu Mountain. I got to know this trail when I was climbing the mountain with my friends last year.

② *Describe a city you would recommend as a nice place to live in (not your hometown).*

I've been to tons of interesting cities since I became an adult, and the city that I strongly recommend people to live in is definitely Changsha, the capital of Hunan. I first visited Changsha when I was studying in high school.

③ *Describe a quiet place you like to visit.*

I've always needed total silence when I want to concentrate on something. One quiet place that I love going to is a pavilion on top of the Yuelu Mountain in my hometown. I got to know this pavilion when I was dining in a restaurant close by.

3. 物品类话题

① *Describe a photo you took that you are proud of.*

I've taken tons of awesome pictures since I entered university, but the one that I've taken the most pride in is a photo of my father admiring the sunset on top of the Yuelu Mountain. I took this photo when my father and I were dining in a restaurant.

②*Describe an interesting novel or story you have read before.*

I've been a big fan of reading since I was a kid, and the story that has left me indelible imprint is "The Miracle Worker" about Hellen Keller. I bought this book when I was visiting a book store in Shanghai.

③ *Describe a song/a piece of music you like.*

I've never been a big fan of music in my life, but I do have a favorite song named "Love Me Hard". I first heard this song when I was strolling in the park.

④ *Describe a traditional product in your country.*

I've been a fan of many traditional products and the one that I am most proud of is the embroidery from my hometown. I bought a piece of embroidery when I was visiting the embroidery town last year.

⑤ *Describe a movie you watched recently and would like to watch again.*

Well, I've been a movie butt for as long as I can remember and a massive hit movie that really appealed to me is "The Miracle Worker". I watched this movie when I was studying in high school.

⑥ *Describe a plant in your country.*

I've never really thought about plants from my country before, but one plant that is very special to me is sun flower. I first saw the sun flower when I was visiting a remote village in my province.

4. 事件类话题

① *Describe a time when you received money on your birthday.*

I've always enjoyed celebrating birthdays and receiving gifts since I was a kid, and the gift that has left me indelible imprint is a red package with money inside from my grandfather. I received it when I was studying in university.

② *Describe a time when you succeeded in doing something that was difficult.*

I've been a hardworking person and have won success in various domains throughout my life and the greatest success that I've been really proud of is being accepted by Central South University. I first got to know this university when I was attending a class meeting.

③ *Describe an occasion when you lost something important.*

I haven't lost many things in my life, but the occasion when I missed something really valuable was when I lost my cellphone. I lost it when I was taking a bus ride to my home.

④ *Describe a time when you disagreed with someone about something.*

I've confronted with lots of disagreements over the years and come up with respective solutions to settle them and one example that I'd like share with you is a disagreement I used to have with my parents. We had this disagreement when we were talking about my major.

⑤ *Describe an important thing you learned* (*not at school or college*).

I've been learning and enhancing my skills in various domains ever since I was born and one of the most important skills that I've learned is swimming. I learned swimming when I was studying in high school.

⑥ *Describe a time when you saw a lot of plastic waste* (*e. g. in a park*).

Well, I haven't been around much white pollution in the city where I live, but I was appalled by the plastic waste scattered over a beach in south China. I visited the beach when I was taking a trip to Shenzhen with my friends.

⑦ *Describe an occasion when someone gave you positive advice or suggestions about your work/study.*

I've taken lots of great suggestions over the years and I'd like to share with you a very important suggestion I got from my mother. My mother gave me this suggestion when I was suffering from pneumonia.

⑧ *Describe a positive change that you made in your life.*

Over the years I've been learning, reflecting on myself and improving in every domain and a very crucial improvement I've been proud of is the transition from sedentary life to active life. I made this transition when I was studying in university.

⑨ *Describe a time when you were stuck in a traffic jam.*

I've been frustrated about traffic congestion over the years but there is a special occasion when I really enjoyed the jam. I came across the jam when I was taking a trip to Fenghuang.

⑩ *Describe a time when someone asked for your help.*

I've always enjoyed helping people out throughout my life and one occasion that has left me indelible imprint was when I was asked to give direction by a kid. I was strolling in a park when the kid came to me for help.

⑪ *Describe a way/change that helps you save a lot of time.*

I've been up to my neck in my study since I entered high school and therefore I've been looking for ways to save my precious time. I ended up coming up with a very effective way when I was studying in high school.

⑫ *Describe a difficult decision that you made and had a good result.*

I've been making all kinds of decisions in my life and the hardest decision I've ever made is about the choice of my major. I eventually chose my major as computer science when I was having a family meeting with my parents.

第三节　Part 2 主体模块

开头模块创设了背景之后,接下来就进入主体部分,讲述事件发生的来龙去脉。考生可以按照答题卡上的提示,依次回答上面的问题,也可以按照时间顺序描述事件的发展。答题卡上的小问题是给考生的提示,并非要严格按照所给问题回答。

对主体模块的描述,就是对人物、地点、事件及物品四类话题中的具体问题进行一分三十秒左右的细节描述。对四类话题的描述既有其共通性也有特殊性,因此本节包含通用模块与分类模块两大部分。通用模块包括名词修饰与举例论证,可广泛运用于四类话题的描述;分类模块则包括人物描述、地点描述、事件描述、未来描述及物品描述五个部分。

一、通用模块

1. 名词修饰

在 Part 2 的回答中,需要提供细节描述,对名词进行细节描述是一个有效的方式,考生可用强语气形容词、介词短语及定语从句等多种方式修饰名词,实现词汇、句式的灵活运用。

策略 1:强语气形容词修饰名词。

在 Part 2 中经常需要对名词进行修饰,最常见的修饰词就是形容词。考生可以学习运用语气强烈的形容词修饰名词。强语气形容词比弱语气形容词更能体现词汇的多样性以及描述的深刻性，考生不需要考虑所描述的状况是否符合事实，只要符合语境，运用自然，尽可能选择更高级的、语气更强的形容词。

下面的形容词中，右边的形容词语气更为强烈，建议在口语交流中尽量用右边的形容词替代左边的形容词。

good — brilliant

very good — incredible/impressive

beautiful — stunning/breathtaking

funny — hilarious

big — massive/huge

interesting — fascinating

hot — boiling

cold — freezing

clean — spotless

bad — terrible/horrible/awful

tired — exhausted

hungry — starving

tasty — delicious/mouthwatering

hard — impossible

需要注意的是，语气强烈的形容词已经表达强烈的语气，已经蕴含"very"之意，因此不要再用"very"来修饰。比如，不能说 very huge、very spotless、very boiling、very delicious，但是可以用 really、so、absolutely 来修饰。

The food was really delicious.

The skyscrapers were so massive.

The weather was absolutely freezing.

策略 2：介词短语修饰名词。

运用介词短语可以对名词的时间或地点进行细节描写，使描述更加丰富细致，也能增加句子的长度和复杂性。比如：

The traffic（in the downtown）（during rush hours）was terrible.

My teacher（at school）（in 5th grade）was the most helpful teacher I had in my childhood.

The café（next to my office）is perfect for my lunch break because it's so close.

The microwave（in my kitchen）has been broken for about 2 months actually.

The staff（at the hotel）is very welcoming.

The view（from our balcony）in the morning was stunning.

The resorts（along the coast of Hainan）（in the summer）are packed with tourists.

下面这段话，如何用介词短语修饰名词呢？

We had a great trip. We went to a delicious local restaurant, then we went on an exhausting hike and there was a beautiful view.

这段话中的主要名词是 trip、restaurant、hike、view，我们可以对这些名词用介词短语做出补充说明：

We had a great trip to the city of Liuyang（地点）during the summer holiday（时间）. We went to a delicious local restaurant near our hotel（地点）, then we went on an exhausting hike up the mountain（地点）in the afternoon（时间）and there was a beautiful view from the top of the mountain（地点）.

经过这样修改，句子内容更加完整丰富，但是句式比较简单，所有句子的开头都是"we"。我们只要变换一下主语，句子就会更具多样性。

We had a great trip（to the city of Liuyang）（during the summer holiday）. The food（at the local restaurant）（near our hotel）was really delicious and the hike（up the mountain）（in the afternoon）was absolutely exhausting but the view（at the top of the mountain）was really beautiful.

策略3：定语从句修饰名词。

在本章第二节描述故事背景的第一句话中，我们的例子中很多使用了定语从句修饰名词。比如：

The river that strikes me the most is Xiang River that runs through my city.

One friend that has left me indelible imprint is Chun Yan, my classmate back in Grade One.

One person that has made far reaching influence on me is my oral English teacher Rebecca.

One teen that has left me indelible imprint is named Amy.

The most important thing I've ever done on my phone is raising fund for my friend.

One of the important skills that I've learned recently is swimming.

定语从句在听、说、读、写中都大量出现，非常重要。

The café（where I like to work）is really close to my home.

The film（that he strongly recommended）was very thrilling.

The snack（that was very famous and delicious）was stinky toufu.

The hotel（where we stayed last summer）was really comfortable and clean.

The food（that they serve in the café）is always fresh and filling.

The reason（why we were so late）was because our taxi drive didn't show up.

Our hosts（who were supposed to meet us）were really late and weren't answering their phones.

与强语气形容词和介词短语修饰名词一样，定语从句给句子增加更多的细节，此外，定语从句把简单句变成了复杂句，增加了句子的复杂性。通常介词短语修饰名词的句子也可以转换为定语从句进行修饰。比如：

We had a great trip（to the city of Liuyang）（during the summer holiday）. The food（at the local restaurant）（near our hotel）was really delicious and the hike（up the mountain）（in the afternoon）was absolutely exhausting but the view（at the top of the mountain）was really beautiful.

如果用定语从句进行修饰，则可以说：

The trip（that we took to the city of Liuyang during the summer holiday）was great. The food (that served in the local restaurant near our hotel) was really delicious and the hike (that we took in the afternoon) was absolutely exhausting but the view (that we saw at the top of the mountain) was really beautiful.

前一段话用了大量的介词短语修饰，后一段话用了大量的定语从句修饰。最好的方式则是把两者结合起来，避免句式的单调与重复。

We had a great trip (to the city of Liuyang during the summer holiday). The food (that served in the local restaurant near our hotel) was really delicious and the hike (up the mountain) (in the afternoon) was absolutely exhausting but the view (at the top of the mountain) was really beautiful.

2. 举例论证

举例论证贯穿雅思口语三个部分的答题中，是雅思口语中最重要的论证与展开方式。举例论证可以增加相关细节，提高答案的逻辑性与可信度。论点、论据如果没有一定的事例进行论证，其表述往往会显得空洞、笼统、抽象。此外，举例论证比单纯讲道理更容易表达，且更有趣味性。举例论证有以下四种常见的方式。

策略 1：因果关系举例论证。

在 Part 2 的描述中，形容词+因果关系的举例论证是最常见的展开方式。形容词是对某人、某地、某事的特质进行描述，在特质描述基础上，加以例子说明。举例论证与形容词之间，既可以用 so、because、therefore、and 等连接词连接，也可以用 which means、it's pretty common to see、where you can 等短语连接，也可以不用连接词，直接开始一个新的句子表达，这是因为上下文语境表达了逻辑上的因果关系。

The museum is full of fascinating exhibits **where you can** admire the various displays of paintings, photos, artifacts, antiques, relics, etc., which are arranged under different themes in chronological order. This is a must-see for tourists, **which means** there are flocks of visitors from all over the country throughout the year. **So it's pretty common to see** the huge lines of visitors in front of the booking office, particularly around 9 o'clock in the morning when the museum opens.

策略 2：条件句举例论证。

条件句是举例论证的一个有效方式。条件从句的构成：If …/When …, sb. will/could/might …。比如：If you study hard, you will pass the exam. 条件句表示在什么情况下将会怎么样。运用条件句可以对主题句进行举例论证。

She is really extroverted and outgoing, so **when we go to parties**, I will always stick with her, because she will help me break the ice with new people and get to know them faster than if I was just by myself.

She is really extroverted and outgoing, so she has lots of friends. **If we go downtown in the evenings**, we will always bump into friends of hers.

He is really introverted and shy, **if we meet new people**, he will look very nervous and rarely joins in.

My friend Amy is a very trustworthy and reliable person. I can trust her with anything and she won't tell anyone. So **when I have some difficulties or problems**, I will turn to her for help and she will always bend over backwards to help me.

My mom always puts other people before herself. **If there is a fundraiser or charity event**, she will always lend a helping hand.

My friend is always there for me in tough times. **If I have a stressful or difficult time**, she will always listen to my problems and help me out.

Changsha is an absolute Mecca for foodies like me, which means there are lots of delicious local snacks and excellent cuisines. **If you talk to the tourists**, they will tell you how impressed they are by the local delicacies.

策略 3：运用记忆模块。

我们在 Part 1 中学习运用过记忆模块，Part 2 的题目均为讲述考生过去的经历以及由此带来的感受等。因此，记忆模块在 Part 2 中非常实用，能够更好地描述过去的事件或感受。

在 Part 2 的故事讲述中，remember doing 是一个非常有效的表达方式。这是因为 doing 表示动作正在进行，能够更生动形象地描述当时的情境。另外，remember doing 后面可以有多个宾语，使表达更为紧凑，内容更为丰富，语言更为优美。

下面两段话，第一段话用了简单的一般过去时，第二段话用了记忆模块 remember doing。第二段话在语言表达上更富有多样性，描述也更为生动有趣。

The water at the beach was crystal clear and warm. So we went snorkeling every day and saw lots of beautiful sea creatures.

The water at the beach was crystal clear and warm. I remember going snorkeling, looking at the seabed, and seeing lots of beautiful sea creatures.

remember doing 的其他例子：

I remember walking into the provincial museum, seeing the old lady from Han Dynasty unearthed 50 years ago and marveling at the great preservation of the mummy.

I remember asking a local driver for directions and being told that I was going in the wrong direction.

我们在 Part 1 中还学习了记忆模块的三个组合表达（**used to**、**remember doing**、**would**），它们共同组成关于过去事件的记忆模块。

I **used to** try tons of new activities when I was little. When I was in elementary school I **would** register in some clubs or training classes almost every summer. I **remember** learning painting, swimming, rock climbing, and even snorkeling, my life was thereby very colourful and fulfilled.

I **used to** be a bookworm/nerd in school. I couldn't go a day without reading. I **remember** every day after school I **would** just stay in my room hour after hour reading whatever interested me, magazines, novels, biographies, etc.

My friend Amy **used to** be shy and introverted. Every time when we bumped into some new people, she **would** feel nervous and keep silent. I remember her hands shaking and her face turning red while making a speech at a birthday party.

二、分类模块

1. 人物描述

　　人物描述最常见的方法是因果描述与例子描述，先对人物进行一个观点性描述，随后以事实或事例论证该观点。

　　She is absolutely open-minded, because she listens to other people's opinions and knows that there are always two sides to an argument.

　　She is very helpful and thoughtful, which means she often puts herself in others' shoes and is always ready to bend over backwards to help people in need.

　　He is so shy and introverted. He is really nervous about meeting new people. I often see his hands shaking when he is at parties.

　　He was very generous. He never earned much money but he gave all his savings to his family or friends who were in need.

　　She is so reliable and trustworthy. I feel like I can trust her with anything and she won't tell anyone.

　　My brother is very inquisitive. He loves asking questions about people, politics and history. He always tries to learn something new.

　　My father is very hardworking. He works day in and day out, hardly taking holidays. He takes business trips on a regular basis and he does his work even when he is on the trains or the planes.

　　My friend is very hilarious. He never fails to crack us up with his funny stories and humorous remarks.

　　My sister has always been good with money. She keeps a weekly budget and only spends her cash on things she needs, and she always checks online for the best price. (此处的"good with money"也可以用"frugal"或"thrifty"代替)

真题范例

Describe a person you like spending time with.

　　(1)开头模块 P：创设背景(现在完成时、一般现在时、过去进行时)。

　　Well, I have several besties who I've enjoyed spending time with over the years. One person who I love to hang out most is my friend Amy. I got to know her when we were attending our mutual friend Tom's birthday.

　　(2)主体模块 D：事件描述(一般现在时)。

　　①进一步描述背景。

　　Amy is a few years older than me and currently works as a middle school English teacher.

　　②形容词+因果论证。

　　I like Amy because she seems to have all the qualities of a good friend. She is very helpful and thoughtful. She often puts herself in others' shoes and is always ready to bend over backwards to help people in need. She is also reliable and trustworthy. I feel like I can trust her with anything and she won't tell anyone. Furthermore, she is hilarious. She has a very good sense of humor and often cracks me up with her funny stories or humorous remarks. It's relaxing and pleasurable to hang out with Amy.

2. 地点描述

地点描述也可以运用以下语言模块描述该地点的外部特征或在该地点展开的活动：

which means …

so there are …

so the traffic is usually …

it's pretty common to see …

where you can try …

the only downside is …

比如：

It's an absolute Mecca for foodies, **which means** there are lots of delicious local snacks and excellent cuisines.

It's a thriving, lively and dynamic city, **where you can see** a wide range of theaters, opera houses, galleries, exhibitions and night clubs, etc. Even in the evenings the streets, shops and pubs are bustling, which creates a great atmosphere.

It's a city with a long history, **so there are** tons of fascinating museums and historical buildings, with the Hunan Provincial Museum as its highlight, which houses the well-preserved Mawangdui Han Tomb, dating back to more than 2000 years.

It features subtropical climate, **which means** it's warm and humid most part of the year, giving a boost to the thriving gardens and mountains, which in turn become good habitat for large number of species.

There are huge beautiful buildings in this metropolitan city of Changsha, so it's very common to see people admiring those buildings and taking pictures of them.

The only downside of the city is the traffic congestion which to a large extent is caused by the huge flocks of tourists.

真题范例

Describe a city you visited that you liked.

(1)开头模块 P：创设背景。

I've been to tons of interesting cities since I became an adult, and the city that I think the world of is definitely Changsha, the capital of Hunan. I got a glimpse of this city through screen when I was watching a tourist program about the city on TV a couple of years ago. And I grew so much attached to it that I visited it the next year.

(2)主体模块 D：事件描述(一般现在时)。

There are tons of reasons why I like this city. To start with, it's an absolute Mecca for foodies like me, ***which means*** there are lots of delicious local snacks and excellent cuisines. The stinky tofu is the most famous local snack, which is crispy outside and tender inside. It's hard not to drool over this special local delicacy. Changsha is a thriving, lively and dynamic city ***where you can see*** a wide range of theaters, opera houses, galleries, exhibitions and night clubs, etc. Even in the evenings the streets, shops and pubs are bustling, which creates a great atmosphere. In addition, Changsha is a city with a long history, ***so there are*** tons of fascinating museums and historical buildings, with the Hunan Provincial Museum as its highlight, which houses the well-preserved Mawangdui Han Tomb, dating back to more than 2000 years. The historical significance is the most arresting feature of Changsha.

对地点的描述如果仅仅是描述该地点的外部特征，可描述的内容会比较有限，考生容易陷入无话可说的境地。对地点的描述如果从活动方面拓展思路，则会有较丰富的素材。比如：

There are lots of delicious restaurants and stalls on both sides of the food street. ***It's very common to see*** diners lining up in huge queues for the food they like, ***which means that*** you have to wait for at least 20 or 30 minutes to get seated. Because the food street is located in the financial center of the city, ***which makes*** this area even more bustling, and the traffic is always terrible. Despite the terrible traffic and long queues, people from all over the country flock here for the excellent local snacks and cuisines, such as Sexy Tea, stinky toufu, crawfish in spice, to name but a few.

There are huge beautiful buildings in this metropolitan city of Changsha, ***where you can*** not only see the modern skyscrapers like International Finance Square and the sky city tower but also find the elegant traditional buildings like Fire Palace and Yuelu Academy. ***So it's pretty common to*** see people admiring those buildings and taking pictures and sharing them on the Wechat moment. ***The only downside*** of the city is the traffic congestion which to a large extent is caused by the huge flocks of tourists.

The museum is full of fascinating exhibits ***where you can*** admire the various displays of paintings, photos, artifacts, antiques, etc., which are arranged under different themes in chronological order. This is a must-see for tourists, ***which means*** there are flocks of visitors from all over the country throughout the year. ***So it's pretty common to see*** the huge lines of visitors in front of the booking office, particularly around 9 o'clock in the morning when the museum opens.

3. 事件描述

在描述个人事件或经历时，考生可编一些富有戏剧性的小插曲或出乎意料的变化（twist），以增加故事的趣味性并有机会运用相关语言模块，讲出更多更长的句子，展示语言表达能力。事件描述常有以下几种策略。

策略 1：正反对比。

曲折的情节是指出乎意料的情况，比如，所设想情况与事实情况完全相反：一开始以为怎么样，结果却与此相反。

（1）设想情况：

at first it seemed/looked …

on the advertisement it seemed/looked …

when we arrived it seemed/looked …

I had heard that …

a lot of people have told me that …

I had thought/heard/read that …

（2）实际情况：

but after reading it, I realized that …

but after watching it, I realized that …

but after spending two weeks there I realized that …

but it turned out to be …

以下是一些完整例句：

At first I thought the book was long and slow, but *after* reading it, *I realized that* it was actually thrilling and fast-paced.

On the advertisement the class sounded really difficult and advanced, but *after* trying it, *I realized that* it was actually more accessible than I imagined.

When we arrived, *the hotel looked* quite run-down and unwelcoming, but after going inside *we realized that* the staff were incredibly welcoming and the room was spotless.

Looking from outside *I had thought* the restaurant was very small but it *turned out to* be spacious and elegant inside.

真题范例

① *Describe your favorite movie.*

I *had heard* that the film was serious and boring, but *after* watching it *I realized* that it was really funny and interesting.

② *Describe a restaurant that you enjoyed going to.*

When I first saw the restaurant it looked really small, but *after* going inside *I realized that* it was very spacious.

③ *Describe a time when you had to give someone advice.*

I had thought my colleague Amy was decisive and self-assured, because she always goes her own way and makes incredible accomplishments, but after a confiding conversation with her, *I realized* she was self-contemptuous and hesitating.

策略 2：使用宾语从句。

在讲述故事时，也可以用表达惊讶、意外、高兴、难过等主观情感的词汇作为主句谓语动词，引导表示感叹的宾语从句，以增加故事的感染力与语言的复杂性。

I was surprised (to find) how spacious the rooms were.

I was amazed (to find) how spacious the rooms were.

I was impressed（to find）how gorgeous this view was.

I was amazed（to find）how welcoming the staff were.

I was surprised（to find）how huge the queue was.

I was surprised（to find）how expensive the tickets were.

I was surprised（to find）how huge the queue was.

I was amazed（to find）how unique that flower was.

I was impressed（to find）how interesting the book was.

I was surprised（to find）how hardworking the students were.

与此类似，还可以用 I couldn't tell、I couldn't believe 或 I wasn't sure 等主句引导相应的宾语从句。

I couldn't tell how big the campus was.

I couldn't believe how much work we had done.

I couldn't tell how beautiful the village was.

I couldn't believe how boiling the weather was.

I couldn't believe how bustling the city was.

I wasn't sure where my tutor was.

I didn't know where my tutor was.

真题范例

① *Describe a time when you made a decision to wait for something.*

I was impressed how delicious the cooking smelled and I decided to wait for the meal.

② *Describe a time when you were very busy.*

I couldn't tell how important the college entrance examination was.

③ *Describe an important event you celebrated.*

I couldn't tell how excited I was when I knew my score. I was so impressed how high my score was.

④ *Describe an occasion when you had a special cake.*

I was impressed how fluffy and creamy the cake was.

策略 **3**：采用副词插入语。

在描述中还可以用表达情感的副词作为插入语（通常置于句首），以增加感情色彩，提高语言难度并体现情节与逻辑上的衔接。此外，情感副词作为插入语有利于激发考生的想象力，能引导考生思考特定情境下的一些让人意外的、开心的、难过的、愚蠢的等各种小插曲。

Sadly, the tickets were already sold out.

Obviously, the reservoir was too dangerous to swim in.

Surprisingly, the apartment was spotless when the tenants left.

Stupidly, I forgot to charge my phone.

Fortunately, the assignment was not too much.

Obviously, this class was really engaging.

真题范例

① *Describe a time when you got lost and needed help.*

The taxi driver said we were at the address, but I couldn't see my hotel anywhere. *Unfortunately* the Google Map on my phone gave some silly directions and I ended up walking up and down the street but just couldn't find my hotel. Just while I was wondering and mumbling to myself in frustration, *suddenly* a passerby came up to me and asked if I needed any help. *Luckily* he was a local resident who had lived all his life in this area.

② *Describe a time when you had to use a foreign language.*

I had taken a few English classes and learned a few words but I couldn't speak much at that time. I was strolling by myself in a park close to where I lived when *suddenly* two foreigners came up to me and tried to say something to me. Despite their somewhat exaggerated body language, I couldn't figure out what they meant. *Luckily* one of them took out a pen and a notebook and sketched a picture of a train.

③ *Describe a time when you saw an animal in the wild.*

I was hiking in the woods with my friends when we saw a snake climbing a tree. *Obviously* that snake didn't notice us. We were *immediately* frozen in horror. *Surprisingly*, the snake changed its direction and moved towards a side branch and then to some small twigs.

④ *Describe a time when you had to wait in a long queue.*

I arrived at the bank, but there was already a long line coming out of the door. I went to the tail of the line and waited for one solid hour. *Fortunately* I got to the desk before the closing time. *Unfortunately*, there weren't enough American dollars for me to buy. *Sadly*, I came home without getting anything from the tedious waiting.

⑤ *Describe a time when you saw a famous person.*

I went to the lift and I saw my favorite singer, ×××. *Amazingly*, she smiled and nodded at me, then asked me which floor I needed. *Unfortunately*, I was too nervous to ask her for an autograph or a picture.

策略 4：使用过去进行时。

我们在本章第一节曾用过去进行时创设故事背景，表达"在干什么的时候发生了什么事"。在主体部分的故事描述中，也可以用过去进行时描写突发的情节，表达"在做某事的时候，突然发生了另外一件事"。

I was walking to a barber shop and suddenly a pack of stray dogs appeared.

My friends and I were having a party when suddenly our parents arrived home.

I was searching online for birthday presents for my husband when he suddenly came in and saw me.

I was jogging in the park when suddenly I felt a pain in my ankle.

I was waiting in line when I suddenly realized that my examination was the day before.

We were hiking along the trail when we suddenly spotted some monkeys jumping through the trees.

I was taking a shower at home when suddenly my phone rang.

I was checking my social media when suddenly a message popped up from an old school friend.

We were talking about our new boss when he suddenly came into the room.

I suddenly noticed the car making a funny noise when I was driving home.

I was replying to some emails when suddenly I heard someone knocking at the door.

I was looking at my phone when suddenly a message from my friend popped up.

过去进行时表达"正在做某事时，另一件事情发生"，另一件事可以是突然发生的，也可以不含有突然之意，或虽有意外，但不需要强调其突然性。比如：

Our train arrived when we were running to the platform.

We were strolling on the street when we heard our favorite song.

I was looking for my hotel when a passer-by told me that I was going the wrong way.

I was cooking dinner in the kitchen when I noticed that I had run out of salt.

I was studying at university when I met Amy for the first time.

真题范例

① *Describe a time when you forgot something important.*

I was taking a shower in the bathroom early in the morning, suddenly the phone rang.

② *Describe a time when you had to give someone advice.*

I was working in my office when suddenly my friend Amy appeared at the door and asked if I could spare her a few minutes.

③ *Describe a time when you met an old friend unexpectedly.*

I was shopping in a local grocery store when suddenly the cashier called out my name.

④ *Describe a time when you got lost and needed help.*

While I was wondering and mumbling to myself in frustration, *suddenly* a passerby came up to me and asked if I needed any help. *Luckily* he was a local resident who had lived all his life in this area.

策略 5：描述真相与结果。

此模块由两个短语构成：turned out ... ended up doing，表示"原来如此+最后如何"，其含义：对某事或某现象从不知情到知情，知情之后发生了什么。

The shopping mall was bustling with thousands of people. It *turned out to* be celebrating its 20 year anniversary and having sale promotions, so we *ended up buying* lots of stuff at very good prices.

The two men were arguing and shouting at each other in the middle of the street. They *turned out to* be fighting over paying for the bill of their dinner. The man *ended up paying* seemed to be really contented.

We were waiting in the traffic for ages. It *turned out* there was a big accident ahead, so we *ended up eating* our lunch in the car.

We were the only ones on the beach. It was completely deserted. We *turned out* to be the last tourists to this beach and we **ended up having** the whole beach to ourselves.

Suddenly, one of the actors from my favorite movie came into the hotel lobby. There **turned out** to be a movie festival in this city, and I **ended up obtaining** an autograph from my adorable movie star.

There was a cluster of people around the podium. They **turned out to** be the admirers of the guest speaker and they **ended up taking** a group photo with him.

I got to the classroom but was surprised to find that the classroom was empty. It **turned out** to be a holiday, so I **ended up taking** a tour in the city.

真题范例

① *Describe a time when you forgot your appointment.*

I was lying lazily on my bed with my eyes closed and mind wandering about when suddenly my phone rang. I picked it up. It **turned out** to be a call from my friend Amy who was waiting for me with a couple of friends at the entrance to the theater! I totally forgot my movie appointment. So my friends **ended up watching** the movie without me.

② *Describe a time when you enjoyed an impressive English lesson.*

My foreign teacher Rebecca organized a coffee hour in our oral English class. I remember eating a cake, drinking coffee and chatting about birthday celebrations. It **turned out** to be Rebecca's first birthday in China. We **ended up singing** the birthday song together and sending birthday wishes.

③ *Describe a time when someone gave you positive advice on your work.*

I had insomnia and unexplained pains and aches. I went to see the doctor. It turned out that I had been overworked. So I ended up winding down and signing for a swimming club in my neighborhood.

策略 6：使用过去完成时。

在 Part 2 的答题中可以设计一些使用过去完成时的情境，以展示语法时态的多样性。比如，当要表示第一次做某事时，可以改说"以前从未做过某事"，随后对某事或某物用一个强语气形容词进行描述，以体现词汇的多样性。比如：

I had never seen the city so early in the morning. It was just gorgeous.

I had never visited the city before. It was just breathtaking.

I had never seen a snake gobble up eggs. It was just horrible.

I had never seen such huge buildings. They were just magnificent.

I had never got such an excellent teacher. He was just amazing.

I had never eaten local curries. They were just incredible.

At that time, I had never tried scuba-diving before. It was just fascinating.

At that time, I had never heard of it before. It was just heart-wrenching.

At that time, I had never bought a product made by Huawei before. It was just impressive.

At that time, I had never thought about trying Yoga before. It was just fantastic.

At that time, I had never taken a flight before. It was just eye-opening.

At that time, I had never read any of her books before. It was just inspiring.

我们可以把以上策略进行综合运用, 凭借想象力, 设计有趣的情节, 运用丰富的语言, 完成雅思口语 Part 2 的经历描述。

真题范例

① *Describe a time when you got lost and needed help.*

The taxi driver said we were at the address, but I couldn't see my hotel anywhere. *Unfortunately* the Google Map on my phone gave some silly directions and I *ended up* walking up and down the street but just couldn't find my hotel. Just while I *was wandering and mumbling* to myself in frustration, *suddenly* a passer-by came up to me and asked if I needed any help. *Luckily* he was a local resident who had lived all his life in this area and he kindly took me to the hotel, which *turned out* to be situated in a very inconspicuous location. You had to take a narrow lane that weaved among the gardens, stalls and cottages.

② *Describe a time when you had to use a foreign language.*

I had taken a few English classes and learned a few words but I couldn't speak much at that time. I *was strolling* by myself in a park close to where I lived when *suddenly* two foreigners came up to me and tried to say something to me. *Despite* their somewhat exaggerated body language, I couldn't figure out what they meant. *Luckily* one of them took out a pen and a note book and sketched a picture of a train. It *turned out* that they had lost their way to the train station. So I *ended up taking* them to the railway station which was just 20 minutes' walk. We did have some communication on our way but it was more like a pantomime with gestures and smiles. All I could say was phrases like "Look, look" "OK, OK" "Good, good". Every English word I blurted out was greeted with enthusiastic response, which immediately livened up the atmosphere.

③ *Describe a time when you saw an animal in the wild.*

I was hiking in the woods with my friends and we saw a snake climbing a tree. *Obviously* that snake didn't notice us. For a moment we were frozen in horror. *Surprisingly*, the snake changed its direction and moved towards a side branch and then to some small twigs. Just when we *were wondering* if the weight of the snake could snap the twigs, we caught sight of a bird nest amid the twigs. The snake *turned out to* be predating on the eggs of the birds. We *ended up* taking a video of the snake preying on the eggs. We *were impressed how* quickly the snake could gobble up an egg.

4. 未来描述

在雅思口语中通常会问及对未来的设想和打算, 比如:

Describe a new food you would like to try.

Describe a film you would discuss with your friends.

Describe a job you would not like to do in the future.

以上问题均是对未来的设想, 都用了虚拟语气。

策略 1：使用虚拟语气。

虚拟语气是指非真实情况，而是虚拟或想象的情境，其语言构成是把动词时态往前推一格，即一般现在时要前推到一般过去时，一般过去时与现在完成时则往前推到过去完成时。题目中的 would，其原型是 will，这是虚拟语气的表达。在回答此类问题时，也要相应地用 would、could、might 这类表示虚拟的动词。

I can't stand working in an office all day, so I **wouldn't** like to work for a bank or have a regular nine-to-five job.

I've always been a big fan of pop music, so I **would** love to attend the live concert if I **had** money.

I actually really enjoy my work at the moment, so I **wouldn't** change my job.

I'm a nature enthusiast, I **wouldn't** like to live in a huge busting city.

I hate big crowds and busy public transport, so I **wouldn't** like to live in the city center.

Most of my friends are not really big fans of horror movies, but I think I **could** change their minds if I showed them this one.

I love drinking tea, so it **would** be really cool to visit a real tea plantation one day.

If I **had** enough money, I **would** invite lots of friends to this ski resort.

If I **could** ask Bill Gates just one question, I **would** ask him for the secrets of running a successful business.

策略 2：采用虚拟+让步。

虚拟语气还可以与让步从句相结合，表达"虽然……但是……"，在英文中，although 与 but 不能同时使用，这点在口语中容易出错，需经过大量练习，避免出现"although … but …"这样的错误。以下句子中 would、could 均表示虚拟假设的情况，而真实情况则用一般现在时表示。

Although I can hardly do it now, with some practice, I think I **could** get the hang of it.

Although I don't speak any Thai, I think I **could** learn enough to survive when I got there.

Although the rent **would** be much higher, it **would** worth it to be so close to the city center.

Although it **would** be stressful, at least it **would** be over quickly because I **would** probably get fired after a few days.

真题范例

① *Describe an ambition that you have had for a long time.*

Although I have no experience in running a business, I imagine that working for myself would be incredibly rewarding and I would learn a lot.

② *Describe a country you would like to live or work in.*

Although I have never been to Japan, I have heard so many wonderful things about it. If I had a chance, I would like to live there for some time, experiencing the local culture and lifestyle.

③ *Describe a change that could improve your local area.*

Although the budget might be a problem, I believe expanding the subway system would be a good way to curb the current traffic congestion.

④ ***Describe a job that you wouldn't like to do in the future.***

Fortunately, I haven't had many jobs that I really didn't like, but one profession that I imagine ***would*** be very unpleasant for me, ***would*** be a kindergarten teacher. I have a 3 year-old nephew, every time when I have to look after him, I am terrified. I can keep him entertained for about 5 minutes before he gets bored and starts running around the house. So I can imagine a whole room filled with 20 or even 30 little kids ***would*** be in complete chaos if I were to care for them. I ***wouldn't*** be able to control them because I don't know any techniques to make them listen to me. I am also terrible at singing or painting, which means the kids ***wouldn't*** like my songs or paintings and I couldn't teach them sing or paint, which are every essential activities in kindergarten. My nephew likes playing football with me, but that's the only thing he likes and obviously I ***couldn't*** just do that all day in the kindergarten. So although it ***would*** be stressful, at least it ***would*** be over quickly should I be the caretaker in a kindergarten, because I ***would*** probably get fired after a few days.

5. 物品描述

策略 1：使用定语从句。

定语从句是最常用的描述物品的方式之一，可以从物品本身或与物品相关的时间、地点、人物等各个角度进行描述。

This is the gift ***that*** I got from my grandfather for my twentieth birthday. （物品）

The gift ***that*** I love most is a smart watch (***which***) I received from my grandfather for my twentieth birthday. （物品）

This is the store ***where/***(***from which***) my grandfather bought the twentieth birthday gift for me. （地点）

This is the restaurant ***where*** I've kept going over the years. （地点）

This is the restaurant whose owner is one of my best friends. （人物）

This restaurant was opened 3 years ago ***when*** I was studying in middle school. （时间）

We had a good meal in the restaurant ***that*** is located right across the street from where I live. （地点）

I have a beautiful dress from Thailand ***that*** I wear for fancy parties and special events. （物品）

It was bought from a street market ***where*** you can buy lots of souvenirs. （地点）

It was my grandfather ***who*** bought it many years ago. （人物）

以上各例从不同的角度，用定语从句对名词(物品)进行修饰补充。

策略 2：形容词连用。

对物品进行详细具体的描述，往往需要涵盖其材质、特色、尺寸、形状、颜色等多个维度。每个维度都可以用形容词进行描述。当多个形容词连用的时候，可按照"看法+尺寸+

颜色＋材料（或产地）"的顺序排列。比如：beautiful black silk dress、cute little orange Japanese sculpture、beautiful blue scarf、cheap little plastic toy.

This is a beautiful black silk dress with stylish red metal buckle that I often wear for fancy parties and special events.

These are interesting wooden cooking utensil with pictures of children and women on them.

It is a little remote control car with studded tyres and a little driver. It is a toy that looks very fun to drive around.

It is a blue Hawaiian shirt with buttons and pictures of palm trees and surfers on it. It looks like a shirt that my dad would wear on vocation.

策略 3：使用介词。

修饰名词的介词有 from、to、on、in、with、by 等。

It is an exquisite hand-painted mask of a human face **with** dark eyes, gray hair and a blonde moustache.

This is the face **of** my grandfather who passed away last year.

It is a handicraft made **by** my uncle who is a professional handicraftsman.

The mask also has my grandfather's name **on** the back.

It is hung **on** one of the walls in our living room which never fails to attract the attention of the visitors.

We once took a family photo **with** the mask on the wall as the background.

The photo was then sent **through** Wechat to my uncle who was overjoyed at it.

According to my uncle the mask was made **of** timber **from** one of the trees which my grandpa planted **on** the mountain **in** our hometown.

This gift **from** my uncle is definitely the lasting memorial to my grandfather, who used to be a successful entrepreneur as well as a remarkable philanthropist.

策略 4：使用强调句。

强调句可以修饰人物、地点、物品等，可以广泛运用于各类问题中，强调其重要性或者特殊性。比如，地点问题可以强调正是在这里遇到了某人；人物问题可以强调这个人对"我"产生了深远的影响；事件问题可以强调通过这件事，"我"懂得/认识/学习了什么；物品问题可以强调这件物品引起"我"的美好记忆，等等。

It was on my twentieth birthday that my grandfather bought this gift for me.（强调时间）

It is in this restaurant that I met my boyfriend.（强调地点）

It is my uncle who made this mask in memory of my grandfather.（强调人物）

It is this mask that keeps taking me back to the sweet memories of my grandfather.（强调物品）

It is this conversation that has totally changed my perspective on foreign language learning.（强调事件）

以上例子显示，在 Part 2 中，几乎每一个问题都可以用强调句，以展示语言的多样性。

🖎 **真题范例**

① *Describe an expensive activity that you do occasionally.*

An activity that costs a lot of money is travelling, particularly trips to the developed countries where people's living condition is high and everything is expensive. I have taken quite a few fascinating trips to different parts of the country or the world over the years. The most luxurious trip (that) I have ever taken is the one to the United States. This trip was actually sponsored by my grandfather who is an entrepreneur. Though this is a trip that really cost me an arm and a leg, I've never regret taking this trip. ***It is through this trip that I experienced American culture and American lifestyle and thereby greatly widened my horizon and deepened my understanding of the States.***

关于物品描述题，很多考生有一个共同的困惑：如何能说满两分钟。如果物品描述仅仅局限于对物品外表特征、功能作用等方面的描述，显然难度会非常大。事实上，对物品的描述可以与人物、事件、地点等题目相结合，使答题内容更加充实完整，语言更加高级丰富，情节更为有趣生动。因此，在物品描述中除了描述物品本身，还可以拓展到对物品出处及相关记忆的描述，对物品的虚拟设想及让步关系等进行描述。在语言层面，可以把前文提及的各种语言模块综合运用于物品描述中。例如：

② *Describe some clothes you like wearing.*

Some clothing that I really like wearing is an outfit that I wore to my friend's wedding. It's a semi-formal outfit of blue trousers, brown leather shoes and a white shirt. I bought it just a few days before the wedding, from a store that is close to where I live. I tried on many outfits in the fitting room before I found this combination that I liked so much. The shirt is a plain white shirt with buttons, which is a good match to the nice Italian leather shoes with thin black laces. Actually, it was my wife who picked out the shoes. So I'm glad she came along. My favorite part is the stylish blue trousers that fit me really nicely. They are just like tailer-made for me. A belt with a big metal buckle really tied everything together. I got quite a few compliments at the wedding and I think I looked quite handsome in my outfit, which was great because I didn't spent a lot of money on it either. Now, I am always in this outfit when I go to weddings or job interviews.

在这个例子中，不仅对喜欢的衣服进行了整体描述和逐一描述，也对买衣服的场景、穿衣服的场合、别人的评价、自己的感受等多方面进行阐述，丰富了描述的内容，也给多样化语言的使用创造了条件。

第四节　Part 2 结尾模块

不管是描述过去经历的开头部分还是细节描述的主体部分，都通过语言模块与框架模块的结合运用，展示考生的语法和词汇的多样性以及内容和结构的完整性、逻辑性。结尾部分可以通过反思模块与让步模块对前文进行总结。反思模块既可以表达对过去的事情的遗憾，也可以表达对未来的真实的或虚拟的愿望。让步模块用"虽然……但是……"的让步模式，对事件进行好坏两个方面的阐述。反思模块与让步模块既起到了对前文进行概括总结与自然收尾的作用，也给考生再次提供展示词汇与语法多样化的机会。

一、反思模块

对前文的总结反思，通常可以用以下短语引入：looking back/upon reflection/in retrospect/to be honest。反思模块可以表达遗憾与愿望。

表达遗憾：I regret …；I could/would/might have …

表达虚拟愿望：I wish …；If … I would …

表达真实愿望：If … I will …

（1）表达遗憾的结尾：

Looking back, I *regret* not learning more about local culture while I was there.

To be honest, I *regret* not going to the beach more often during my holiday.

Upon reflection, I *regret* booking a hotel so close to the main tourist areas, where it was so noisy.

The taxi takes 20 minutes to the airport. The bus takes 1 hour. I took the bus and missed my flight. I *should have* taken the taxi.

It *would have been* amazing to see the animals in the wild, but unfortunately, we didn't visit the wildlife park.

I *could have* waited for you, but I had a meeting in the afternoon.

I *should have* asked for help, but I was just too shy to ask.

Thinking about it now, I *should have* listened to my parents. They always give me good advice.

Looking back, I *should have* studied harder and participated in more social activities in the university so that I could be more competitive in the job market.

In retrospect, I *should have* studied harder at school. If I had studied harder, I might have gone to some top university and would earn a higher salary than what I am making now.

If not for the pandemic, I *would have* traveled a lot all over country with my friends over the years.

反思模块通过回顾过去，表达遗憾，从而创设一个运用虚拟语气的场景，引申出对未来的期望。但回顾过去并不局限于表达遗憾，也可以表达庆幸和欣慰，比如：

If I hadn't attended the party, I *wouldn't* know my friend Xiaoming.

If I hadn't listened to the lecture, I *wouldn't have* known so much about healthy lifestyle and *wouldn't* live so healthily.

（2）表达虚拟愿望的结尾：

To be honest, I *wish I hadn't* bought such an expensive dress.

Looking back, I *wish we had* gone to more museums.

Upon reflection, I *wish I had* made a bigger effort to meet new people.

If I had the chance, I *would* go back to that same restaurant by the beach and watch another sunset.

If I had enough money, I *would* invite lots of friends to this ski resort.

If I went there again, I *would* explore more local villages.

If I could ask Bill Gates just one question, I *would* ask him for the secrets to running a successful business.

If I could go back there again, I *would* love to take my wife and show her the beautiful sunsets.

（3）表达真实愿望的结尾：

In the future, I will do more research before my trip.

Looking forward, I will try to stay calm in that situation.

Next time if I finish work late, I will take a taxi instead of the bus.

In the future, if my computer breaks again, I will ask my friend to help me.

二、让步模块

让步模块 even though/although 所引导的从句表达不足之处，主句则引导积极的方面。例如：

Even though the weather wasn't perfect, the city was beautiful.

Even though not everyone likes Amy, I think she is hilarious.

Even though I wouldn't go there again, I have some good memory about this city.

Although I got a replace for free, I was really annoyed that my laptop broke so quickly.

Even though the flight was really long and tedious, my trip to Japan was amazing.

Even though we are not as close as we used to be, I still consider Amy one of my best friends.

Although the museum needs some repairs and renovation, the exhibits are some of the most fascinating in my country.

The medicine really wiped me out, although it definitely stopped my fever.

反思模块与让步模块也可以结合起来用于 Part 2 的总结性结尾，比如：

Even though we are connected on Facebook and we occasionally exchange festival greetings, I haven't met Rebecca for decades. I wish I could visit her in near future and express my gratitude to her in person.

Even though the flight was really long and tedious, my trip to Japan was amazing. If I had the chance, I would love to go back and see more historical cities like Kyoto one day.

第五节　Part 2 真题实训

每季度雅思口语考试 Part 2 题库共有 50 多道题，内容涵盖人物、物品、地点、事件四个方面。每道题的开头均可运用现在完成时与过去进行时模块，结尾模块则通过反思及让步运用虚拟语气。虽然题目不同，但开头与结尾的语言模块与逻辑框架大同小异，具有较强的相通性和相似性。但主体模块则需要具体的事例，需要符合题目要求的内容与情节。如果考前准备不充分，在考场上很容易陷入无话可说的境地。由于每季的题库庞大，考生无法也不需要每道题都准备故事情节。我们可以把50多道题进行关联组合，以尽量少的素材涵盖尽可能多的题目，以减少素材准备的时间和精力。

以2022年9月到12月雅思口语考试Part 2为例，该题库包含58道题，其中人物10道题、物品17道题、地点6道题、事件25道题。这58道题可进行整合归类，用7个背景素材串联起来。

一、题目整合

2022年9—12月雅思口语考试Part 2的题库具体分类如下：

1. 人物(10题)

① Describe a person you know who is from a different culture.

② Describe a person who is fashionable.

③ Describe a person you know who loves to grow vegetables/fruits.

④ Describe your favorite childhood friend.

⑤ Describe an interesting neighbor.

⑥ Describe a family member you want to work with in the future.

⑦ Describe a popular/well-known person in your country.

⑧ Describe a person you enjoyed talking with.

⑨ Describe a person you follow on social media.

⑩ Describe a person who makes contribution to the society.

2. 物品(17题)

(1)具体物品(8题)。

① Describe a photo you took and you are proud of.

② Describe an object that you think is beautiful.

③ Describe a traditional product in your country.

④ Describe an invention that changed the world.

⑤ Describe something you received for free.

⑥ Describe a toy you got in your childhood.

⑦ Describe a piece of clothing that someone gave to you.

⑧ Describe a gift you would like to buy for your friend.

(2)抽象物品(9题)。

① Describe a movie you watched recently and would like to watch again.

② Describe a program you like to watch.

③ Describe an important thing you learned (not at school or university).

④ Describe a story or a novel that you have read and you found interesting.

⑤ Describe something you do to keep fit and healthy.

⑥ Describe something that surprised you and made you happy.

⑦ Describe something that helps you to focus on study/work.

⑧ Describe a song or piece of music you like.

⑨ Describe a story someone told you and you remember.

3. 地点(6 题)

① Describe a popular place for doing sports (e. g. stadium).

② Describe the home of someone you know well and you often visit.

③ Describe a quiet place where you like to spend your time.

④ Describe an important river/lake in your country.

⑤ Describe a place in the countryside that you visited.

⑥ Describe a city that you think is interesting.

4. 事件(25 题)

① Describe a problem you had while shopping online or in a store.

② Describe a time when you made a decision to wait for something.

③ Describe a time when you received money on your birthday.

④ Describe a time when you had an argument with a friend.

⑤ Describe an outdoor activity you did in a new place recently.

⑥ Describe a time when you forgot an appointment.

⑦ Describe a time when you shared something with others.

⑧ Describe a time when you needed to search for some information.

⑨ Describe a time when you saw a lot of plastic waste (e. g. in a park, on the beach, etc.).

⑩ Describe a time when you enjoyed an impressive English lesson.

⑪ Describe a time when you used your cellphone to do something important.

⑫ Describe a time when someone gave you positive advice on your work.

⑬ Describe an occasion when you lost something in a public place.

⑭ Describe a contest/competition you would like to participate in.

⑮ Describe an important event you celebrated.

⑯ Describe a positive change you made in your life.

⑰ Describe a special day out that didn't cost you much.

⑱ Describe a time when you helped a child.

⑲ Describe a time when you were caught in a traffic jam.

⑳ Describe a time when you were very busy.

㉑ Describe a recent change in life that helps you save a lot of time.

㉒ Describe an occasion when you had a special cake.

㉓ Describe a time you visited a new place.

㉔ Describe a happy event you organized.

㉕ Describe a long walk you have been on.

把以上题目进行整合，可分为 7 类主题背景：户外活动、服装、生日聚会、英语课、名人、繁忙生活、电话(表 3-1)。

表 3-1 Part 2 主题题库

主题	主题模块	串联题目
户外活动 (14)	House & garden	① Describe a person you know who loves to grow vegetables/fruits. ② Describe the home of someone you know well and you often visit. ③ Describe your favorite childhood friend.
	Hiking & picnic	④ Describe a place in the countryside that you visited. ⑤ Describe an outdoor activity you did in a new place recently. ⑥ Describe a long walk you have been on. ⑦ Describe a time when you saw a lot of plastic waste.
	Scenery & relaxation	⑧ Describe a popular place for doing sports (e. g. stadium). ⑨ Describe something you do to keep fit and healthy. ⑩ Describe a quiet place where you like to spend your time. ⑪ Describe a song or a piece of music you like. ⑫ Describe an important river/lake in your country.
	City charm	⑬ Describe a city you think is interesting.
服装 (12)	Qipao & fashion model	① Describe a person who is fashionable. ② Describe a person you follow on social media. ③ Describe a toy you got in your childhood. ④ Describe a gift you would like to buy for your friend. ⑤ Describe a problem you had while shopping online. ⑥ Describe a time when you made a decision to wait for something. ⑦ Describe a time that you had an argument with a friend.
	Qipao & Xiang Embroidery	⑧ Describe an object that you think is beautiful. ⑨ Describe a traditional product in your country.
	Qipao & play	⑩ Describe a piece of clothing that someone gave to you. ⑪ Describe a contest/competition you would like to participate in. ⑫ Describe a time when you shared something with others.

续表

主题	主题模块	串联题目
生日聚会 （10）	Birthday decoration & sentimental reaction & gourmet dishes & birthday noodle & birthday cake & traffic jam	① Describe a happy event you organized. ② Describe an important event you celebrated. ③ Describe a time when you were caught in a traffic jam. ④ Describe a photo you took and you are proud of. ⑤ Describe a time when you needed to search for some information. ⑥ Describe a special day out that didn't cost much. ⑦ Describe something that surprised you and made you happy. ⑧ Describe an occasion when you had a special cake. ⑨ Describe a time when you received money on your birthday. ⑩ Describe something you received for free.
英语课 （6）	Life scenarios in classroom & birthday party in classroom & reflection and feeling	① Describe a person you know who is from a different culture. ② Describe a time when you enjoyed an impressive English lesson. ③ Describe a time when someone gave you positive advice on your work. ④ Describe a person you enjoyed talking with. ⑤ Describe an interesting neighbor. ⑥ Describe a family member you want to work with in the future.
名人 （6）	Celebrity story	① Describe a person who makes contribution to the society. ② Describe a popular/well-known person in your country. ③ Describe a story or a novel you have read and you found interesting. ④ Describe a story someone told you and you remember. ⑤ Describe a movie you watched recently and would like to watch again. ⑥ Describe a program you like to watch.
繁忙生活 （5）	Busy life & wake-up call & exercise	① Describe a time when you were very busy. ② Describe a positive change you made in your life. ③ Describe a time when you forgot an appointment. ④ Describe an important thing you learned (not at school or university). ⑤ Describe a change in life that helps you save a lot of time.
电话 （4）	Looking for my way & attending a conference	① Describe a time when you used your cellphone to do something important. ② Describe a time when you helped a child. ③ Describe an occasion when you lost something in a public place. ④ Describe an invention that changed the world.

二、解题思路

根据 PDF 的框架思路，每道题以现在完成时开头，以虚拟语气结尾，体现语言形式的多样性。以下答案的开头结尾遵循统一的结构和思路，不再展开分析，仅针对主体部分主题模块进行分析、拓展与运用。

（一）户外活动

2022 年 9—12 月雅思口语考试关于户外活动的题库如表 3-2 所示。

表 3-2　户外活动题库

主题	主题模块	串联题目
户外活动 （14）	House & garden	① Describe a person you know who loves to grow vegetables/fruits. ② Describe the home of someone you know well and you often visit. ③ Describe your favorite childhood friend.
	Hiking & picnic	④ Describe a place in the countryside that you visited. ⑤ Describe an outdoor activity you did in a new place recently. ⑥ Describe a long walk you have been on. ⑦ Describe a time when you saw a lot of plastic waste.
	Scenery & relaxation	⑧ Describe a popular place for doing sports (e. g. stadium). ⑨ Describe something you do to keep fit and healthy. ⑩ Describe a quiet place where you like to spend your time. ⑪ Describe a song or a piece of music you like. ⑫ Describe an important river/lake in your country.
	City charm	⑬Describe a city you think is interesting.

1. House & garden

1）串联题目

（1）Describe a person you know who loves to grow vegetables/fruits.

（2）Describe the home of someone you know well and you often visit.

（3）Describe your favorite childhood friend.

2）主题模块

A. House

She lives in an old wooden house surrounded by thriving orchards and vegetable gardens which she has tended to in her entire life.

She lives in an old wooden house, which is almost 70 years old. So it has gone through quite a bit of renovations. The floors, electrical appliances, furniture have been updated or replaced.

B. Garden（1）

I used to live with my grandma when I was a little kid. I remember when I was a child every morning when I got up, I would find my grandma working in the orchards or gardens, pruning, watering, raking, etc. I remember sitting under the trees, eating all the fruits, melons, persimmons, kiwis, dragon fruits, to name just a few.

C. Garden（2）

Every time when I visit her, she will treat me with lots of veggies and fruits: cabbages, lettuce, peanuts, corns, oranges and so on. The veggies go straight from the garden to the pan and then to the table. Everything is just so organic, fresh and tasty.

3）模块解析

模块 A 描述地点，模块 B、C 分别用过去时和现在时描述菜园活动，突出语法和词汇的多样性。语法层面运用了一般现在时、一般过去时、现在完成时；运用了定语、状语、宾语、条件等从句；运用了记忆模块的三个组合表达（used to …，remember doing 以及 would）。词汇层面运用了跟菜园相关的主题词汇，比如：thriving orchards and vegetable gardens，pruning，watering，raking，melons，persimmons，kiwis，dragon fruits，cabbages，lettuce，peanuts，corns，oranges 等。

4）模块运用

（1）Describe a person you know who loves to grow vegetables/fruits.

喜欢种菜的人：房子及旁边的菜园（A），在菜园的过去（B）和现在（C）的生活经历。

（2）Describe the home of someone you know well and you often visit.

经常拜访的人：房子及旁边的菜园（A），在菜园的过去（B）和现在（C）的生活经历。

（3）Describe your favorite childhood friend.

儿时伙伴：儿时伙伴家的房子旁边是菜园（A），菜园的生活经历（B）。

5）参考答案

（1）*Describe a person you know who loves to grow vegetables/fruits.*

● *You should say*：

① *Who this person is*；

② *What he/she grows*；

③ *Where he/she grows those vegetable/fruits*；

④ *And explain how you feel about this person.*

I've come across quite a few green fingers in my life and the person who loves gardening most is definitely my grandmother.

My grandmother is a farmer in my hometown, a remote village in Zhejiang province along the east coast of the country. She lives in an old wooden house surrounded by thriving orchards and vegetable gardens which she has tended to in her entire life. I used to live with my grandma when I was a little kid. I remember when I was a child every morning when I got up, I would find my grandma working in the orchards or gardens, pruning, watering, raking, etc. I remember sitting under the trees, eating all the fruits, melons, persimmons, kiwis, dragon fruits, to name just a few.

Even though my grandma is in her late 80s now, she continues to do gardening. Every time when I visit her, she will treat me with lots of veggies and fruits: cabbages, lettuce, peanuts, corns, oranges and so on. The veggies go straight from the garden to the pan and then to the table. Everything is just so organic, fresh and tasty. In recent years due to grandma's old age, I have tried to persuade her give up gardening. Grandma has turned a deaf ear to my naggings, saying that gardening was her passion which had kept her happy and healthy. I think she is right. If not for gardening, she probably wouldn't be in such great health condition.

(2) Describe the home of someone you know well and you often visit.

☞ You should say:

① Whose home it is;

② How often you go there;

③ What it is like;

④ And explain how you feel about the home.

Honestly, I've been up to my neck in my study. I don't have time visiting anybody frequently except my grandmother's home, which I visit every now and then.

My grandmother is a farmer in my hometown, a remote village in Zhejiang province along the east coast of the country. She lives in an old wooden house, which is almost 70 years old. So it has gone through quite a bit of renovations. The floors, electrical appliances, furniture have been updated or replaced.

In front of the house are several thriving orchards and vegetable gardens. I used to live with my grandma when I was a little kid. I remember when I was a child every morning when I got up, I would find my grandma working in the orchards or gardens, pruning, watering, raking, etc. I remember sitting under the trees, eating all the fruits, melons, persimmons, kiwis, dragon fruits, to name just a few. This is exactly the reason why I have so much attachment to grandma's home. I have ponds of favorite memories out there.

Even though my grandma is in her late 80s now, she continues to do gardening. Every time when I visit her, she will treat me with lots of veggies and fruits: cabbages, lettuce, peanuts, corns, oranges and so on. The veggies go straight from the garden to the pan and then to the table. Everything is just so organic, fresh and tasty.

It is a shame though that due to my tight schedule and the long distance, I am not able to visit my grandma as often as I want to. I wish I could visit my grandma more often.

(3) Describe your favorite childhood friend.

☞ You should say:

① Who he/she is;

② Where you met each other;

③ *What you often did together*;

④ *And explain what made you like him/her.*

I've lost touch with most of my childhood friends but there is one special friend whom I am still in contact with. Her name is Chunyan, I got to know her when I was studying in Grade One in an elementary school that was located in Chunyan's village.

I think I was 6 or 7 years old at that time, and we used to be the best friends. Every day after school we would hang out together, collecting mushrooms and wild berries, catching fish and shrimps, having picnics, to name just a few. I even had quite a few sleep overs in Chunyan's home, which was an old wooden house surrounded by thriving orchards. I remember sitting under the fruit trees with Chunyan, eating all the fruits, melons, persimmons, kiwis, dragon fruits.

Chunyan is definitely my best childhood friend but unfortunately my family moved to the city of Yongkang and then I lost contact with her until 3 years ago when I happened to visit Chunyan's hometown and I asked people about her. Surprisingly, I was told she had gone to Hunan University, which is only 3 kilometers away from my university. So I ended up meeting Chunyan in her university. Interestingly neither of us recognized each other at the first sight, but once we did, we were so excited. We screamed, cheered and hugged each other. We hung out together for the rest of the day, catching up with each other and taking lots of selfies, which I shared on my Wechat moment, along with an account of our story. I got lots of likes.

Even though we were out of touch for many years, we are now close to each other. We are actually planning on our tourist trips for next summer. I wish I had resumed our contact earlier so that we would have spent more quality time together.

6) 模块拓展

以上各题的主体部分大量套用主题模块，并增加了过去完成时的运用。在对儿时伙伴的回答中，也可以把儿时伙伴描述为在农村种菜，但在真实生活中，考生的儿时伙伴更大的可能是仍在上学。以上学为背景，描述与儿时伙伴的再次重逢，用了 surprisingly、interestingly、ended up doing 等语言表达。此题中提到拍照发朋友圈并得到很多点赞，非常接近生活，可用于描述人物、事件、地点、物品等任何可以拍照的情境。

2. Hiking & picnic

1) 串联题目

（1）Describe a place in the countryside that you visited.

（2）Describe an outdoor activity you did in a new place recently.

（3）Describe a long walk you have been on.

（4）Describe a time when you saw a lot of plastic waste.

2) 主题模块

A. Phone call

One day just when I was having breakfast, I received a phone call from my cousin, inviting me to a picnic with a group of hometown fellows. Even though I had heard of the picnic place for quite a few times, I had never visited it.

B. Hiking & picnic place

We hiked up the winding trail on the mountain in front of the village for around 6 or 7 kilometers and got to the community picnic spot with a tinkling spring on the right and a flat and open space on the left, just large enough for a couple of picnic tables. Next to the spring was a small cabin which housed the camping stoves and cook wares.

C. Picnic & food

A couple of hours had passed by when we got to this picnic place and we were hungry. We dug some bamboo shoots and picked some wild mushrooms from the mountain and we cooked them with the chicken, tomatoes, and pickled vegetables（此句型也可转换为记忆模块：I remember digging bamboo shoots, picking wild mushrooms and cooking them with chicken, tomatoes and pickled vegetables）. It was the best delicacy I had ever tried. I took lots of selfies and shared them on the Wechat moment. I got lots of likes.

D. White pollution

Disposable cups and plates were piled on the dinning tables, cans, packages and plastic bags were scattered all over the ground, some had been swept by the wind down to the slope. The once crystal clear brook was floated with bottles and cans. The food leftover was giving out disgusting smell.

3) 模块解析

模块 A 引入活动，模块 B、C 描述活动地点及活动内容，模块 D 描述白色污染。这些模块在语法层面，运用了一般过去时、过去进行时、过去完成时，这里不仅运用了定语、状语、条件、让步等从句。在词汇方面运用了野炊相关的主题词汇，比如：winding trail, community picnic spot, tinkling spring, flat and open space, picnic tables, small cabin, camping stoves, cook wares, dig bamboo shoots, pick wild mushrooms, chicken, tomatoes, pickled vegetables, best delicacy I had ever tried 等。

4) 模块运用

（1）Describe a place in the countryside that you visited.

野炊的地方：电话邀请（A），走路上山到野炊地方（B），野炊并享受美食（C）。

（2）Describe an outdoor activity you did in a new place recently.

户外活动：走路上山到野炊地方（B），野炊并享受美食（C）。

（3）Describe a long walk you have been on.

远足：电话邀请（A），走很远的山路到野炊地方（B），野炊并享受美食（C）。

（4）Describe a time when you saw a lot of plastic waste.

白色污染的地方：电话邀请（A），来到野炊地方（B），到处都是白色污染（D）。

5）参考答案

（1）*Describe a place in the countryside that you visited.*

☞ *You should say*：

① *Where it is*；

② *When you visited this place*；

③ *What you did there*；

④ *And explain how you feel about this place.*

I'd like to share with you a very special place I've visited last spring. It is a self-cooking picnic place back in my hometown, a remote village in Zhejiang province along the east coast.

One day just when I was having breakfast, I received a phone call from my cousin, inviting me to a picnic with a group of hometown fellows. Even though I had heard of the picnic place for quite a few times, I had never visited it. So I agreed. We hiked up the winding trail on the mountain in front of the village for around 6 or 7 kilometers and got to the community picnic spot with a tinkling spring on the right and a flat and open space on the left, just large enough for a couple of picnic tables. Next to the spring was a small cabin which housed the camping stoves and cook wares.

A couple of hours had passed by when we got to this picnic place and we were hungry. We dug some bamboo shoots and picked some wild mushrooms from the mountain and we cooked them with the chicken, tomatoes, and pickled vegetables. It was the best delicacy I had ever tried. I took lots of selfies and shared them on the Wechat moment. I got lots of likes.

As for how I feel about this place. Well, it is definitely a fabulous place. The only downside is that it is too far away from the village, which deters the older people like my grandparents from visiting. If it were close by, the senior residents could also enjoy this public amenity.

（2）*Describe an outdoor activity you did in a new place recently.*

☞ *You should say*：

① *What the activity is*；

② *Who invited you to participate in it*；

③ *Whether you asked for help during the activity*；

④ *And explain what change you had in the activity.*

I am a nature enthusiast and I've had tons of outdoor activities over the years. I'd like to share with you a picnic I had with my friends a couple of months ago in a newly constructed self-cooking picnic spot back in my hometown, a remote village in Zhejiang province along the east coast.

We hiked up the winding trail on the mountain in front of the village for around 6 or 7 kilometers and got to the community picnic spot with a tinkling spring on the right and a flat and open space on the left, just large enough for a couple of picnic tables. Next to the spring was a small cabin which housed the camping stoves and cook wares.

A couple of hours had passed by when we got to this picnic place and we were hungry. We dug some bamboo shoots and picked some wild mushrooms from the mountain and we cooked them with the chicken, tomatoes, and pickled vegetables. It was the best delicacy I had ever tried. I took lots of selfies and shared them on the Wechat moment. I got lots of likes.

As for how I feel about this activity. This is certainly fantastic experience, but I feel bad my parents didn't join us due to my father's health condition. If my parents had been there, the picnic would have been perfect for me.

(3) *Describe a long walk you have been on.*

☞ *You should say*:

① *When this happened*;

② *Where you walked*;

③ *Who you were with*;

④ *And explain how you felt about this long walk.*

Even though I am a nature enthusiast and I love outdoor activities, walking has never been my favorite form of exercise simply because it is boring. However, last summer I took quite a bit of walking while I was having picnic with a group of friends in my hometown, a remote village in Zhejiang province along the east coast.

One day just when I was having breakfast, I received a phone call from my cousin, inviting me to a picnic with a group of hometown fellows. Even though I had heard of the picnic place for quite a few times, I had never visited it. So I agreed. And it turned out to be a long walk involving at least 7 or 8 kilometers for one-way. It took us nearly half an hour to get to the foot of the mountain then we hiked up the winding trail on the mountain. Following a long and gradual slope, we eventually got to the self-cooking picnic spot with a tinkling spring on the right and a flat and open space on the left, just large enough for a couple of picnic tables. Next to the spring was a small cabin which housed the camping stoves and cook wares.

A couple of hours had passed by when we got to this picnic place and we were hungry. We ended up cooking, eating and having a great day in the wildness and walking back in late evening. So altogether I walked for around 15 kilometers, which was very good exercise. If I lived close to my hometown, I would definitely go for lots of walks like this.

(4) *Describe a time when you saw a lot of plastic waste* (*e. g. in a park, on the beach, etc.*)

☞ *You should say*:

① *Where you saw the plastic waste*;

② *When you saw the plastic waste*;

③ *What you did*;

④ *And explain how you felt about this experience.*

Honestly, I haven't seen much white pollution over the years except one occasion when I was appalled by the plastic waste scattered over a picnic spot back in my hometown, a remote village in Zhejiang province along the east coast.

One day when I was having breakfast, I received a phone call from my cousin, inviting me for a picnic on the mountain. I agreed happily as I had picnicked there many times and never failed to have fun. So we hiked up the mountain and got to the self-cooking picnic spot. To our great surprise it was nothing like what it used to be. Disposable cups and plates were piled on the dinning tables, cans, packages and plastic bags were scattered all over the ground, some had been swept by the wind down to the slope. The once crystal clear brook was floated with bottles and cans. The food leftover was giving out disgusting smell. We blew up at this sight, because the picnic spot was by the village and was supposed to be exclusive to the village. Who had made all the mess? Later on, it turned out that some outsiders got to know this picnic spot from the Wechat moment of one of the villagers and found their way here for the picnic. They enjoyed the facilities but left the mess to us! So we ended up cleaning up the place and putting up a sign requesting picnickers clean up after each use.

Looking back, I think we should have prohibited the outsiders to use the picnic spot, but the villagers were just too kind and generous to make the prohibition.

6) 模块拓展

对野炊地点、野炊活动及食物的描述可用于多种场合。关于食物的表达不仅可用于日常生活对话，也可运用于各类口语题目，比如，涉及地点的题目(美食街;喜欢的餐馆、田园生活)，涉及人物的题目(擅长烹饪的人)，涉及事件的题目(有趣的事、愉快的一天)，涉及节日的题目(节日做饭聚餐)等。

3. Scenery & relaxation

1) 串联题目

(1) Describe a popular place for doing sports (e.g. stadium).

(2) Describe something you do to keep fit and healthy.

(3) Describe a quiet place where you like to spend your time.

(4) Describe a song or a piece of music you like.

(5) Describe an important river/lake in your country.

2) 主题模块

A. Beautiful scenery & quiet place

The scenery along the way is so beautiful: the lush trees, the clear water and the fragrant flowers. It is very quiet out there, with no hustle and bustle of the city, no horns. All you can hear is the sound of nature, the chirping of the birds and the rustling of the tree.

B. Physical & mental benefits

This is a very popular place because jogging by the river brings physical and mental benefits.

Physically, jogging is low impact cardio exercise that fits everybody: young or old, male or female. It burns calories, builds muscles, improves heart rates and helps people stay healthy and energetic.

Mentally, it is relaxing and soothing. Your mind will be slowly relaxing away from the day-to-day worries of work or study and is allowed to drift off to appreciate the beauty of nature. That is just the right type of silent meditation that your mind needs, or as people say, just "unplug" from the world of electronics.

Every time when I jog along the river while admiring the stunning views, breathing the fresh air and basking in the morning sun, I am completely energized and feeling terrific.

C. Wish for good weather

It is a shame that we are not able to jog by the river when weather is not good, particularly during the winter days when we have much snow and rain. I really wish we had more sunny days so that we could jog by the river more frequently.

D. Music & environment

It was sung by a beautiful lady whose voice was rather deep and resonant. The song had really catching tune so that I could sing along easily even though I am kind of tone deaf.

What really struct us was its philosophical lyrics which went something like "Every creature is our sibling; Every species is a child of mother nature."

"Human being is no more than a species in nature. For another toss of coin, we could have been fungi or insects or any other species that are known or unknown to human." I couldn't agree more with her on that.

3) 模块解析

模块 A 描述风景及安静，模块 B 说明运动促进身心健康，模块 C 以虚拟语气表达愿望。模块 A、B 是对客观事实的描述，运用一般现在时，未涉及多种时态，但在语言层面提供了丰富的主题词汇与句型。模块 D 从歌曲主题引申到环境保护，既运用了虚拟语气，又为环保主题积累素材。

4) 模块运用

（1）Describe a popular place for doing sports (e. g. stadium).

湘江边：描述江边的风景（A），并说明江边跑步促进身心健康（B）。

（2）Describe something you do to keep fit and healthy.

江边跑步：描述江边风景（A），并说明跑步对身心健康的影响（B）。

（3）Describe a quiet place where you like to spend your time.

山顶的亭子：描述山顶的风景（A），在亭子里专注学习，学习之余散步放松（B）。

（4）Describe a song or a piece of music you like.

山顶茶馆喝茶时听的歌：描述周边风景（A），引入音乐与环保主题模块（D）。

（5）Describe an important river/lake in your country.

长江的支流——湘江：描述江边风景（A）及湘江给当地居民提供休闲娱乐场所（B）。

以上题目把地点（安静场所、运动场所）、物品（集中注意力的东西）与事件（保持健康的运动）结合起来，聚焦于对户外场景及户外活动的描述。户外活动需要有好天气，因此结尾部分均可以用虚拟语气表达对好天气的愿望（C）。

5）参考答案

（1）*Describe a popular place for doing sports*（*e. g. stadium*）.

☞ *You should say*：

① *Where it is*；

② *When you went there*；

③ *What you did there*；

④ *And explain how you feel about this place.*

I've been a sporty person and have been to tons of sports arenas over the years and one of the most popular places is the trail by the Xiang River across my school where people jog or stroll for exercise. This trail was constructed when I was studying in high school.

This area is very popular, particularly among the residents who live close by. The scenery along the way is so beautiful: the lush trees, the clear water and the fragrant flowers. It is very quiet out there, with no hustle and bustle of the city, no horns, all you can hear is the sound of nature, the chirping of the birds and the rustling of the tree. Every time when I jog along the river while admiring the stunning views, breathing the fresh air and basking in the morning sun, I am completely energized and feeling terrific.

This is a very popular place because jogging by the river brings physical and mental benefits. Physically, jogging is low impact cardio exercise that fits everybody. young or old, male or female. It burns calories, builds muscles, improves heart rates and helps people stay healthy and energetic. Mentally, it is relaxing and soothing. Your mind will be slowly relaxing away from the day-to-day worries of work or study and is allowed to drift off to appreciate the beauty of nature. That is just the right type of silent meditation that your mind needs, or as people say, just "unplug" from the world of electronics.

Yes, this is a very popular place for doing sport. It is a shame that we are not able to jog by the river when weather is not good particularly during the winter days when we have much snow and rain. I really wish we had more sunny days so that we could jog by the river more frequently.

（2）*Describe something you do to keep fit and healthy.*

☞ *You should say*：

① What it is；

② When you do it；

③ Who you do with；

④ And explain why you think this method is important.

I've been a sporty person and I've done lots of sports and games to maintain health. One of the exercises I often do is strolling along the walking trail by the Xiang River across my school.

I often start my day with morning joggings on the tree-lined scenic path along the river. I often do it by myself so that I can totally immerse myself in nature without being interrupted by anybody. The scenery along the way is so beautiful: the lush trees, the clear water and the fragrant flowers. It is very quiet out there, with no hustle and bustle of the city, no horns, even no phone signals, all I can hear is the sound of nature, the chirping of the birds and the rustling of the tree. Every time when I jog along the river, admiring the stunning views, breathing the fresh air and basking in the morning sun, I am completely energized and feeling terrific.

I think jogging by the river brings me physical and mental benefits. Physically, jogging is low impact cardio exercise that burns calories, builds muscles, improves heart rates and helps me stay healthy and energetic. Mentally, it is relaxing and soothing. My mind will be slowly relaxing away from the day-to-day worries of my study and is allowed to drift off to appreciate the beauty of nature. That is just the right type of silent meditation that my mind needs, or as people say, just "unplug" from the world of electronics.

It is a shame though that I am not able to jog by the river when weather is not good particularly during the winter days when we have much snow and rain. I really wish we had more sunny days so that I could enjoy outdoor jogging more frequently.

(3) Describe a quiet place where you like to spend your time.

☞ *You should say:*

① *Where it is;*

② *How often you go there;*

③ *What you do there;*

④ *And explain how you feel about this place.*

Well, I've been to lots of quiet places over the years and a very special place that I'd like to visit is an exquisite pavilion on top of the Yuelu Mountain, a renowned tourist attraction in my city. I got to know this place when I was hiking up the mountain many years ago.

The pavilion is right on top of the mountain. It is very quiet out there, with no hustle and bustle of the city, no horns, even no phone signals. All I can hear is the sound of nature, the chirping of the birds and rustling of the trees. I often go there to work or study simply because it is so quiet out there and I can fully concentrate on what I am doing. It helps me to "unplug" myself from the world of electronics. You know I can't help checking my social media constantly when there is access to Internet. So the pavilion is just perfect for concentration. It has a stone table in the middle with benches built to the sides. I often sit on one of the benches for hours reading books or working on my laptop. When I am mentally tired, I will get up, take a stroll and admire the stunning views. It is very relaxing and refreshing. My mind will be slowly relaxing away from my work and is allowed to drift off to appreciate the beauty of nature.

It is a shame though that I am not able to visit the pavilion when weather is not good particularly during the winter days when we have much snow and rain. I really wish we had more sunny days so that I could use the pavilion more frequently.

（4）*Describe a song or piece of music you like.*

☞ *You should say*：

① *What the song or music is*；

② *What kind of song or music it is*；

③ *Where you first heard it*；

④ *And explain why you like it.*

Well, honestly speaking, I've never been really into music but there is one special song that has left me indelible imprints. I first heard this song when I was hanging out with my friend Amy in a tea house on top of the Yuelu Mountain, the renowned tourist attraction in my city.

The tea house happened to be celebrating its 10 years' anniversary, so there were some special events going on, one of which was the live music concert by a live band and some singers. Amy and I were really struck by a song titled "We Are a Family". It was sung by a beautiful lady whose voice was rather deep and resonant. The song had really catching tune so that I could sing along easily even though I am kind of tone deaf. However, what really struct us was its philosophical lyrics which went something like "Every creature is our sibling; Every species is a child of mother nature."

This lyrics really resonated with us deeply, particularly because we were totally immersed in nature with the stunningly beautiful surroundings: the lush trees, the fragrant flowers, the birds and butterflies … It was very peaceful and quiet. We hummed the song while sipping the tea and admiring the stunning views. It was so relaxing and refreshing. Suddenly my friend Amy said "Well, human being is no more than a species in nature. For another toss of coin, we could have been fungi or insects or any other species that are known or unknown to human." I couldn't agree more with her on that.

（5）*Describe an important river/lake in your country.*

☞ *You should say*：

① *Where it is*；

② *How big/long it is*；

③ *What it looks like*；

④ *And explain why it is important.*

I've seen lots of significant rivers in different parts of the country over the years but the one that is most special to me is the Xiang River, one of the principal tributaries of the Yangtze running across Hunan and Guangxi province before flowing into the Dongting Lake and merging into the Yangze.

The river plays a crucial role in the development and prosperity of the two provinces it flows through because it is the main water resources for agricultural, industrial and household purposes.

In addition, Xiang River provides the local residents with recreation and entertainment. Take myself as an example, I often start my day with morning joggings along the tree-lined scenic path along the river. Every time when I jog along the river while admiring the stunning views, breathing the fresh air and basking in the morning sun, I am completely energized and feeling terrific, very relaxing and refreshing. In the middle of the river there is an orange oasis with a huge sculpture of Chairman Mao overlooking the river where he used to swim. This is the iconic landmark of the city.

The river nourishes the ecosystem it runs through, and the scenic spots along the river as well as the orange oasis are the renowned tourist attractions in my city that attract people from all over the country.

Surprisingly though there aren't many water activities on the river, so far I have just noticed sporadic cases of boating and fishing. If activities like canoeing, kayaking or rafting were developed, the river would bound to be more popular and appealing to the residents as well as to the tourists.

6) 模块拓展

主题模块 A 关于风景及安静的段落可用于大量话题，尤其是关于事件及地点的话题，均可提及风景。主题模块 B 关于运动对人的身心健康的影响，是雅思口语考试的热点话题，在三个部分的考题中均高频出现。此模块关于有益于身心健康的描述可用于户外运动、旅游健身等话题。

主题模块 C 设计了虚拟语气的情境，可用于任何户外活动的结尾段落，表达愿望。

主题模块 D 不仅运用了虚拟语气以及较高级的主题词汇，也对环保问题提出自己独特的见解，可运用于 Part 1 及 Part 3 关于环保的讨论。

4. City charm

1) 串联题目

Describe a city that you think is interesting.

2) 主题模块

A. Food

It's an absolute Mecca for foodies like me, which means there are lots of delicious local snacks and excellent cuisines. The stinky tofu is the most famous local snack, which is crispy outside and tender inside.

B. Dynamism

Changsha is a thriving, lively and dynamic city where you can see a wide range of theaters, opera houses, galleries, exhibitions and night clubs, etc. Even in the evenings the streets, shops and pubs are bustling, which creates a great atmosphere.

C. Nature

The city presents the stunning sceneries: the lush trees, the thriving gardens, walking trails, exquisite pavilions and many more, with the Xiang River and Yuelu Mountain, the most renowned tourist attractions, as the highlight of the scenery.

D. History

Changsha is a city with a long history, so there are tons of fascinating museums and historical buildings, with Hunan Provincial Museum as its highlight, which houses the well-preserved Mawangdui Han Tomb, dating back to more than 2000 years.

3) 模块解析

以上模块以因果关系、定语从句进行了大量例子论证。对城市的描述从美食美景、城市活力、自然风光及城市历史四个方面展开。每个方面进行举例论证，把抽象概念具体化，降低了题目难度，且条理清晰。

4) 模块运用

(1) Describe a city you think is interesting.

有趣的城市：美食(A)，活力(B)，风景(C)，历史(D)。

5) 参考答案

(1)*Describe a city that you think is interesting.*

☞ *You should say*：

① *Where it is*；

② *What the city is famous for*；

③ *Why it is interesting*；

④ *And explain how you feel about it.*

I've been to many cities of the country, be it metropolitan cities or small, quiet cities. The most interesting city I think is Changsha, the capital of Hunan province. I first got to know this city while I was watching a documentary about Changsha through TV many years ago. Then I went to University in Changsha and experienced the charm of the city in person.

There are tons of reasons why I like this city. To start with, it's an absolute Mecca for foodies like me, which means there are lots of delicious local snacks and excellent cuisines. The stinky tofu is the most famous local snack, which is crispy outside and tender inside. Changsha is a thriving, lively and dynamic city where you can see a wide range of theaters, opera houses, galleries, exhibitions and night clubs, etc. Even in the evenings the streets, shops and pubs are bustling, which creates a great atmosphere.

In addition, Changsha is a great combination of nature and history. The city presents the stunning sceneries: the lush trees, the thriving gardens, walking trails, exquisite pavilions and many more, with the Xiang River and Yuelu Mountain, the most renowned tourist attractions, as the highlight of the scenery. At the same time, Changsha is a city with a long history, so there are tons of fascinating museums and historical buildings, with the Hunan Provincial Museum as its highlight, which houses the well-preserved Mawangdui Han Tomb, dating back to mroe than 2000 years.

Changsha is a city of fun that draws visitors from all over the country, however, internationally it is not so well-known, which, I think, is partly due to the insufficient English introduction of this city through media. Should more effort be made to let the world know Changsha, I bet tourists from all over the world would flock to this city.

6）模块拓展

本书前文分类模块的地点描述中，对美食、博物馆、建筑及交通阻塞等主题均有详细介绍及真题讲解，此处不再赘言。

（二）服装

2022 年 9—12 月，雅思口语考试关于服装的题库如表 3-3 所示。

表 3-3 服装题库

主题	主题模块	串联题目
服装 （12）	Qipao & fashion model	① Describe a person who is fashionable. ② Describe a person you follow on social media. ③ Describe a toy you got in your childhood. ④ Describe a gift you would like to buy for your friend. ⑤ Describe a problem you had while shopping online. ⑥ Describe a time when you made a decision to wait for something. ⑦ Describe a time that you had an argument with a friend.
	Qipao & Xiang Embroidery	⑧ Describe an object that you think is beautiful. ⑨ Describe a traditional product in your country.
	Qipao & play	⑩ Describe a piece of clothing that someone gave to you. ⑪ Describe a contest/competition you would like to participate in. ⑫ Describe a time when you shared something with others.

本主题下的 12 道题均以旗袍为主线，把对旗袍的描述运用于每一道题中，根据题目特点，增加关于湘绣及戏剧表演的主题模块。

1. Qipao & fashion

1）串联题目

（1）Describe a person who is fashionable.

（2）Describe a person you follow on social media.

（3）Describe a toy got in your childhood.

（4）Describe a gift you would like to buy for your friend.

（5）Describe a problem you had while shopping online.

（6）Describe a time when you made a decision to wait for something.

（7）Describe a time that you had an argument with a friend.

2）主题模块

A. Qipao & shopping

It happened three years ago when I was looking for a fancy dress in a mall for my friend's wedding. I had wandered for a solid hour in the huge mall before I caught sight of a very stylish lady in a gorgeous blue silk Qipao dress which was sleeveless, ankle-long, and very well-cut. It just hugged her body completely like a second skin and accentuated her hour-glass figure. Just when I was appreciating her outfit enviously, she took a few steps towards me with such charming smile and warmly invited me into the store. She turned out to be the seller and fashion model of the clothing store. So I ended up buying that Qipao and adding her as my Wechat friend.

B. Fashion model

As a fashion model, Amy often wears the fashionable clothes in her store to attract customers. She often wears the formal clothes like bodycon dresses, suits, skirt suits, etc. and she has a wide range of accessories to match with different clothing: shoes, necklaces and earrings of different designs and colours. Anyway, she always looks very feminine and presentable.

3）模块解析

以上主题在语法层面运用了一般过去时、一般现在时、过去进行时、过去完成时。在语言层面，运用了服装及饰品的主题词，运用了 turned out ...、ended up doing ...表达真相与结果。

4）模块运用

（1）Describe a person who is fashionable.
服装店的模特：被穿旗袍的模特吸引而买旗袍（A），模特穿时尚衣服推销商品（B）。

（2）Describe a person you follow on social media.
服装店的模特：被穿旗袍的模特吸引而买旗袍（A），模特穿时尚衣服自拍发朋友圈（B）。

（3）Describe a toy you got in your childhood.
穿旗袍的芭比娃娃：描述旗袍（A），给芭比娃娃穿时尚衣服（B）。

（4）Describe a gift you would like to buy for your friend.
给朋友买旗袍：好朋友商城试穿旗袍很好看（A），但家境贫寒，买不起（B）。

（5）Describe a problem you had while shopping online.
被网上模特穿旗袍的广告吸引而买旗袍（A），但因质量问题退货遇到困难。

（6）Describe a time when you made a decision to wait for something.

商城试穿旗袍很好看(A)，但是尺码太小需要调货。

（7）Describe a time that you had an argument with a friend.

商城试穿旗袍很好看(A)，但是觉得太贵不值得买，朋友觉得应该买。

5) 参考答案

（1）*Describe a person who is fashionable.*

☞ *You should say：*

① *Who he/she is；*

② *What he/she does；*

③ *What kind of clothes he/she wears；*

④ *And explain why you think this person is fashionable.*

I've come across quite a few fashionable people in my life and my real fashion icon is Amy, a seller in a chic clothing store. I got to know Amy when I was shopping in her store.

It happened three years ago when I was looking for a fancy dress in a mall for my friend's wedding. I had wandered for a solid hour in the huge mall before I caught sight of a very stylish lady in a gorgeous blue silk Qipao dress which was sleeveless, ankle-long, and very well-cut. It just hugged her body completely like a second skin and accentuated her hour-glass figure. Just when I was appreciating her outfit enviously, she took a few steps towards me with such charming smile and warmly invited me into the store. She turned out to be the seller and fashion model of the clothing store. So I ended up buying that Qipao and adding her as my Wechat friend.

As a fashion model, Amy often wears the fashionable clothes in her store to attract customers. She often wears the formal clothes like bodycon dresses, suits, skirt suits, etc. and she has a wide range of accessories to match with different clothing: shoes, necklaces and earrings of different designs and colours. Anyway, she always looks very feminine and presentable.

However, Amy has moved to work in another city. If she were still in my city, I would continue to be a frequent visitor of her store.

（2）*Describe a person you follow on social media.*

☞ *You should say：*

① *Who he/she is；*

② *How you knew him/her；*

③ *What he/she posts on social media；*

④ *And explain why you follow him/her on social media.*

Honestly I haven't got much time to follow people on social media over the years, but there is one person I will check on Wechat moment every now and then. That is my fashion icon Amy, a seller in a chic clothing store. I got to know Amy when I was shopping in her store.

It happened three years ago when I was looking for a fancy dress in a mall for my friend's wedding. I had wandered for a solid hour in the huge mall before I caught sight of a very stylish lady in a gorgeous blue silk Qipao dress which was sleeveless, ankle-long, and very well-cut. Just when I was appreciating her outfit enviously, she took a few steps towards me with such charming smile and warmly invited me into the store. The lady turned out to be the seller and fashion model of that store. The Qipao she was in was the commodity carried by the store. So I ended up buying that Qipao and adding her as my Wechat friend.

Ever since then I have followed Amy on her Wechat moment because she often posts the clothes in her store and sometimes she posts her own selfies, wearing the clothes and accessories she is selling. By following her on the social media, I can catch up with the latest clothing in her store and make purchases. I like Amy's taste and style in clothing. She often wears the formal clothes like bodycon dresses, suits, skirt suits, etc. and she has a wide range of accessories to match with different clothing: shoes, necklaces and earrings of different designs and colours.

Over the years Amy has been my fashion icon that I follow closely on social media and on clothing. She always looks so feminine and presentable. I wish I had as good an eye on fashion as Amy.

(3) *Describe a toy you got in your childhood.*

☞ *You should say*:

① *What it was*;

② *When you got it*;

③ *How you got it*;

④ *And explain how you felt about it.*

Even though I had lots of toys when I was a kid, I haven't been able to recall what toys I had except a Barbie doll that was given to me by my aunt for my birthday.

The Barbie was tall and slim, with long and curly hair. When I first saw her, she was in a gorgeous blue silk Qipao that was sleeveless, ankle-long with two side slits. The Qipao was very well-cut and fitting. It just hugged her body completely and well-accentuated her hour-glass figure. She looked very feminine and presentable. The real standout of the Barbie was that she was lifelike. When I patted her, she would cry and her eyes would blink. As for how I feel about the Barbie, well, I was on top of the world at this gift. The Barbie came with a wardrobe filled with her clothes and accessories. So I used to be crazy about dressing her up with all the stylish clothes, bodycon dresses, suits, skirt suits and matched them with accessories, shoes, necklaces and earrings of different colours and designs. Every evening I would fall asleep with the Barbie in my arms. I remember holding the Barbie, walking along the winding paths through the village and collecting compliments.

Yes, that was my favorite toy, but it was a shame I no longer have the doll and neither do I have a photo of it. If I still had the doll, I would keep it as a house decoration and a good souvenir.

(4) *Describe a gift you would like to buy for your friend.*

☞ *You should say*:

① *What gift you would like to buy*;

② *Who you would like to give it to*;

③ *Why you want to buy this gift for him/her*;

④ *And explain why you would like to choose that gift.*

I've bought lots of gifts for different friends over the years. There is one particular gift that I would like to buy for my friend Amy. That is a Qipao, the traditional Chinese women's gown.

It happened two weeks ago when I was hanging out with Amy in the mall. We had wandered for a solid hour before we got to a chic clothing store where Amy tried on a blue silk Qipao. She looked gorgeous in it. It was sleeveless, ankle-long, with two side slits. The real standout of the dress was that it was very well-cut and fitting, just hugged her body completely and well-accentuated her hour-glass figure. It was just like tailor-made for her. However, after being told that it cost 500 RMB, Amy took it off and put it back. Then she whispered to me "well, I can't afford it" but her eyes kept wandering at the Qipao. The way she looked at the Qipao has lingered in my memory.

Amy is from a poor family in a remote village. I understand this dress is too luxurious for her. I want to buy this dress for her because I know she loves it and she looks so good in it. In addition, Amy has been my best friend over the years who has given me tremendous support and help whenever I have any difficulty in my personal and professional life. I want to buy this dress for her as her birthday gift. I bet she would do the same for me if she were in my shoes.

（5）*Describe a problem you had while shopping online.*

☞ *You should say*:

① *When it happened*;

② *What you bought*;

③ *What problems you had while shopping online*;

④ *And explain how you felt about it.*

I've been a compulsive online shopper over the years and have had lots of pleasant online shopping experience. However, there was one time when I had some difficulty in returning and refunding the commodity that I had bought on Taobao, the most famous platform for online shopping in China.

One day when I was browsing online, suddenly an advertisement popped up on the screen. It was a bodycon dress that immediately captivated me. It was very well-cut and stuck completely to the body of the model, which well complimented. In addition, I liked the colour and the material. It was a blue silk dress, very feminine and presentable. So I ended up buying it without hesitation. However, when I received it after a few days I could hardly squeeze myself in because it was way too small at the hip but too big at the waist. On top of that, it was definitely not made of silk as had been claimed. It seemed to be made of polyester. I immediately decided to return and refund the product. I could have done that easily as Taobao has the 7-day unconditional return policy but as I was just in the middle of something when the dress arrived so I forgot to return it within 7 days. Two weeks had passed when I realized that I hadn't return the dress yet. The seller declined my request to return, but I argued that the dress was not made of silk and that a faulty item deserved a full refund beyond the 7-day timeline. Anyway, to make a long story short, eventually I contacted the customer service of Taobao and got a full refund.

Looking back, if I had returned it within the 7 days, I wouldn't have got into all the trouble of refunding. That is a good lesson for me.

（6）Describe a time when you made a decision to wait for something.

☞ *You should say*：

① *When it happened*；

② *What you waited for*；

③ *Why you made the decision*；

④ *And explain how you felt about the decision.*

Well, I've been fully occupied with my work and have hated waiting over the years, however, there was one exception that I chose to wait for a dress delivered to me from Shanghai.

It took place last summer when my best friend Amy and I were shopping in a chic clothing store. I really liked a gorgeous blue silk Qipao that I tried on. It was sleeveless, ankle-long, with two side slits. It had a standing collar with a long line of exquisite handmade buttons coming from the collar all the way down to the right hip. The real standout of the dress was that it was very well-cut and fitting. It just hugged my body completely and well-accentuated my hour-glass figure. Just when I was ready to pay for it, somehow I felt that my shoulders were kind of restricted out of tightness, but unfortunately I was told that the store had run out of the bigger size of this item and the only choice would be to order one from its chain store in Shanghai. However, the delivery service was being suspended in Shanghai. I was between two minds whether I should take the one I was on or whether I should wait. Then my friend said, "You won't feel comfortable if it limits your movement." So I decided to wait for the dress from Shanghai. I ended up waiting for 2 months before I eventually got the dress.

Looking back, I think I made the right decision, because I gained a couple of pounds during the winter and if I had bought the one of the smaller size, I wouldn't have been able to wear it the following summer.

（7）Describe a time when you had an argument with a friend.

☞ *You should say*：

① *When it happened*；

② *Why you argued*；

③ *How you resolved this argument*；

④ *And explain how you felt about this experience.*

Well, honestly speaking, I hardly have had any arguments with my friends over the years, but if I have to talk about one, I would talk about a gentle argument with my friend Amy. Amy likes to splurge on clothes while I am more frugal with my budget. Three years ago we had an argument regarding whether I should buy an expensive Qipao dress that looked gorgeous on me.

One day Amy and I were shopping in a chic clothing store. I tried on a blue silk Qipao. It looked just fantastic. It was sleeveless, ankle-long with two side slits. The real standout of the dress was that it was very well-cut and fitting. It just hugged my body completely and well-accentuated my hour-glass figure. However, it was very expensive. It would cost me nearly 3000 RMB. So I took it off and put it back. Amy exclaimed, "You look so nice in this dress. Why don't you buy? You can't always find a good dress like this. You should buy it." And I said, "Well, I don't think it worthwhile to spend that much money on a dress." And she went something like "but you can afford it, can't you?" And I argued, "Yes, but I would rather save the money. With 3000 RMB, I could do a lot of things." Amy couldn't understand me and tried to persuade me to buy it. I simply turned a deaf ear to her suggestion.

Looking back, I am glad I was not persuaded by Amy. If I had bought the Qipao, I wouldn't have been able to afford the new laptop to replace the old one when it collapsed a couple of weeks later.

6) 模块拓展

本主题以旗袍为背景,根据题目要求编故事。前三道题与两段主题模块的吻合度比较高,可以大量套用。后面四道题,则需要在描述旗袍的基础上,根据题意设问并解答问题。比如,给朋友买旗袍,为什么要给朋友买?网上购买旗袍,碰到了什么问题,如何解决?旗袍试穿效果很好,为什么要等待?为什么与朋友意见不同?考生针对以上问题,做出合理解释即可。有的问题比较复杂,难以用几句话解释清楚。这时可以用"to make a long story short"跳过一些中间的步骤,比如"Anyway, to make a long story short, eventually I contacted the customer service of Taobao and got a full refund."类似的表达还有"ended up doing",比如"So I ended up buying that Qipao and adding her as my Wechat friend."

此外,用记忆模块的三个表达方式(used to …、would …、remember doing …)讲故事,可以让表达生动形象、言简意赅,同时充分体现词汇和语法的多样性。例如:

So I **used to** be crazy about dressing her up with all the stylish clothes, bodycon dresses, suits, skirt suits and matched them with accessories, shoes, necklaces and earrings of different colours and designs. Every evening I **would** fall asleep with the Barbie in my arms. I **remember holding** the Barbie, **walking along** the winding paths through the village and **collecting compliments**.

2. Qipao & Xiang Embroidery

1) 串联题目

(1) Describe an object that you think is beautiful.

(2) Describe a traditional product in your country.

2）主题模块

A. *Xiang Embroidery*

The real standout of the dress was the hand-made embroidery in the front with the patten of a phoenix, which is an auspicious animal in my culture. It was absolutely an incredible work of art. I ended up buying this dress, which cost me an arm and a leg. It was worthwhile, though, as I wore it for many years and I wore it to many special occasions, like weddings, parties, presentations, etc. I remember every time when I wore it to those occasions, I would get lots of compliments.

The designs were often the auspicious animals such as dragon, phoenix, fish or the natural sceneries as mountains, rivers, or temples, and they came with profuse colours, for instance, red, scarlet, pink, purple, dark blue, and bottle green, to name but a few. Everything was handmade and lifelike.

3）模块解析

此模块在旗袍描述的基础上，增加对湘绣的描述。把对湘绣的描述与旗袍描述结合起来。在词汇层面，运用了与湘绣相关的主题词汇，如描述颜色、图案的词汇，以及评价词汇如 handmade、lifelike、incredible work of art、compliment、cost an arm and a leg。在语法层面，运用了过去将来时、一般过去时、定语从句、状语从句等。

4）模块运用

（1）Describe an object that you think is beautiful.

描述旗袍，最突出的是旗袍上的湘绣（A）。

（2）Describe a traditional product in your country.

描述湘绣，最突出的是湘绣馆的旗袍（A）。

对物品的描述如果仅仅描述物品本身，内容比较有限，描述的难度也比较大。可以通过描述活动（购买旗袍、游览湘绣之乡）作为物品描述的拓展。但作为物品描述题，其侧重点应围绕物品。为此，可以把两道题进行结合。在描述旗袍后，说说旗袍上的湘绣。在描述湘绣后，说说湘绣馆的旗袍。

5）参考答案

（1）***Describe an object that you think is beautiful.***

☞ *You should say*：

① *What it is*；

② *Where you saw it*；

③ *What it looks like*；

④ *And explain why you think it is beautiful.*

I've admired lots of pretty objects in my life and one of the beautiful things that has left indelible imprints on me is an exquisite embroidered Qipao. I caught sight of it when I was hanging out with my best friend Amy in a shopping mall a few years ago.

It happened three years ago when I was looking for a fancy dress in a mall for my friend's wedding. I had wandered for a solid hour in the huge mall before I caught sight of a very stylish lady in a gorgeous blue silk Qipao dress which was sleeveless, ankle-long and very well-cut. It just hugged her body completely like a second skin and accentuated her hour-glass figure. The lady turned out to be the seller and fashion model of that store. The Qipao she was in was the commodity carried by the store. So I tried on the Qipao. I was amazed how beautiful I looked in this dress. It fitted me so well that looked like tailor-made for me. The real standout of the dress was the hand-made embroidery in the front with the patten of a phoenix, which is an auspicious animal in my culture. It was absolutely an incredible work of art. I ended up buying this dress, which cost me an arm and a leg. It was worthwhile, though, as I've worn it for three years and I wore it to many special occasions, like weddings, parties, presentations, etc. I remember every time when I wore it to those occasions, I would get lots of compliments.

I still have this dress in my closet, however, I can't squeeze myself in currently as I have gained quite a few pounds over the years. I really wish I could be as slim as I used to be so that I could wear this beautiful Qipao.

（2）Describe a traditional product in your country.

☞ *You should say*：

① *What it is*；

② *When you tried this product for the first time*；

③ *What it is made of*；

④ *And explain how important this product is.*

Honestly I've been too busy to pay much attention to the traditional artifacts over the years, but there is one product that I purchase every now and then as gifts for my family and friends. It is Xiang Embroidery, or Hunan Embroidery, as Xiang is the abbreviation for the province of Hunan.

I first got to know the embroidery 3 years ago when my family and I were taking a tourist trip to Shaping, the embroidery village in the outskirts of my city. Our guide showed us around the biggest exhibition hall where we had the jaw-dropping experience of admiring the stunning embroideries with different patterns, colours and styles.

(Optional paragraph: The main street of Shaping was lined with stores, studios or exhibitions of embroidery. Almost every family was involved in the business related with embroidery. The designs were often the auspicious animals such as dragon, phoenix, fish or the natural sceneries as mountains, rivers, or temples, and they came with profuse colours, for instance, red, scarlet, pink, purple, dark blue, and bottle green, to name but a few. Everything was handmade and lifelike. There was also the double-sided embroidery, the embroidery that carried different patterns on the front and reverse side. It is said only a tiny handful of embroiders can produce double-sided embroidery.)

Something that really caught my eyes was a gorgeous blue silk Qipao. It was sleeveless, ankle-long, with two side slits. The real standout of the dress was the hand-made embroidery in the front with the patten of a phoenix. It was absolutely an incredible work of art. I tried it on and I was amazed how beautiful I looked in this dress. It fitted me so well that looked like tailor-made for me.

Unfortunately, I was not able to afford it. If I had enough money, I would have bought this dress.

6) 模块拓展

对湘绣的描述也可以拓展运用到人物、物品、事件等话题，比如绣湘绣的人、湘绣的照片、湘绣作为礼物、学习刺绣、让你集中注意力的事、有趣的经历等。

3. Qipao & play

1) 串联题目

(1) Describe a piece of clothing that someone gave to you.

(2) Describe a contest/competition you would like to participate in.

(3) Describe a time when you shared something with others.

2) 主题模块

A. Performance

I was amazed how gorgeous Amy looked in the play. She walked and behaved like a traditional lady, taking elegant small steps in Qipao and covering half of her face with an exquisite round silk fan, very presentable and feminine. The play won a great success and the applause from the audience simply brought down the house. Amy even won a nick name as "Qipao" lady.

3) 模块解析

本模块运用了表达感叹的宾语从句(I was amazed how gorgeous Amy looked in the play)，运用了俚语(bring down the house)，使用了表达美丽的主题词汇(gorgeous、elegant、exquisite、presentable、feminine)，并对穿旗袍的女性的舞台表现进行细节描述，内容充实有趣。

4) 模块运用

(1) Describe a piece of clothing that someone gave to you.
妈妈送给我旗袍，让我参加戏剧表演(A)。

（2）Describe a contest/competition you would like to participate in.

想参加时装比赛，因为穿着旗袍表演戏剧非常成功（A）。

（3）Describe a time when you shared something with others.

我和朋友商场试穿旗袍很好看，但是朋友没买（参考"Describe a gift you would like to buy for your friend"），朋友借我的旗袍表演戏剧（A）。

说明为什么想参加一个比赛，如果列举理由，比较落于俗套，而谈论过去发生的故事会更有趣味，因此，此题从参加戏剧比赛的成功引申到时装比赛。

5) 参考答案

（1）Describe a piece of clothing that someone gave to you.

☞ *You should say*：

① *What it is*；

② *Who gave it to you*；

③ *When you got it*；

④ *And explain why this person gave you this piece of clothing.*

Honestly I haven't received many items of clothes since I went to university but I received a very beautiful Qipao dress from my mother when I was studying in university.

My mother sent me this tailor-made Qipao because I was going to act as a lady from Qing Dynasty in a play that was to put on in our school English festival. It was a gorgeous blue silk Qipao that was sleeveless, ankle-long with two side slits. It had a standing collar with a long line of exquisite handmade buttons coming from the collar all the way down to the right hip. The real standout of the dress was that it was very well-cut and fitting, just hugged my body completely which well-accentuated my hour-glass figure. When I made my first appearance in the rehearsal everybody exclaimed, "Wow, you turn out to have such a good figure." Well, I had never worn Qipao or anything as tight as that before. In the play I was required to walk and behave like a traditional lady, taking elegant small steps and covering half of my face with an exquisite round silk fan, very feminine. To make a long story short, anyway, our play won a great success and the applause from the audience simply brought down the house. I even won a nick name as "Qipao" lady in my class.

I still have this dress in my closet, however, I can't squeeze myself in currently as I have gained quite a few pounds over the years. I really wish I could be as slim as I used to be so that I could wear this beautiful Qipao.

（2）Describe a contest/competition you would like to participate in.

☞ *You should say*：

① *What the contest is about*；

② *Where the contest will take place*；

③ *When it will be held*；

④ *And explain why you would like to participate in it.*

I've taken lots of contests in my life and the next one I would like to take is the fashion contest in my university. I was suggested to participate in this contest by quite a few of my friends who had watched a play in which I acted as a lady from Qing Dynasty. The play was put on at our school new year gala 3 years ago. I was dressed in a blue silk Qipao that was sleeveless, ankle-long with two side slits. It was very well-cut and fitting, just hugged my body completely which well-accentuated my hour-glass figure. And I walked and behaved like a lady from old times, taking those elegant small steps and covering half of my face with an exquisite round silk fan. I looked very feminine and presentable. This play turned out to be a great success and I ended up getting a nick name as "Qipao" lady. Ever since then I have been suggested repeatedly by my friends that I take part in the university fashion contest that is held in May every year. I think I have a good chance of winning in this contest, but the problem is that I have gained quite a few pounds over the years and now I can hardly squeeze into the Qipao. I wish I could lose some weight and be fit enough for the Qipao.

So yes, I would like to participate in the fashion contest but not until I lose the few pounds I have gained.

（3）*Describe a time when you shared something with others.*

☞ *You should say：*

① *What you shared；*

② *Who you shared it with；*

③ *Why you shared it；*

④ *And explain how you felt about sharing it.*

Though I've been a very sharing person in my life, I don't like to share with people my personal things, like clothing or cosmetic stuff. However, there was one exception. I shared with my best friend Amy my beautiful Qipao while I was studying in high school.

Amy and I were both captivated by this beautiful Qipao while we caught sight of it in the local shopping mall. It was a gorgeous blue silk Qipao that was sleeveless, ankle-long with two side slits. Amy and I both tried it on and it fitted both of us just perfectly. I bought it immediately but Amy didn't because she was not able to afford it. I felt bad when Amy looked at my newly bought dress enviously and I blurted out, "We can share the dress." Amy said, "No, no, no! It's your dress."

A couple of weeks later, Amy was going to act as a lady from Qing Dynasty in a play that was to put on in our school English festival, certainly my Qipao would be the best costume for her. So I lent her my dress. I was amazed how gorgeous Amy looked in the play. She walked and behaved like a traditional lady, taking elegant small steps in Qipao and covering half of her face with an exquisite round silk fan, very presentable and feminine. The play won a great success and the applause from the audience simply brought down the house. Amy even won a nick name as "Qipao" lady.

I am very happy and proud that my Qipao has gained Amy this reputation. I still have this dress in my closet, however, I can't squeeze myself in currently as I have gained quite a few pounds over the years. I would give this Qipao to Amy, should she be slim enough. However, I am out of touch with Amy now.

6) 模块拓展

描述旗袍的主题模块只适用于女生，男生可以用其他服装替代，比如第三章第二节中关于服装的描述。

It's a semi-formal outfit of blue trousers, brown leather shoes and a white shirt. I bought it just a few days before the wedding, from a store that is close to where I live. I tried on many outfits in the fitting room before I found this combination that I liked so much. The shirt is a plain white shirt with buttons, which is a good match to the nice Italian leather shoes with thin black laces. Actually, it was my wife who picked out the shoes. So I'm glad she came along. My favorite part is the stylish blue trousers that fit me really nicely. They are just like tailer-made for me. A belt with a big metal buckle really tied everything together. I got quite a few compliments at the wedding and I think I looked quite handsome in my outfit. Now, I am always in this outfit when I go to a wedding or a job interview.

以上段落在词汇层面，包含了男士服装搭配、服装与服饰等主题词汇；在语法层面，运用了一般现在时、一般过去时、过去完成时，采用了定语从句、状语从句、强调句等句型；在内容层面，提到了购买衣服、选择衣服、描述衣服、评价衣服等多方面内容。

(三) 生日聚会

2022 年 9—12 月雅思口语考试生日聚会题库如表 3-4 所示。

表 3-4　生日聚会题库

主题	主题模块	串联题目
生日聚会（10）	Birthday decoration & sentimental reaction & gourmet dishes & birthday noodle & birthday cake & traffic jam	① Describe a happy event you organized. ② Describe an important event you celebrated. ③ Describe a time when you were caught in a traffic jam. ④ Describe a photo you took and you are proud of. ⑤ Describe a time when you needed to search for some information. ⑥ Describe a special day out that didn't cost much. ⑦ Describe something that surprised you and made you happy. ⑧ Describe an occasion when you had a special cake. ⑨ Describe a time when you received money on your birthday. ⑩ Describe something you received for free.

1）主题模块

A. *Birthday decoration*

We held a surprise party for my father, which means we had got everything ready before we brought in my father. We reserved a private dinning room in our favorite restaurant named "Grandma's Kitchen" in a neighboring village, which we decorated with birthday banners, balloons, light strings and ribbons. We got a two-tiered chocolate fruit cake toppled with berries, cherries, strawberries and pineapples. The whole family, uncles, aunts and cousins, were sitting at the table when I eventually took my father to the party.

B. *Sentimental reaction*

Of course, it was a great pleasant surprise for him. I remember him gasping in surprise, laughing softly and repeatedly saying, "Oh, this is lovely, so lovely."

I was seized by great joy and surprise. I gasped and exclaimed, "Wow, this is lovely, so lovely."

No sooner had we got home after the party than I read a sentimental message on my father's Wechat moment, expressing his gratitude and happiness for this event. However, unfortunately I didn't have a photo to go with it. We simply forgot to take photos. It was such a shame. We should have snapped some photos to capture those special moments in life.

C. *Gourmet dishes*

We ended up singing the birthday song and enjoying all the gourmet dishes ranging from beef and pork to sea food and chicken. We ate to our heart's content as the foods were absolutely out of the world, more delicious than any other dishes I had ever eaten.

D. *Birthday noodle*

The noodle was cooked with chicken broth, mushrooms and pickled vegetables. It was absolutely out of the world and was more delicious than any other noodle I had ever eaten. It turned out that the chef of this restaurant had some secret recipe for noodle cooking passed down from his ancestors.

E. *Birthday cake*

A two-tiered chocolate fruit cake toppled with berries, cherries, strawberries and pine-apples was in the middle of the table. What really struck me was that the birthday cake was baked by my aunt from scratch. Certainly, that had made the cake very special, but what had made it even more special was the design of the cake, some daisies were dotted around the edge of the cake, cause my aunt knew daisy was my favorite flower and my English name. So, this cake was very personal and sentimental which conveyed so much love and care.

I remember blowing off the candles on the cake and making a wish before we ate the cake. The cake was incredibly fluffy and tasty. It was definitely the best cake I had ever tried.

F. Traffic jam

I was held up by the traffic jam on my way to the restaurant. It was a one-hour bus ride from my place to the restaurant. Just half way to the restaurant, the bus stopped and lined up behind a long queue of vehicles. We couldn't see the starting point of the line. Word came that there was an accident in the front that had blocked the road. We waited and waited, but there was just no sign of moving on. The minutes dragged on and I was on pins and needles. There was no turning back, no moving on. I was just totally got stuck in the traffic. The traffic wasn't cleared until around 6 PM.

2) 模块解析

模块 A 开头采用了过去完成时，中间部分使用生日装饰及生日蛋糕的主题词汇，结尾部分采用了过去进行时。模块 B 通过动作、表情描述情感，使语言生动真实，运用了情感主题词汇；运用了倒装、过去完成时、一般现在时、虚拟语气、现在分词表示伴随等，充分体现了语法的多样性和复杂性。模块 C、D 运用了一些好的表达方式，如 ended up doing something、eat to our heart's content、absolutely out of the world、turned out。模块 E 运用了跟蛋糕相关的主题词汇：two-tiered chocolate fruit cake、bake it from scratch、fluffy and ststy、blow off the candle 等。描述蛋糕的特殊性，可以就蛋糕上的图案进行发挥，思路更加开阔，话题更加自由，出时也便于引入一些表达情感和心意的主题词汇，比如：personal and sentimental、convey love and care 等。模块 F 运用了大量描述交通阻塞的语言表达，使用了一般过去时及过去完成时。

3) 模块运用

(1) Describe a happy event you organized. / Describe an important event you celebrated.
筹办爸爸的惊喜生日派对(A)，爸爸很感动，发朋友圈纪念(B)。

(2) Describe a time when you were caught in a traffic jam.
筹办爸爸的惊喜生日派对(A)，碰到交通阻塞(F)。

(3) Describe a photo you took and you are proud of.
筹办爸爸的惊喜生日派对(A)，爸爸很感动，发朋友圈纪念(B)。我抢拍爸爸的照片。

(4) Describe a time when you needed to search for some information.
筹办爸爸的惊喜生日派对(A)，网上找生日聚会的餐馆。有个餐馆评价很高，菜很好吃，尤其是长寿面(C、D)，还给老人打折。

(5) Describe a special day out that didn't cost much.
筹办爸爸的惊喜生日派对(A)，餐馆的菜很好吃，尤其是长寿面(C、D)，还给老人打折。

(6) Describe something that surprised you and made you happy.
家人给我筹办惊喜生日派对(A)，我很感动，发朋友圈纪念(B)，菜很好吃，尤其是长寿面(C、D)。

（7）Describe an occasion when you had a special cake.

家人给我筹办惊喜生日派对(A)，蛋糕很特别(E)，我很感动，发朋友圈纪念(B)。

（8）Describe a time when you received money on your birthday.

家人给我筹办惊喜生日派对(A)，派对上给我红包。我很感动，发朋友圈纪念(B)。

（9）Describe something you received for free.

家人给我筹办惊喜生日派对(A)，菜很好吃，餐馆送我们一份免费的长寿面(C、D)，我很感动，发朋友圈纪念(B)。

4）参考答案

（1）*Describe a happy event you organized. / Describe an important event you celebrated.*

☞ *You should say:*

① *What the event was;*

② *When you had it;*

③ *Who helped you to organize it;*

④ *And explain how you feel about it.*

I have celebrated lots of special occasions in my life and one of the most joyful and special celebrations I have ever had was my father's 50th birthday party.

My mother and I actually held a surprise party for my father, which means we had got everything ready before we brought in my father. We reserved a private dinning room in our favorite restaurant named "Grandma's Kitchen" in a neighboring village, which we decorated with birthday banners, balloons, light strings and ribbons. We got a two-tiered chocolate fruit cake toppled with berries, cherries, strawberries and pineapples. The whole family, uncles, aunts and cousins, were sitting by the table when I eventually took my father to the party. Of course, it was a great pleasant surprise for him. I remember him gasping in surprise, laughing softly and repeatedly saying, "Oh, this is lovely, so lovely." We ended up singing the birthday song and enjoying all the gourmet dishes ranging from beef and pork to sea food and chicken. We ate to our heart's content as the foods were absolutely out of the world, more delicious than any other dishes I had ever eaten. The last dish was the longevity noodle cooked with ginger, chicken and mushroom, which conveyed our wish for the health and longevity of my father.

No sooner had we got home after the party than I read a sentimental message on my father's Wechat moment, expressing his gratitude and happiness for this event. However, disappointedly there were no photos attached. We simply forgot to take photos. It was such a shame. We should have snapped some photos to capture those special moments in life.

（2）*Describe a time when you were caught in a traffic jam.*

☞ *You should say:*

① *When it happened;*

② *Where it happened;*

③ *How you passed the time while waiting;*

④ *And explain how you felt when you were in that traffic jam.*

Well, living in this big city of Changsha, I have gone through lots of traffic jams, and the most frustrating one took place when I was heading to my father's birthday party.

My sister and I had planned a surprise party for my father, which means we would have to get everything ready before my father was brought in. We reserved a private dinning room in our favorite restaurant named "Grandma's Kitchen" in a neighboring town. We had planned that my sister and I would get to the restaurant at 5 pm on that day, putting up the birthday decorations, the birthday banners, balloons, light strings and ribbons and that all the family, uncles, aunts and cousins, would arrive before 6 pm to greet my father who would be brought in at 6: 30.

However, I was held up by the traffic jam on my way to the restaurant. It was a one-hour bus ride from my place to the restaurant. Just half way to the restaurant, the bus stopped and lined up behind a long queue of vehicles. We couldn't see the starting point of the line. Word came that there was an accident in the front that had blocked the road. We waited and waited, but there was just no sign of moving on. The minutes dragged on and I was on pins and needles. There was no turning back, no moving on. I was just totally got stuck in the traffic. The traffic wasn't cleared until around 6 pm. When I got there everybody was waiting for me, including my father. Fortunately all the decorations had been put up by my sister alone but I missed the chance of seeing my father's reaction at the sight of the surprise party. It was said that he choked with joy.

I felt really bad at the jam. I wish I had been there to decorate the room and to greet everybody rather than having everybody waiting for me.

(3) *Describe a photo you took and you are proud of.*

☞ *You should say:*

① *When you took it;*

② *Where you took it;*

③ *What is in this photo;*

④ *And explain why you are proud of it.*

Honestly speaking, I know little about photography, nothing about focusing or filtering, so technically I haven't taken any high-quality photos, but if I have to choose the best photo I've ever taken, I would like to talk about the photo I took for my father while we were celebrating his 50th birthday.

My mother and I actually held a surprise party for my father, which means we had got everything ready before we brought in my father. We reserved a private dinning room in our favorite restaurant named "Grandma's Kitchen" in a neighboring village, which we decorated with birthday banners, balloons, light strings and ribbons. We got a two-tiered chocolate fruit cake toppled with berries, cherries, strawberries and pineapples. The whole family, uncles, aunts and cousins, were sitting by the table when I eventually took my father to the party. Of course, it was a great pleasant surprise for him. I remember him gasping in surprise, laughing softly and repeatedly saying, "Oh, this is lovely, so lovely." He looked so happy. He even looked kind of shy because he had tears in his eyes. So I quickly snapped a photo and captured this special moment. I then forwarded the photo to the family Wechat group.

No sooner had we got home after the party than I saw the photo posted on my father's Wechat moment that went with a very sentimental message, expressing his gratitude and happiness for this event. Looking back I was very proud of myself for taking this photo that has kept bringing back the sweet memories over the years.

(4) *Describe a time when you needed to search for some information.*

☞ *You should say*：

① *What information it was*；

② *When you searched for it*；

③ *How you searched for it*；

④ *And explain why you needed to search the information.*

I would like to share with you my experience of searching for a restaurant for my father's birthday party. A couple of year ago in an early morning when I was having breakfast, I received a phone call from my sister, suggesting that we hold a surprise party for our father's 50th birthday in the coming summer. That was certainly a great idea. My sister happened to be up to her neck in a project at that time so I was responsible for finding a good restaurant.

I went online, searching and browsing for the restaurants all over the city. I visited the websites of dozens of restaurants and then screened and narrowed down to 5 of them. Just when I was comparing carefully and thoroughly the menus, settings and ratings of those restaurants, suddenly an advertisement popped up for a restaurant named "Grandma's Kitchen" on top of the Yuelu Mountain. Then I read the ratings and went through the pictures of dishes in the restaurants. Everything looked just perfect. The restaurant had a very good rating at 4.8 out of 5. Many raters mentioned that the food there was out of the world, particularly the longevity noodle which was cooked with some secret recipe passed down from the ancestor of the chef. In my culture longevity noodle is a must for birthday celebrations to convey good wishes for the birthday person. To make a long story short, I chose this restaurant which turned out to be a great choice. Actually it has become our family favorite restaurant ever since then.

(5) *Describe a special day out that didn't cost much.*

☞ *You should say*：

① *When the day was*；

② *Where you went*；

③ *How much you spent*；

④ *And explain how you feel about that day.*

Well, with the ever-increasing inflation over the years I have been complaining about the rocketing price of almost everything, however there was one occasion when we had a very good deal for a dinner party. We had this party while we were celebrating for my grandfather's 80th birthday.

The party was held in a private dinning room in a restaurant named "Grandma's Kitchen" back in my hometown. There were nearly 20 people attending this banquet including all the family members, some relatives and my grandfathers' close friends. My father ordered up to 20 dishes ranging from beef and pork to sea food, chicken and various veggies. I remember we singing the birthday song and enjoying all the gourmet dishes. We ate to our heart's content as the foods were absolutely out of the world, more delicious than any other dishes I had ever eaten. The last dish was the longevity noodle cooked with ginger, chicken and mushroom, which conveyed our wish for the health and longevity of my grandfather.

Surprisingly, when the bill came we were told that the birthday parties for seniors at or beyond 80 were entitled to a senior discount of 40 percent of the total bill. We couldn't believe our ears! This was just too good to be true! So we ended up paying only 740 RMB, which was amazingly inexpensive for 20 dishes!

As for how I feel about this day, we were certainly happy for the very good price and super tasty food but what really struck us was how the restaurant paid their respect for the senior citizens in their own way. We were really appreciative for that.

No sooner had we got home after the party than I posted a sentimental message on my Wechat moment, expressing my gratitude to this restaurant and calling on people to dine in this restaurant. However, unfortunately I didn't have a photo to go with it. We simply forgot to take photos. It was such a shame. We should have snapped some photos to capture those special moments in life.

（6）*Describe something that surprised you and made you happy.*

☞ *You should say*：

① *What is it*；

② *How you found out about it*；

③ *What you did*；

④ *And explain whether it made you happy.*

I've got lots of pleasant surprises in my life and one of the things that surprised me with joy was my 20th birthday party that my family held for me.

I had thought my mom would cook a big dinner at home for my birthday, which was our usual way to celebrate birthdays. However, just when I was working out in the gym in the afternoon I received a phone call from my mother saying that we would eat out for my birthday in our favorite restaurant named "Grandma's Kitchen" in a neighboring village. When I got there, I was ushered into a private dinning room and I was seized by great joy and surprise. The whole family, uncles, aunts and cousins, were sitting by the table, smiling at me and the room was decorated with birthday banners, balloons, light strings and ribbons. A two-tiered chocolate fruit cake toppled with berries, cherries, strawberries and pineapples was in the middle of the table. I gasped and exclaimed, "Wow, this is lovely, so lovely." We ended up singing the birthday song and enjoying all the gourmet dishes ranging from beef and pork to sea food and chicken. We ate to our heart's content as the foods were absolutely out of the world, more delicious than any other dishes I had ever eaten. The last dish was the longevity noodle cooked with ginger, chicken and mushroom, which was our traditional food for birthday celebrations as the long noodle indicates long life.

No sooner had we got home after the party than I posted a sentimental message on my Wechat moment, expressing my gratitude and happiness for this event. However, unfortunately I didn't have a photo to go with it. We simply forgot to take photos. It was such a shame. We should have snapped some photos to capture those special moments in life.

(7) ***Describe an occasion when you had a special cake.***

☞ *You should say*：

① *When this happened*；

② *Where this happened*；

③ *Who gave you the cake*；

④ *And explain why it was a special cake.*

I've got lots of cakes in my life and the most special one was the birthday cake that my aunt baked from scratch for my 20th birthday.

I had thought my mom would cook a big dinner at home for my birthday, which was our usual way to celebrate birthdays. However, just when I was working out in the gym in the afternoon I received a phone call from my mother saying that we would eat out for my birthday in our favorite restaurant named "Grandma's Kitchen" in a neighboring village. When I got there, I was ushered into a private dinning room and I was seized by great joy and surprise. The whole family, my parents, uncles, aunts and cousins, were sitting by the table, smiling at me and the room was decorated with birthday banners, balloons, light strings and ribbons. A two-tiered chocolate fruit cake toppled with berries, cherries, strawberries and pineapples was in the middle of the table. I gasped and exclaimed, "Wow, this is lovely, so lovely." What really struck me was that the birthday cake was baked by my aunt from scratch. Certainly, that had made the cake very special, but what had made it even more special was the design of the cake, some daisies were dotted around the edge of the cake, cause my aunt knew daisy was my favorite flower and my English name. So this cake was very personal and sentimental which conveyed so much love and care.

I remember blowing off the candles on the cake and making a wish before we ate the cake. The cake was incredibly fluffy and tasty. It was definitely the best cake I had ever tried.

No sooner had we got home after the party than I posted a sentimental message on my Wechat moment, expressing my gratitude and happiness for this event, particularly for the cake. However, unfortunately I didn't have photos to go with it. We simply forgot to take photos. It was such a shame. We should have snapped some photos to capture those special moments in life.

(8) ***Describe a time when you received money on your birthday.***

☞ *You should say*：

① *When it happened*;

② *Who gave you the money*;

③ *Why he/she gave you the money*;

④ *And explain how you felt about it.*

There have been many occasions when I received money as birthday gifts. For example, when I was celebrating my 20th birthday, I received money from everybody who attended the party. I actually made quite a fortune at the party. Let me share with you this special occasion.

I had thought my mom would cook a big dinner at home for my birthday, which was our usual way to celebrate birthdays. However, just when I was working out in the gym in the afternoon I received a phone call from my mother saying that we would eat out for my birthday in our favorite restaurant named "Grandma's Kitchen" in a neighboring village. When I got there, I was ushed into a private dinning room and I was seized by great joy and surprise. The whole family, my parents, uncles, aunts and cousins, were sitting by the table, smiling at me and the room was decorated with birthday banners, balloons, light strings and ribbons. We ended up eating the birthday cake, singing the birthday song and enjoying all the gourmet dishes ranging from beef and pork to sea food and chicken. The highlight of the party was the shower of red envelopes with money inside, which is our traditional way to send money gift. Right after I made the birthday wish, my mom took the lead giving me her red envelope, and then everybody followed and I was accepting red envelopes from everybody, probably 14, 15 envelopes in total, I think. It was really very touching and impressive that I was cared for and loved by such a huge extended family.

No sooner had we got home after the party than I posted a sentimental message on my Wechat moment, expressing my gratitude and happiness for this event. However, unfortunately I didn't have a photo to go with it. We simply forgot to take photos. It was such a shame. I should have snapped some photos to capture those special moments in life.

(9) *Describe something you received for free.*

☞ *You should say*:

① *What it was*;

② *Who you received it from*;

③ *Why you received it for free*;

④ *And explain how you felt about it.*

Well, I've received lots of free gifts over the years. I would like to share with you an occasion when I received the longevity noodle for free from the restaurant where we were holding my 20th birthday party.

The party was held in a private dinning room in a restaurant named "Grandma's Kitchen" back in my hometown. There were nearly 20 people attending this birthday banquet including the family members, some relatives and my close friends. And I ordered up to 20 dishes ranging from beef and pork to sea food, chicken and various veggies. Just when we were talking and eating, suddenly the waiter came in with a big pot of noodle, saying that it was longevity noodle, a gift from the restaurant to wish for the health and longevity of the birthday person. We were overjoyed at the gift and the nice wish. The waiter then served everybody with a bowl of noodle. The noodle was cooked with chicken broth, mushroom and pickled vegetable. It was absolutely out of the world and was more delicious than any other noodle I had ever eaten. It turned out that the chef of this restaurant had some secret recipe for noodle cooking passed down from his ancestors.

No sooner had we got home after the party than I posted some photos and a sentimental message on my Wechat moment, expressing my gratitude to this restaurant and called on people to dine in this restaurant. We ended up coming back frequently mostly for the noodle. If the restaurant hadn't sent us the gift of the longevity noodle, we wouldn't have visited the restaurant so frequently. It seems delivering free gift is an effective promoting strategy in the business world.

5) 模块拓展

关于生日的主题模块：生日的装饰、庆祝、美食、红包、长寿面、蛋糕等模块可以单独也可以组合起来运用于很多话题。比如，特殊场合的庆祝、难忘的事、难忘的人、文化传统、节日美食、喜欢的餐馆、新的地方、早起的一天、昂贵的物品（如蛋糕）、难忘的一餐饭等。关于到家就发朋友圈表示感谢或感想的语句，可用于人物、物品、事件、地点各个方面的很多话题。

(四) 英语课

2022 年 9—12 月雅思口语考试英语课题库如表 3-5 所示。

表 3-5　英语课题库

主题	主题模块	串联题目
英语课 (6)	Life scenarios in classroom & birthday party in classroom & reflection and feeling	① Describe a person you know who is from a different culture. ② Describe a time when you enjoyed an impressive English lesson. ③ Describe a time when someone gave you positive advice on your work. ④ Describe a person you enjoyed talking with. ⑤ Describe an interesting neighbor. ⑥ Describe a family member you want to work with in the future.

1) 主题模块

A. Life scenarios in classroom

She is very professional and innovative as a language teacher. She used to say, "People can only learn to swim by swimming, likewise, you can only learn to speak English by speaking." In order to make the conversations real and meaningful, Rebacca converted the classrooms into different scenarios like hospital, tea house, restaurant, grocery store, etc. by using pictures, decorations, costumes and realia.

B. Birthday party in classroom

Once Rebecca brought to the class a beautiful two-tiered fruit cake. It turned out to be her first birthday in China. The classroom immediately heated up with cheers and clapping. Everybody was thrilled! Then we were taught some English words and expressions related with birthday celebration. And we ended up eating the cake, using the newly learned expressions and sentences at the birthday party and singing the birthday song. I remember everybody was so impressed how interesting and engaging this class was.

C. Reflection and feeling

I think part of the reason why Amy is so interesting and innovative is that she had studied abroad for many years in education and in applied linguistics before she became a teacher. I was blessed to have her in my life as my neighbor and teacher, without whose help I probably wouldn't have been here for this IELTS test.

2) 模块解析

主题模块 A、B 在事件描述中运用了 turned out to be …、ended up doing …，这一语言表达有助于省略一些无须交代的细节，更快捷简练地描述事件的发生发展；运用了以情感词汇为主句谓语动词引导的宾语从句(everybody was so impressed how interesting and engaging this class was)，此句型增加了故事的感染力及语言的复杂性。此外，以上模块运用了大量与英语学习及生日派对相关的主题词汇。

主题模块 C 运用了过去完成时、一般过去时，虚拟语气，定语从句、状语从句等，体现了语法的多样性。

3) 模块运用

(1) Describe a person you know who is from a different culture.
英语外教的教学方法：在课堂创建生活情境(A)，举办生日派对(B)。

(2) Describe a time when you enjoyed an impressive English lesson.
英语外教的课堂：在课堂创建生活情境(A)，举办生日派对(B)。

(3) Describe a time when someone gave you positive advice on your work.
朋友建议我在课堂创建生活情境(A)，我在课堂举办生日派对(B)。

(4) Describe a person you enjoyed talking with.
朋友建议我在课堂创建生活情境(A)，跟她交流很有趣，思考她这么有趣的原因(C)。

(5) Describe an interesting neighbor.
邻居给我上很有趣的英语课，在课堂上创建生活情境(A)，思考她这么有趣的原因(C)。

(6) Describe a family member you want to work with in the future.
堂妹带我去她的英语课堂，在课堂上庆祝生日(B)，思考她教学这么有创意的原因(C)。

4) 参考答案

（1）*Describe a person you know who is from a different culture.*

☞ *You should say*：

① *Who he/she is*；

② *Where he/she is from*；

③ *How you knew him/her*；

④ *And explain how you feel about this person.*

I have made quite a few foreign friends since I went to university and the one that has exerted the most far-reaching influence on me is definitely my oral English teacher Rebecca Jernigan from America. I learned a lot from her when I was attending her classes or participating the extracurricular activities she organized.

As for how I feel about her. Well, she is very professional and innovative as a language teacher. She used to say, "People can only learn to swim by swimming, likewise, you can only learn to speak English by speaking. " In order to make the conversations real and meaningful, Rebacca converted the classrooms into different scenarios like hospital, tea house, restaurant, grocery store, etc. by using pictures, decorations, costumes and realia. Once Rebecca brought to the class a beautiful two-tiered fruit cake. It turned out to be her first birthday in China. The classroom immediately heated up with cheers and clapping. Everybody was thrilled! Then we were taught some English words and expressions related with birthday celebration. And we ended up eating the cake, using the newly learned expressions and sentences at the birthday party and singing the birthday song. I remember everybody was so impressed how interesting and engaging this class was.

Such was very sweet memory about Rebecca, who has left huge footprints in my life, particularly in my journey of English learning. Unfortunately, I haven't met Rebecca for ages ever since she returned to America. I wish I could meet Rebecca one day and tell her that I talked about her in my IELTS test.

（2）*Describe a time when you enjoyed an impressive English lesson.*

☞ *You should say*：

① *When and where you had the lesson*；

② *Who gave the lesson*；

③ *What the lesson was about*；

④ *And explain why you enjoyed the lesson.*

I have had lots of interesting English classes in my life and the one that has left me indelible imprints was an oral English class delivered by my American oral English teacher Rebecca Jernigan. I attended this class when I was studying in university.

Rebecca is a very professional and innovative language teacher. She used to say, "People can only learn to swim by swimming, likewise, you can only learn to speak English by speaking. " In order to make the conversations real and meaningful, Rebacca used to convert the classrooms into different scenarios like hospital, tea house, restaurant, grocery store, etc. by using pictures, decorations, costumes and realia. Once Rebecca brought to the class a beautiful two-tiered fruit cake. It turned out to be her first birthday in China. The classroom immediately heated up with cheers and clapping. Everybody was thrilled! Then we were taught some English words and expressions related with birthday celebration. And we ended up eating the cake, using the newly learned expressions and sentences at the birthday party and singing the birthday song. I remember everybody was so impressed how interesting and engaging this class was.

The sweet memory about this special English class will come flooding back to me every time when I think of my teacher Rebecca. Unfortunately, I haven't met her for ages ever since she returned to America. I wish I could visit her one day and tell her that I talked about her English lesson in my IELTS test.

（3）*Describe a time when someone gave you positive advice on your work.*

☞ *You should say*:

① *When it happened*;

② *Who the person is*;

③ *How the advice affected you*;

④ *And explain how you felt about it.*

There have been many occasions in my life when people gave me constructive suggestions on my work. I would like to talk about my oral English teacher Rebecca Jernigan who was from America and who used to give me some good advice when I was teaching oral English in a language training center for my internship.

I remember I used to complain to Rebacca that my students were just so reluctant to speak and I was at a loss how to make my class engaging and interactive. Rebecca gave me some very good suggestion about making the conversations real. She said, "People can only learn to swim by swimming, likewise, students can only learn to speak English by speaking. " In order to carry out some real and meaningful conversations, she suggested that I convert the classrooms into different scenarios like hospital, tea house, restaurant, grocery store, etc. by using pictures, decorations, costumes and realia. So I took her suggestion. Surprisingly this strategy worked just wonderfully in my class. Students were thrilled and ready to talk in those simulated situations. Interestingly, I even had my birthday party in my English class. I remember bringing to the class a beautiful two-tiered fruit cake and being greeted with the cheering and clapping of the class. We ended up eating the cake, speaking English and singing the birthday song.

Such was very sweet memory that will come flooding back to me every time when I think of my teacher Rebecca. I benefited a lot from her suggestion, without which my class wouldn't have been so engaging and interesting.

（4）*Describe a person you enjoyed talking with.*

☞ *You should say*:

① *Who he/she is*;

② *When you talked*;

③ *What you talked about*;

④ *And explain why you enjoyed talking with this person.*

There are lots of people in my life who I've had delightful conversations with. The one whom I enjoyed talking with the most is definitely my friend Amy, a middle school English teacher in Changsha. I got to know Amy when I was teaching in an English training center for my internship.

I remember I used to complain to my father that my students were just so reluctant to speak and I was at a loss how to make my class engaging and interactive. My father then introduced his friend's daughter Amy to me, who is a very successful and popular teacher in her school. Then Amy and I had our first talk in a cafeteria and what she said was eye-opening and inspiring to me. She said, "People can only learn to swim by swimming, likewise, students can only learn to speak English by speaking." She then gave me lots of ideas on how to carry out some real and meaningful conversations. For example, she suggested that I convert the classrooms into different scenarios like hospital, tea house, restaurant, grocery store, etc. by using pictures, decorations, costumes and realia. So I took her suggestions. Surprisingly this strategy worked just wonderfully in my class. Students were thrilled and ready to talk in those simulated situations.

Amy and I have been great friends ever since then and every time when I talk with her, I can learn a lot from her. I think part of the reason why Amy is so interesting and innovative is that she had studied abroad for many years in education and in applied linguistics before she became a teacher. I was blessed to have her in my life as my friend. Unfortunately, I haven't met Amy for a couple of years since she moved to work in Shanghai. Hopefully I can meet her one day and thank her in person and tell her that I talked about her in my IELTS test.

（5）*Describe an interesting neighbor.*

☞ *You should say*:

① *Who this person is*;

② *How you knew this person*;

③ *What he or she did*;

④ *And explain why you think this person is interesting.*

I've got quite a few interesting neighbors in my life but the one that is most interesting and inspiring is definitely Amy, an English teacher in Central South University, one of the prestigious universities in China. I got to know Amy when I was attending her English class for the kids in the neighborhood.

I used to hate English very much and I had never done well in English exam until I attended Amy's class. She was very humorous and hilarious who never failed to crack up everybody with her witty quips or interesting language games. She used to say, "People can only learn to swim by swimming, likewise, you can only learn to speak English by speaking." Therefore, Amy used to convert the classrooms into different scenarios like hospital, tea house, restaurant, grocery store, etc. by using pictures, decorations, costumes and realia. Once she brought to the class a beautiful two-tiered fruit cake. It turned out to be her first birthday in China. We ended up eating the cake, speaking English and singing the birthday song. I remember every time when I left her class I would look forward to the next class and certainly my interest as well as my score in English were both enhanced greatly.

I think part of the reason why Amy is so interesting and innovative is that she had studied abroad for many years in education and in applied linguistics before she became a teacher. I was blessed to have her in my life as my neighbor and teacher, without whose help I probably wouldn't have been here for this IELTS test.

（6）*Describe a family member you want to work with in the future.*

☞ *You should say*：

① *Who he/she is*；

② *What he/she did*；

③ *What kind of work you would like to do with him/her*；

④ *And explain how you feel about him/her.*

I would like to be a middle school math teacher when I graduate. Even though I have quite a few family members working in this profession, my cousin Amy is the one I like to collaborate with the most.

Amy is a very talented and innovative middle school English teacher. I once visited her class and I was impressed how interesting and engaging her class was. It was actually Amy's birthday and she invited me to join her birthday party in her class. We brought to the class a beautiful two-tiered fruit cake, birthday banners, candles, and some snacks and drinks. The kids were thrilled, cheering and clapping. Amy started with teaching some English words and expressions related with birthday celebration. And then we ended up eating the cake, using the newly learned expressions and sentences at the birthday party and singing the birthday song. Amy used to say, "People can only learn to swim by swimming, likewise, students can only learn to speak English by speaking." Therefore, she often converts the classrooms into different scenarios like hospital, tea house, restaurant, grocery store, etc. by using pictures, decorations, costumes and realia. I really love Amy's innovative ideas and experiential way of teaching. Even though my major is math, I think Amy's teaching philosophy and methodologies are transferrable in the teaching of other disciplines.

I think part of the reason why Amy is so interesting and innovative is that she had studied abroad for many years in education and in applied linguistics before she became a teacher. I am proud to have Amy in my family.

5）模块拓展

关于英语课和英语老师的主题模块可以用于大量话题，比如提供建议/劝告的人、有趣的人、有创新思维的人、喜欢的人、教授中文的老师（只要把模块中的英文改为中文即可）、外语说得好的人、成功的人、乐于助人的人、受欢迎的人、有趣的对话、难忘的会议、给人启发的演讲、有趣的经历等。

(五)名人

2022 年 9—12 月雅思口语考试名人题库如表 3-6 所示。

表 3-6　名人题库

主题	主题模块	串联题目
名人 (6)	Celebrity story	① Describe a person who makes contribution to the society. ② Describe a popular/well-known person in your country. ③ Describe a story or a novel you have read and you found interesting. ④ Describe a story someone told you and you remember. ⑤ Describe a movie you watched recently and would like to watch again. ⑥ Describe a program you like to watch.

1)主题模块

A. *Celebrity story*

The school Zhang set up is in Huaping, a poverty-stricken area where lots of girls were deprived of education and forced to work or to get married at very young age. Going to university was simply out of the question for them. Zhang Guimei wanted to set up a free public high school for girls, to change their fate and break their poverty chain. She spent the summer and winter vacations in public places to raise funding but she raised only 10,000 RMB, which was nowhere near enough to start a school. Eventually she got enough funding from government and enterprises after her story was reported by a journalist. The school was set up in 2008 and ever since then Zhang Guimei has been a workaholic, sparing no effort to run the school and serve the students. She works day in and out despite the fact that she is battling against many diseases. Her hard work is paid off, so far the school has sent over 2,000 girls to universities, who, upon graduation, have scattered all over the country, blooming in different professions. This wouldn't have been possible without Zhang's contribution and dedication.

2)模块解析

本模块运用了一般过去时、现在完成时、一般现在时、虚拟语气、定语从句、状语从句、插入语、动名词、分词等多样化的语言形式。在词汇与表达层面，运用了一些比较好的表达方式，如 poverty-stricken area、be deprived of、out of the question、break poverty chain、nowhere near enough、spare no effort、work day in and out、pay off 等。

3) 模块运用

（1）Describe a person who makes contribution to the society. /Describe a popular or well-known person in your country.

名人及对社会的贡献：张桂梅事迹(A)。

（2）Describe a story or a novel you have read and you found interesting. /Describe a story someone told you and you remember.

听说过的故事：张桂梅事迹(A)。

（3）Describe a movie you watched recently and would like to watch again.

看过的电影：张桂梅事迹(A)。

（4）Describe a program you like to watch.

喜欢的节目是《东方之星》：张桂梅事迹(A)。

此处也可以把电视节目描述为地方性电视台并根据已有的素材杜撰一个节目。

4) 参考答案

（1）*Describe a person who makes contribution to the society. /Describe a popular or well-known person in your country.*

☞ *You should say*：

① *Who he/she is*；

② *What he/she has done*；

③ *Why he/she is popular*；

④ *And explain how you feel about him/her.*

Well, I've come across tons of celebrities through various media over the years and the person I would like to talk about most is Zhang Guimei who set up China's first and only free public high school for girls. I got to know her from my friend Amy who told me her story when we were talking about the top 10 people that moved China in 2020 broadcasted by CCTV news.

The school Zhang set up is in Huaping, a poverty-stricken area where lots of girls were deprived of education and forced to work or to get married at very young age. Going to university was simply out of the question for them. Zhang Guimei wanted to set up a free public high school for girls, to change their fate and break their poverty chain. She spent the summer and winter vacations in public places to raise funding but she raised only 10,000 RMB, which was nowhere near enough to start a school. Eventually she got enough funding from government and enterprises after her story was reported by a journalist. The school was set up in 2008 and ever since then Zhang Guimei has been a workaholic, sparing no effort to run the school and serve the students. She works day in and out despite the fact that she is battling against many diseases. Her hard work is paid off, so far the school has sent over 2,000 girls to universities, who, upon graduation, have scattered all over the country, blooming in different professions. This wouldn't have been possible without Zhang's contribution and dedication.

I've been very inspired by Zhang Guimei's dedication to education ever since I heard about her story. I wish one day I could meet her in person and express my respect and admiration to her.

（2）Describe a story or a novel that you have read and you found interesting. / Describe a story someone told you and you remember.

☞ *You should say*：

① *When you read it*；

② *What the story or novel was about*；

③ *Who wrote it*；

④ *And explain why you found it interesting.*

I've heard lots of stories from many people over the years and one of the stories that has left me indelible imprints is the story about Zhang Guimei who set up China's first and only free public high school for girls in some mountainous area. My friend Amy told me this story when we were talking about the top 10 people that moved China in 2020 broadcasted by CCTV news.

The school Zhang set up is in Huaping, a poverty-stricken area where lots of girls were deprived of education and forced to work or to get married at very young age. Going to university was simply out of the question for them. Zhang Guimei wanted to set up a free public high school for girls, to change their fate and break their poverty chain. She spent the summer and winter vacations in public places to raise funding but she raised only 10,000 RMB, which was nowhere near enough to start a school. Eventually she got enough funding from government and enterprises after her story was reported by a journalist. The school was set up in 2008 and ever since then Zhang Guimei has been a workaholic, sparing no effort to run the school and serve the students. She works day in and out despite the fact that she is battling against many diseases. Her hard work is paid off, so far the school has sent over 2,000 girls to universities, who, upon graduation, have scattered all over the country, blooming in different professions. This wouldn't have been possible without Zhang's contribution and dedication.

I've been very inspired by Zhang Guimei's story. I wish one day I could meet her in person and express my respect and admiration to her.

（3）Describe a movie you watched recently and would like to watch again.

☞ *You should say*：

① *What it was about*；

② *Where you watched it*；

③ *Why you like it*；

④ *And explain why you would like to watch it again.*

I've been up to my neck in my work and study for as long as I can remember and I haven't watched many movies over the years, but recently I've watched a very special movie that has left me indelible imprints. The movie is titled "A Female School Principal on the Mountain", which is about Zhang Guimei who set up China's first and only free public high school for girls in some mountainous area. I watched this movie from my laptop a couple of weeks ago when I was having my winter holiday.

The school Zhang set up is in Huaping, a poverty-stricken area where lots of girls were deprived of education and forced to work or to get married at very young age. Going to university was simply out of the question for them. Zhang Guimei wanted to set up a free public high school for girls, to change their fate and break their poverty chain. She spent the summer and winter vacations in public places to raise funding but she raised only 10, 000 RMB, which was nowhere near enough to start a school. Eventually she got enough funding from government and enterprises after her story was reported by a journalist. The school was set up in 2008 and ever since then Zhang Guimei has been a workaholic, sparing no effort to run the school and serve the students. She works day in and out despite the fact that she is battling against many diseases. Her hard work is paid off, so far the school has sent over 2, 000 girls to universities, who, upon graduation, have scattered all over the country, blooming in different professions. This wouldn't have been possible without Zhang's contribution and dedication.

I've been so touched and inspired by Zhang's story that I would like to watch it again when I have time. I wish one day I could meet Zhang in person and express my respect and admiration to her.

（4）Describe a program you like to watch.

☞ *You should say*：

① *What it is*；

② *What it is about*；

③ *Who you watch it with*；

④ *And explain why you like to watch it.*

I've been up to my neck in my work and study for as long as I can remember and I haven't watched many programs over the years, but recently I've been really into watching a local TV program called "Oriental Stars" that airs at 8 pm every Tuesday evening. This program introduces celebrities in our society who have made great contributions to the community or the country. I usually watch it with my roommate Amy and we both enjoy watching it. Through this program we've got to know the inspiring stories about the famous people in our era, such as Yuan Longping, the father of hybrid rice, who spared no effort to feed the world, or Zhong Nanshan, the medical scientist who led us in the anti-virus campaign.

A few weeks ago we watched a story about Zhang Guimei who set up China's first and only free public high school for girls in Huaping, a poverty-stricken area where lots of girls were deprived of education and forced to work or to get married at very young age. Zhang Guimei wanted to set up a free public high school for girls, change their fate and break their poverty chain. She spent the summer and winter vacations in public places to raise funding but she raised only 10, 000 RMB, which was nowhere near enough to start a school. Eventually she got enough funding from government and enterprises after her story was reported by a journalist. The school was set up in 2008 and ever since then Zhang Guimei has been a workaholic, sparing no effort to run the school and serve the students. She works day in and out despite the fact that she is battling against many diseases. Her hard work is paid off, so far the school has sent over 2,000 girls to universities, who, upon graduation, have scattered all over the country, blooming in different professions. This wouldn't have been possible without Zhang's contribution and dedication.

I love watching this program because I am always inspired and touched by those heroes in our era and they are definitely my role models.

5) 模块拓展

名人事迹可以用于描述人物的题目,以及用于描述获取名人事迹的途径,如书籍、报纸、电影、电视等;可以用于物品类题目,比如,跟名人的合影或签名(从物品引入名人事迹)、想实现的愿望(受名人激励所引发的愿望);可以用于地点类题目,比如名人的故居故乡、名人去过的地方;可以用于事件类题目,比如基于名人激励带来的"我"的积极改变、相关的建议等。

(六) 繁忙生活

2022 年 9—12 月雅思口语考试繁忙生活题库如表 3-7 所示。

表 3-7　繁忙生活题库

主题	主题模块	串联题目
繁忙生活(5)	Busy life & wake-up call & exercise	① Describe a time when you were very busy. ② Describe a positive change you made in your life. ③ Describe a time when you forgot an appointment. ④ Describe an important thing you learned (not at school or university). ⑤ Describe a change in life that helps you save a lot of time.

1) 主题模块

A. *Busy life*

I remember staying up late and getting up early. Every day after I got back from school I would rush to my room, shut myself indoors and continue doing my assignments which seemed to be endless. I remember being criticized by my class head teacher for taking lunch too slowly and wasting too much precious time which could otherwise have been spent on studying. Truth be told, I used to be like a nerd, burying myself in books, leaving little time for relaxation or entertainment.

I was just like a high-geared machine, working day and night. I remember staying up late and getting up early, attending classes and tutorials, doing assignments, memorizing facts and dealing with quizzes and exams. Every day after I got back from school I would rush to my room, shut myself indoors and continue doing my assignments which seemed to be endless.

I would have hectic days, working day and night like a high-geared machine. I remember staying up late and getting up early, reviewing lessons, doing assignments and memorizing facts. I remember every day after class I would study in the library and bury myself in books. I spent nearly all my spare time in the library with my phone silenced. As usual I grabbed a bite after the afternoon class and spent the whole evening in the library.

I remember getting up at 6:30 in the morning, taking a shower, having breakfast and hitting the road before 7 am to avoid the heavy traffic, then in the afternoon on my way back home I would often be caught in the traffic jams and get home late. Every day was just hectic.

B. Wake-up call

Eventually the stressful work and sedentary lifestyle made a toll on my overall health and I ended up suffering from insomnia and other physical complains.

My father had a good talk with me by my sick bed in hospital, saying that my sickness was a wake-up call that I had to respond to and that it was not worthwhile to burn candles at both ends.

My parents stopped me from overworking and requested that I integrate exercise into my daily routine. So I did.

C. Exercise

Physically, swimming burns calories, builds muscles, improves heart rates and helps me stay healthy and energetic. Mentally, swimming is relaxing and soothing. While swimming, my mind will be slowly relaxing away from the day-to-day worries of work or study and is allowed to drift off to the fun of water. That is just the right type of relaxation that my mind needs, or as people say, just "unplug" it from the world of electronics. And academically, my study efficiency and academic performance have been improved accordingly.

2) 模块解析

主题模块 A 中的几个段落大量运用了记忆模块的三个句式（remember doing ..., would ..., used to ...）对忙碌的点点滴滴进行具体生动的描述，运用了多样化的语法和词汇。语法方面，运用了一般过去时、过去将来时、虚拟语气、现在分词、过去分词、定语从句、状语从句等；词汇方面展示了表达"忙碌"的主题词汇，如：stay up late and get up early, nerd, bury myself in books, no time for relaxation or entertainment, high-geared machine, work day and night, hectic days, grab a bite 等。

主题模块 B、C 运用了一些俗语，如：make a toll, end up doing something, respond to wake up call, burn candles at both ends 等；进一步补充了表达忙碌的词汇，如：stressful work, sedentary lifestyle, physical complains, burn candles at both ends, overwork 等。以上模块对忙碌、生病、锻炼分别进行详细描述，融入相关主题词汇。

3）模块运用

（1）Describe a time when you were very busy.

忙于备考（A），累病了（B），去锻炼（C）。

（2）Describe a positive change you made in your life.

忙于备考（A），累病了（B），去游泳（C）。

（3）Describe a time when you forgot an appointment.

忙于备考（A），忘记约会。

（4）Describe an important thing you learned（not at school or university）

忙于备考（A），累病了（B），去学游泳（C）。

（5）Describe a change in life that helps you save a lot of time.

忙于备考（A），累病了（B），在学校附近租房节省通勤时间。

4）参考答案

（1）*Describe a time when you were very busy.*

☞ *You should say：*

① *When it happened；*

② *Where you were；*

③ *What you did；*

④ *And explain why you were very busy.*

Well, honestly speaking, I've been pretty busy for as long as I can remember. Particularly I was up to my neck in study while I was preparing for college entrance examination.

It was really hard time for me cause I knew I had to score high to be accepted to my ideal university, which means I had to do excellently in all of the required courses. For the last semester before the examination every teacher expected us to spend more time on the subject he or she was teaching, as a result, we were given lots of tutorials, assignments, quizzes, exams, etc. I remember staying up late and getting up early. Every day after I got back from school I would rush to my room, shut myself indoors and continue doing my assignments which seemed to be endless. I remember being criticized by my class head teacher for taking lunch too slowly and wasting too much precious time which could otherwise have been spent on studying. Truth be told, I used to be like a nerd, burying myself in books, leaving little time for relaxation or entertainment.

Eventually the stressful work and sedentary lifestyle made a toll on my overall health and I ended up suffering from insomnia and other physical complains. Fortunately, my parents stopped me from overworking and requested that I integrate exercise into my daily routine. So I did. As a result, my physical and emotional condition improved, so was my work efficiency and academic performance. Fortunately, I entered my dream university, Central South University.

Looking back, I am happy my parents insisted that I strike a balance between work and play. Otherwise, I don't think I would have been able to do well in the entrance examination.

（2）Describe a positive change you made in your life.

☞ *You should say*：

① *What the change was*；

② *When it happened*；

③ *How it happened*；

④ *And explain why it was a positive change.*

I have had lots of great changes in my life, one of the best changes I have ever had is the change from sedentary lifestyle to sporty lifestyle. This took place when I was preparing for college entrance examination 3 years ago.

For the last semester before the examination, I was just like a high-geared machine, working day and night. I remember staying up late and getting up early, attending classes and tutorials, doing assignments, memorizing facts and dealing with quizzes and exams. Every day after I got back from school I would rush to my room, shut myself indoors and continue doing my assignments which seemed to be endless. Eventually the stressful work and sedentary lifestyle made a toll on my overall health and I ended up suffering from insomnia and other physical complains. Once I got a cold which never seemed to get better and eventually was developed into pneumonia. My father had a good talk with me by my sick bed in hospital, saying that my sickness was a wake-up call that I had to respond to and that it was not worthwhile to burn candles at both ends. Right after I discharged from hospital, my parents stopped me from overworking and suggested that I integrate exercise into my daily routine. They registered me in a swimming club which I used to visit every other day. Gradually my physical and emotional condition improved, so did my study efficiency and academic performance. Fortunately, I entered my dream university, Central South University.

Looking back, I am happy my parents insisted that I strike a balance between work and play. Otherwise, I don't think I would have been able to do well in the entrance examination.

（3）Describe a time when you forgot an appointment.

☞ *You should say*：

① *What the appointment was for*；

② *Who you made it with*；

③ *Why you forgot it*；

④ *And explain how you felt about the experience.*

Well, I am basically a punctuate person and I've kept almost all of my appointments over the years but once I missed a dinner party because I had totally forgot about it.

It happened 3 years ago one day when I was having breakfast suddenly I got a phone call from my friend Lily, saying that our mutual friend Amy was visiting Changsha the coming weekend and asking me whether I would join the dinner party to welcome Amy. I agreed happily. However, it happened to be the end of the semester when I was preparing for the final examination, which means I would have hectic days, working day and night like a high-geared machine. I remember staying up late and getting up early, reviewing lessons, doing assignments and memorizing facts. I remember every day after class I would study in the library and bury myself in books. I spent nearly all my spare time in the library with my phone silenced. Then on Friday evening I just totally forgot about my dinner appointment. As usual I grabbed a bite after the afternoon class and spent the whole evening in the library. When I finished my day in the library, I checked my phone. To my great surprise, I saw numerous missed calls from Lily. Then I realized I had missed the dinner party.

As for how I felt about this experience, well, even though I was well understood and forgiven by my friends, I felt bad forgetting about the appointment. If I had set an event reminder on my phone, I wouldn't have forgot about the appointment.

(4) ***Describe an important thing you learned*** (***not at school or university***).

☞ *You should say*：

① *What it is*；

② *When you learned it*；

③ *How you learned it*；

④ *And explain why it was important.*

Well, basically I am a very passionate and curious learner. I've been learning and enhancing my skills in various domains ever since I was born and one of the important skills that I've learned is swimming. I learned swimming when I was studying in high school.

This all started from the collapse of my health. I used to be like a high-geared machine, working day and night in my high school. Eventually the stressful work and sedentary lifestyle made a toll on my overall health. I ended up being hospitalized for pneumonia, which, according to my father, was a wake-up call from my body that I had to respond to. So I decided to learn swimming. Shortly after I recovered from my ailment, my father signed me up for a swimming club in a gym close to where we lived. He even hired a private instructor to teach me swim. At first I was very scared of water because I had some awful drowning experience in my childhood. I was told on the first session to hold my breath and let my body float at the surface of water with my face fully immersed in water. Interestingly, I didn't sink as I had expected! Then step by step I learned the pulling, kicking, gliding and breathing separately before I was instructed to coordinate all those elements together. It just took 7 or 8 sessions and I learned to swim.

As for why I think it was important, the learning of swimming was very rewarding as it has benefitted me in multiple ways. Physically, swimming burns calories, builds muscles, improves heart rates and helps me stay healthy and energetic. Mentally, swimming is relaxing and soothing. While swimming, my mind will be slowly relaxing away from the day-to-day worries of work or study and is allowed to drift off to the fun of water. That is just the right type of relaxation that my mind needs, or as people say, just "unplug" it from the world of electronics. And academically, my study efficiency and academic performance have been improved accordingly.

I am very happy that I learned swimming, otherwise I wouldn't be so healthy, neither would I be successful in my study.

（5）*Describe a recent change in life that helps you save a lot of time.*

☞ *You should say*：

① *What it is*；

② *What you have done*；

③ *How it helps you save time*；

④ *And explain how you feel about this change.*

Well, honestly speaking, I've been pretty busy for as long as I can remember. Particularly nowadays when I am up to my neck in writing my graduation thesis. Therefore, I have figured out lots of time saving strategies. One of the most useful strategies was moving to live close to school.

I used to live nearly 8 kilometers away from my school, so I had to spend over an hour every day commuting to and from school. I remember getting up at 6：30 in the morning, taking a shower, having breakfast and hitting the road before 7 am to avoid the heavy traffic, then in the afternoon on my way back home I would often be caught in the traffic jams and get home late. Every day was just hectic. I used to be like a high-geared machine, working day and night, dealing with all the tasks related with my paper writing：reading, researching, data collecting and analyzing. I hardly had any time for relaxation and entertainment. Eventually the stressful work and sedentary lifestyle made a toll on my overall health. I ended up being hospitalized for pneumonia, which, according to my parents, was a wake-up call from my body that required immediate response. Therefore, my parents made a decision. They rented an apartment just across from my school so that I could save the commuting time.

So now I don't have to get up so early, which means I can sleep for an extra hour. In the afternoon with the time saved from commuting, I can now work out in the gym. My life quality is greatly enhanced and I am happier and healthier. If I hadn't moved house, I wouldn't have got those good changes in my life！

5）模块拓展

本主题密切围绕忙碌、生病和锻炼三个方面展开，三者之间互为因果，因忙碌而生病，因生病而锻炼，因锻炼而身体健康、工作学习效率提升。现代生活竞争激励，工作学习的压力大，健康状况下降，健身锻炼越来越引起人们的重视，与此相关的问题是雅思口语考试的高频问题，频繁出现在雅思口语考试的三个部分中，比如对生活方式、兴趣爱好、身心健康问题、运动锻炼等方面的讨论。

（七）电话

2022 年 9~12 月雅思口语考试电话题库如表 3-8 所示。

表 3-8　电话题库

主题	主题模块	串联题目
电话 (4)	Looking for my way & attending a conference	① Describe a time when you used your cellphone to do something important. ② Describe a time when you helped a child. ③ Describe an occasion when you lost something in a public place. ④ Describe an invention that changed the world.

1) 主题模块

A. *Looking for my way*

Interestingly my GPS gave some silly directions and I ended up walking up and down the street but just couldn't find my hotel. It was late evening, and darkness had shrouded everything. I was kind of stressed and scared. I wanted to ask the way, but there were no pedestrians. Obviously I had to rely on the phone to reach someone who could give me assistance. I called the front desk of the hotel. Unfortunately the clerk who answered my phone couldn't figure out where I was through my description. So I added him as my Wechat friend and I sent him my location through Wechat and then somebody from the hotel came to pick me up. I turned out to be just 200 meters away from the hotel. If not for the phone, I would have had difficulty finding my way in the strange city.

B. *Attending a conference*

Cellphone has been an essential part in my life and it has played a crucial role in many situations.

I was kind of stressed and lonely and every day I would use my phone to stay connected with my family and to navigate and explore the neighborhood.

For example, I relied on my smart phone throughout my trip to Guangzhou for a conference. I made online reservations for the train, the hotel and I made conference registration through Internet. When I got to the city, I used Baidu app on my phone to get a taxi. And when I got off the taxi I couldn't see my hotel anywhere. Then I used the GPS for navigation to find my hotel. Throughout my stay, I used the phone to explore the neighborhood, to stay in touch with my family and friends.

2) 模块解析

以上模块运用了多个表达情感的副词插入语,比如 interestingly、unfortunately、obviously;运用了一般过去时、过去完成时、现在完成时、虚拟语气及多种形式的主从复合句;运用了 turned out to …、ended up doing …表达真相与结果。

3) 模块运用

(1) Describe a time when you used your cellphone to do something important.
用手机导航找宾馆没找到,后加微信发定位(A)。

（2）Describe a time when you helped a child.

小孩跟妈妈走散了，找不到路，加孩子妈妈微信发定位（A）。

（3）Describe an occasion when you lost something in a public place.

广州出差的时候用手机探索新的环境（A），但是手机丢了。

（4）Describe an invention that changed the world.

手机在职业生活和个人生活中发挥的作用，个人生活以广州出差开会为例（B）。

4）参考答案

（1）Describe a time when you used your cellphone to do something important.

☞ You should say：

① When it happened；

② What happened；

③ How important the cellphone was；

④ And explain how you felt about it.

Well, cellphone has been an essential part in my life and it has played a crucial role in many situations. For example, I used cellphone to find my way when I was taking a business trip in Guangzhou nearly 10 years ago.

It was my first trip to Guangzhou and I took a taxi from the railway station to my hotel in late evening. About one hour later the taxi driver said I was at the address, but when I got off the taxi I couldn't see my hotel anywhere. Then I used the GPS on my phone for navigation. Interestingly the GPS gave some silly directions and I ended up walking up and down the street but just couldn't find my hotel. It was late evening, and darkness had shrouded everything. I was kind of stressed and scared. I wanted to ask the way, but there were no pedestrians. Obviously I had to rely on the phone to reach someone who could give me assistance. I called the front desk of the hotel. Unfortunately the clerk who answered my phone couldn't figure out where I was through my description. So I added him as my Wechat friend and I sent him my location through Wechat and then somebody from the hotel came to pick me up. I turned out to be just 200 meters away from the hotel.

If not for the phone, I would have had difficulty finding my way in the strange city.

（2）Describe a time when you helped a child.

☞ You should say：

① When it happened；

② Who you helped；

③ How you helped him/her；

④ And explain how you felt about it.

Well, I haven't got many chances to help kids over the years but there was one particular occasion when I helped a poor little girl find her way. I met her when I was strolling on a park close to where I lived.

I was heading home after a couple of hours' walking at the park when I suddenly caught sight of a little girl crying for her mother, walking up and down the trail. I immediately realized that she had got separated from her mother. It was late evening, and darkness had shrouded everything. The little girl looked very stressed and scared. I went up to her, crouched down and asked if she remembered her mother's phone number. I ended up calling her mother who was desperately searching for her daughter. However, her mother couldn't figure out where we were through my description. So I added her as my Wechat friend and I sent her my location through Wechat and then the mother came to pick up the little girl. It turned out that the mother and daughter had looked for each other for nearly one hour. They were certainly overjoyed while meeting each other and they both expressed their heartfelt thanks to me.

Looking back it was really risky for little kids to get separated from their parents in public places. It would have been a nightmare if there had been some bad guys around. Anything could have happened. Hopefully the mother could learn a good lesson from this experience.

(3) *Describe an occasion when you lost something in a public place.*

☞ *You should say:*

① *What you lost;*

② *When and where you lost it;*

③ *What you did to find it;*

④ *And explain how you feel about this experience.*

Honestly speaking, I've been really careful with my stuff and have rarely lost valuable things over the years but there was one exception. I lost a cellphone when I was taking a business trip to Guangzhou.

It was my first trip to Guangzhou, I was kind of stressed and lonely and every day I would use my phone to stay connected with my family and to navigate and explore the neighborhood. However, I lost it on a bus which was overcrowded. I remember I was in a loose winter coat, unfortunately I forgot to zip up the pocket it was in. It might have fallen out of my pocket during the ride when the bus hit a big bump in the road or it might have been pinched by some pickpockets. I remember being surrounded by a group of young and noisy guys who stayed on the bus just for a few minutes and got off the bus all together. Anyway, I didn't realize I had lost my phone until I got home. So I borrowed a phone and dialed my number for numerous times, but unfortunately, the phone had been powered off. I knew somebody had got it and powered it off.

I was devastated. It was my first iPhone which had cost me an arm and a leg. Anyway, I just blamed myself and regretted not taking good care of it. If I had been more careful, I wouldn't have lost it.

(4) *Describe an invention that changed the world.*

☞ *You should say:*

① *What the invention was;*

② *What it can do;*

③ *How popular it is*；

④ *Why it is an important invention.*

There are lots of inventions that have brought fundamental changes to the human civilization. One of the most important inventions I think is Internet that has changed the world tremendously.

Internet has been an essential part in our personal and professional life. Professionally, every profession today relies heavily on Internet. If for some reason, any institutions, such as the banks, hospitals, schools or malls, were off grid, they would immediately stop operation. This is also true for most of the working professionals or students today. Take myself as an example, when I am out of the Internet, I just don't know how to continue with my work. I need Internet for making researches, for online meetings, for submitting documents, for searching for information, sharing data, just everything.

Personally, with Internet, we have smart home, smart phone, smart city. Our life is so much easier and more comfortable with Internet. For example, I relied on my smart phone throughout my trip to Guangzhou for a conference. I made online reservations for the train, the hotel and I made conference registration through Internet. When I got to the city, I used Baidu app on my phone to get a taxi. And when I got off the taxi I couldn't see my hotel anywhere. Then I used the Baidu map for navigation to find my hotel. Throughout my stay, I used the phone to explore the neighborhood, to stay in touch with my family and friends, to make cashless payment, to check the conference detail, to name just a few.

I simply can't imagine what our life or our world would be like without Internet, which has certainly been an indispensable part in our life.

5) 模块拓展

本模块围绕手机的运用拓展到生活中与手机相关的经历和故事。用手机找路、找人、发送位置等生活细节及生活小插曲可以运用到其他话题描述中，比如，有趣的人(迷路的时候给"我"带路聊天的人)、外国人(在国外迷路的时候给"我"带路的人)、生活中必不可少的物品、昂贵的物品、新的地方、度假的地方(迷路)、浪费时间的事(刷手机)等。

第四章　Part 3 模块解析及运用

第一节　Part 3 框架模块 ORDER

一、Part 3 题型分析

在 Part 3 中，考官与考生进行 4 到 7 分钟的讨论，这是最有挑战性的一部分。此部分的问题涵盖范围很广，不拘泥于题库范围。考官在 Part 3 中有绝对的自主权，可以根据 Part 2 的内容进行拓展性提问，也可以根据自己的喜好灵活提问，问题数量不固定，问题内容没有限制。此部分的考题很难在考前准备，而且是即兴回答，没有思考的时间，因此，Part 3 的难度是三个部分中最高的。

考官为了了解考生的最高英语水平，会逐步加大问题难度，会问到抽象的、复杂的、较偏的问题，这是为了让高水平的考生有机会表达复杂的想法，有机会使用多样化的语言结构和词汇来表达意见。因此，针对一些刁钻古怪的问题，未能很好地回答并不会影响考生的成绩，相反，能被问到难题本身就是对考生英语水平的认可。

Part 3 的问题虽然题库很大，随机性强，题目无法预测，但依然有一定的出题规律及高频话题。Part 3 最常见的问题有五大类别：

① 观点陈述：Do you think the seasons still influence people's behavior?

② 意见建议：What can people do to make a greener city?

③ 进行对比：How has transportation changed since your grandparents were young?

④ 推测未来：Do you think the hobbies people have will be different in the future?

⑤ 讨论本国：Do people in your country mostly buy or rent their own homes?

Part 3 主要考查内容与语言两个层面：在内容上，论证是否充分合理，有说服力；在语言上，话语是否具有连贯性、准确性，词汇及语法是否有多样性，语音语调是否具有较强的可理解性等。

二、Part 3 ORDER 模块简介

在回答 Part 3 时，由于没有思考时间，考生往往不知从何说起，或者答题无条理，说了一大堆，但言之无物，没有说到点子上。ORDER 模块可以帮助考生言简意赅、清晰明

了、有理有据地回答 Part 3 的问题。

ORDER 是 opinion、reason、describe、example、restatement 五个单词的首字母组合。五个单词首字母分别代表回答 Part 3 问题的五个步骤。

(1) O（观点模块）：阐明观点。应开门见山，直接回答问题，阐述自己的观点意见。

Yes, I think so. Absolutely!

Generally speaking, I believe …

There are a lot of people who believe that … but I think …

In regards to A, I think … whereas with B I guess …

(2) R（理由模块）：说明原因。针对前面的观点，说明理由。

This is due to the fact that …

Because …

(3) D（描述模块）：描述倾向、趋势、建议等。

People enjoy …

People have been used to …

By doing that, people can …

(4) E（举例模块）：通过事例进行论证。

It's common to see people …

For example …

I've learned from many different resources that …

(5) R（总结模块）：重申观点。

So I think those are the reasons why …

So in my opinion those are the most popular outdoor activities.

I think those are the two tips parents can consider doing to help their children stay healthy.

以 ORDER 模块回答 Part 3 的问题，有助于使回答逻辑清晰、条理清楚、衔接紧凑。

在回答较难的问题，一时不知如何回答的时候，可以先说以下表达，以争取时间组织后面的语言：

Well …

Let me think …

I'm not an expert but …

That's a good question.

That's an interesting question.

I've never thought about it before.

第二节　Part 3 观点模块

一、疑问句分类

英语中的问句分为一般疑问句和特殊疑问句两大类，前者称为封闭式问题，后者为开放式问题。

(一) 开放式问题

Why do you think friendship is important?

What do you think are the most important qualities for friends to have?

What benefits do children get from doing sports?

What factors do people consider when buying presents for other people?

开放式问题的回答以"我认为"加观点进行回答：

I believe + opinion

I guess + opinion

I suppose + opinion

I guess + opinion

(二) 封闭式问题

Do you think life will be more stressful in the future?

Do you think men and women enjoy different kinds of movies?

Do people in your country like music?

Is it important to arrive at parties on time in your country?

封闭式问题用"是"与"否"进行肯定与否定回答，也可以折中回答(一定程度上)：

Absolutely/Definitely/Of course.

Yes/I think so.

To an extent/To some extent/It depends …

Absolutely not/Definitely not.

请用相关语言模块简要对以下封闭式问题提出你的观点：

① Do you think happiness is good for health?

_____

② Do you think people who have fixed routines are not creative?

_____

③ Do you think your notion of happiness is changing over time?

_____

④ Do you think Chinese people are family-oriented?

_____

参考答案：

① Absolutely! Happiness plays an important role in maintaining good health.

② No, I don't think so. Definitely not.

③ Yes, I think my concept of happiness changes with time.

④ Yes, to a large extent.

不管是开放式还是封闭式问题，都可以从以下三个方法中选择合适的方法表达观点。

二、常见方法

（一）笼统表达

在 Part 3 中，有些问题是针对整体情况的提问，对这类题目，考生只要给出笼统的观点就可以，不需展开太多细节。

1. 语言素材

Generally speaking, I think …

Broadly speaking, I suppose …

On the whole, I believe …

Without going into too much detail, I guess …

2. 真题范例

① *Is eating out expensive in your country*?

Well, generally speaking, I believe eating out is rather affordable in my country.

② *Are people friendly in your neighborhood*?

Broadly speaking, I think the people in my local area are happy to chat and ready to help anytime.

③ *How reliable do you think information on the Internet is*?

Well, on the whole, I guess what we learn from Internet is not always trustworthy.

④ *Who is the head of the family in your culture*?

Well, generally speaking, I think more often than not, the man is the head of the family.

⑤ *Do you think it is easy for famous people to earn a lot of money*?

Yes, on the whole, I think it is way easier for the celebrity to make fortune than people from other professions.

3. 练习

请用笼统表达对以下问题提出你的观点。

① Do you think examinations are the best way to assess a student's ability?

_____

② Why do people choose to live in old buildings?

_____

③ What do you think is the most important quality in a friend?

_____

④ Why do people like different types of movies at different stages in life?

_____

⑤ Is it important for young children to spend time with their grandparents?

参考答案：

① Generally speaking, I don't think examinations do a good job in evaluating students' capabilities.

② Generally speaking, I think most people choose to live in old buildings simply because the new buildings are too expensive for them.

③ On the whole, I believe honesty is the most essential quality in friendship.

④ Broadly speaking, people's taste in music changes with time, which, I think, is the reflection of their changes in personality and physical condition.

⑤ On the whole, I believe it is crucial for kids to spend time with their grandparents.

（二）分类表达

分类表达就是对人、物、事件的不同情况和特质等进行分类表达。这样不仅有利于快速建立一套完整的逻辑结构，也可以丰富答题角度，尽量做到全面客观，具体问题具体分析。分类表述需要把两个类别分开表述，分别阐述观点、原因、论证。

我们可以从人物、时间、地点及事件等维度进行分类，对不同类别的人、事、物进行比较。

（1）人物维度：性别对比（female & male）、年龄对比（old & young）、贫富对比（rich & poor）。

（2）地点维度：城乡对比（country & city）、公司对比（big & small company）、南北方对比（south & north）、国内外对比（motherland & foreign country）、国家对比（developed & developing country）。

（3）时间维度：过去现在对比（past & present）、现在未来对比（present & future）。

（4）事件维度：娱乐类型对比（genres of entertainment）、室内外对比（indoor & outdoor）

在以上对比中，最常见的是性别、年龄、过去现在、现在未来对比。

1.语言素材

In regards to A, I think …whereas with B …

When talking about A, I believe …, when it comes to B, I guess …

In terms of A, I suppose … Looking at B, I believe …

If you mean A, I believe …, but if you are talking about B, then I guess …

（1）分类表达的主语可以是名词，特指某一类人、物或地点，比如：

① **In regards to** older people, I think … whereas **with** the young generation, I guess …

② **When talking about** ebooks, I believe … **when it comes to** the physical books, I think …

③ **In terms of** big companies, I suppose … **Looking at** the small companies, I believe …

④ **If you mean** children, I guess … **but if you're talking about** teenagers, I think …

（2）分类表达的主语也可以是动名词，特指某类活动或行为动作事件，比如：

When talking about reading books, I believe …

When it comes to watching movies, I guess …

In terms of learning from elderly, I suppose …

Looking at learning from youngsters, I believe …

Looking at doing extreme sports, I think …

If you mean going abroad, I guess …

In regards to taking part time jobs, I suppose …

2. 真题范例

① *Do young and old people have the same attitudes towards old buildings*?

In regards to elderly people, I think they have a greater appreciation of history and more respect for old buildings, *but if you are talking about the younger generation*, then I guess they don't have such a great emotional attachment to the past yet.

② *What are the differences between learning about history from book and from films/ movies*?

Well, *in regards to learning history from books*, *I think* that involves lots of imagination, analyzation and digestion, because the readers can always pause and read back and forth for digestion and pondering, *whereas in terms of watching movies*, the viewers can take advantage of the audio-visual effect, making the process of learning more entertaining and amusing, but they just don't have the opportunity for deep thinking while watching.

③ *Which one is better when making complaint, by talking or writing*?

Well, it is hard to tell. Each has its own pros and cons. As I see it, *in regards to making a verbal*, face to face complaint, people can take advantage of the verbal cues, eye contact, smiles, which really facilitate effective communication, *whereas in terms of written complaints*, you avoid the stressful and direct confrontation that might arise and also you can read over your letter and think back and forth and craft carefully to make it less offensive.

④ *What's the difference between learning face-to-face with teachers and learning by oneself*?

I think there are several differences between the two. First of all, *with students in a classroom*, they can rely on their teacher for answers and extra information. If they have a doubt or need any help, they can raise their hand and their teacher can give them an immediate answer. Secondly, they are given the benefit of working in groups. If they collaborate on a project, students can help each other and learn from each other at the same time. *In regards to studying* on their own, however, they have to be more independent and self-reliant. If they study by themselves, they don't have a teacher there to give immediate feedback or support, so they may have to go on the Internet to find the specific answers they need. Those are two key differences that I am aware of.

3.练习

请用分类表达模块回答以下问题：

① *Are women more fashionable than men*?

Yes, generally speaking, I guess women are more stylish than men. _____

_____, it's true that they tend to be more obsessed to the clothes, accessories, cosmetics, etc., on which they spend more time and more money than men. _____, I suppose they seem to be more interested in video games, high tech, gadgets, those kinds of stuff. This may be related with the gender differences in their innate natures or in the cultural and social impact? I am not pretty sure. It is more than just a gender stereotype, it is actually a common phenomenon that women are more fashionable than men.

② *Which do you think are better: indoor or outdoor games*?

Generally speaking, I think both indoor and outdoor games have their intrinsic pros and cons and the two should be complemented to each other to help us lead a healthy and active lifestyle. _____, they are reliable because you can play them regardless how the weather is outside, rainy or snowy. _____ I suppose it's healthier and more entertaining as you can get some fresh air or even get totally immersed in the nature if you go hiking or mountain climbing.

③ *Who are more likely to make complaints, old people or young people*?

Well, broadly speaking, I assume that young people tend to make complaints more easily. _____, they have weathered the roller coaster in life, the ups and downs, through which they obtained experience and wisdom and learned to be calm and composed when facing frustrations. _____, they are more radical and fretful when compared to elderly people, which is characterized by their "young blood".

④ *Who can influence children more, teachers or parents*?

I believe both teachers and parents are equally significant and indispensable along the path of the young generation. They should collaborate to foster the growth of the kids. _____, they exert a great influence on the kids because they play the role as a teacher, whom the students tend to respect and look up to, which paves the way for effective education. _____ _____, they spend much time with their children and they are like the textbooks of their kids. As we say, "Actions speak louder than words." The parents constantly impact their children with their behaviors, their way of doing things.

⑤ *What are the differences between young people and old people when they use cellphones*?

Broadly speaking, there are striking differences between the old and young regarding the use of cellphones. _____, they are digital natives with higher digital proficiency and more reliance on the devices. They are hooked on their phones a great amount of time, doing everything on cellphones, such as playing games, shopping, texting, posting, streaming music, etc. _____, they are digital immigrants with limited digital proficiency, who may use the phone for some basic functions, such as making calls, texting or making digital payment.

> 参考答案:
> ① In regards to women; Whereas with men
> ② In terms of/When talking about indoor activities; When it comes to/Looking at outdoor games
> ③ In regards to old people; Whereas with young generation
> ④ In regards to teachers; Whereas with parents
> ⑤ In regards to young people; Whereas with old people

(三)让步表达

让步表达是指承认某种观点的同时,提出自己不同的观点,对两个相反的观点进行表述对比。让步表达分为两种类型:

(1)以大众观点为让步。通过"有些人认为"来提出对立面的观点,随后陈述自己的观点。

(2)以自我表述为让步。通过"即便","虽然"等表达让步的词引出对立面观点,继而提出自己的观点。此模块在 Part 1 的高级表达及 Part 2 的结尾中均有涉及。

1. 语言素材

A lot of people seem to think that (opinion A), but I (contrasting idea) …

Some people say (opinion A), but I (contrasting idea) …

There are a lot of people who believe that (opinion A), but I (contrasting idea) …

Although/Even though …, I (don't) think …

While/Despite the fact that …, I (don't) think …

2. 真题范例

① *Do you think ebooks will replace paper books in the future*?

There are a lot of people who believe that paper books are out of date and that they should be completely abandoned in favor of digital formats, *but I don't think* that is a realistic solution.

② *Do you think television has a positive effect on a child's attitudes towards learning*?

Well, *there are a lot of people who believe that* TV makes kids stupid because they watch silly cartoons all the time, *but I don't think that is necessarily true.*

③ *Are art classes important for children*?

Yes, definitely. *There are a lot of people who believe that* kids should only lean academic skills like maths and science, *but I think* art classes are absolutely necessary for the overall development of the kids.

④ *Do you think it is necessary to make environmental protection a standardized subject at school*?

Yes, definitely! *There are probably a lot of people who think* that students already learn about the environment in science, ***but I think learning*** a subject focusing on environmental protection would certainly make a difference in their awareness of the systematic learning about environmental protection.

⑤ ***Do you think people should have to pay to visit museums***?

Yes, certainly. ***Although*** I think some museums in my country are far too expensive, ***I don't think*** that museums should be completely free for everyone.

⑥ ***Do you think the Internet is a good place to get news***?

Despite the fact that there is a lot of misleading and fake information online, ***I still think*** the Internet is a good place for news and updates on current events.

⑦ ***Do we really need teachers to learn something***?

Despite the fact that online learning is very convenient and economical, ***I still think*** teachers are a vital part of learning anything new.

⑧ ***Is music an important subject at school***?

Even though I really enjoyed learning music at school, I don't think it helped me succeed or find work as an adult, so I don't think it's that important.

3. 练习

请用让步表达回答以下问题：

① ***Do you think only old people have time for leisure***?

_____

_____ ,

but I think young people also have much spare time for relaxation and recreation.

② ***Do you think negative feedback is more important than positive feedback***?

_____

_____ ,

but I think that negative feedback plays a more significant role in prompting for desired behavior.

③ ***Is it important to have the same hobbies and interests when making friends***?

_____

_____ ,

but I believe this is not necessarily true. People of different hobbies can also make friends, complimenting each other and learning from each other and in the long run they may even pick up each other's hobbies.

④ ***Do you think people should pay for higher education by themselves***?

_____

_____ ,

but I think people should pay for their higher education.

① There are a lot of people who think that young people today are under such great pressure in this competitive world that they simply have no leisure time

② Some people think that encouragement or positive feedback weighs more than negative feedback in achieving success

③ Many people believe that birds of the same feather flock together and that only people with similar interests can become friends

④ Although I know higher education is so expensive that many people simply can't afford it

三、小结

在观点模块 O 中，常用的观点表达方法如表 4-1 所示。

表 4-1　观点模块 O 常用表达方法

类别	语言素材	范例
笼统表达	Generally speaking, I think …; Broadly speaking, I suppose …; On the whole, I believe …	① *Is eating out expensive in your country*? *Well*, *generally speaking*, I believe eating out is rather affordable in my country. ② *Are people friendly in your neighborhood*? *Broadly speaking*, I think the people in my local area are happy to chat and ready to help anytime. ③ *How reliable do you think information on the Internet is*? *Well*, *on the whole*, I guess what we learn from Internet is not always trustworthy.
分类表达	In regards to A, I think … whereas with B …; When talking about A, I believe …, when it comes to B, I guess …; In terms of A, I suppose … Looking at B, I believe …;	① *What kind of music do young people and old people like*? Generally speaking, people at different ages have different preferences when it comes to music. *In regards to elderly people*, I think they prefer the peaceful and soothing music such as folk music or country music, which well suits their tendency of seeking for calm and peace or recalling the past, *whereas with the young generation*, I guess they are fond of exciting and loud music, such as pop music, rock and roll and hip-hop. I suppose this is because young people are more energetic and they like to chase the fashion.
	If you mean A, I believe …, but if you are talking about B, then I guess …	② *What do young people do for fun*? *If you mean children*, *then I guess* they like to play with their friends and also surf the Internet on their tablets or phones, *but if you are talking about teenagers*, then I think they are more mature and independent, so they tend to go out more with each other. I think those are some common ways young people enjoy themselves.

续表4-1

类别	语言素材	范例
让步表达	There are a lot of people who believe that … but I …; Some people say … but I …; Although/Even though …, I (don't) think …; While/Despite the fact that …, I (don't) think …	① *Do you think ebooks will replace paper books in the future*? *There are a lot of people who believe that* paper books are out of date and that they should be completely abandoned in favor of digital formats, *but I don't think that is a realistic solution.* ② *Do you think television has a positive effect on a child's attitudes towards learning*? *Some people say that* TV makes kids stupid because they watch silly cartoons all the time, *but I don't think that is necessarily true.* ③ *Do you think people should have to pay to visit museums*? Yes, certainly. *Although I think some museums in my country are far too expensive, I don't think that* museums should be completely free for everyone. ④ *Do you think the Internet is a good place to get news*? Yes, I think so. *Despite the fact that* there is a lot of misleading and fake information online, *I still think* the Internet is a good place for news and updates on current events.

第三节　**Part 3** 理由模块

第一句话以多样化的句式和词汇清晰明确地阐明观点之后，接下来就应该陈述理由，论证观点。很多考生往往千篇一律地用 because 说明理由，无法向考官展示语言多样性与复杂性，其实考生可以用原因短语，也可以用原因从句来陈述理由。

一、常用方法

(一) 原因从句

1. 语言素材

because + 从句…
since+ 从句…
as + 从句…
due to the fact that + 从句…

2. 真题范例

① *Why do some people start their own business*?
I suppose that's *because* they don't like working for other people, or they want to work in an

industry they are more passionate about.

② *Do people in your country like to take public transportation*?

Yes, definitely. ***This is due to the fact*** that we have a very good public transportation system all over the country, particularly the extensive subway system and railway system, which are very fast, reliant and economical.

③ *Is it necessary for people to be patient*?

Yes, definitely. People should learn to be patient. ***This is because*** being patient can actually enhance rather than depress the efficiency. As the saying goes, "More haste, less speed."

④ *Why do some people like to share news on social media*?

I think it's ***due to the fact*** that people like to connect with their friends and family by updating the news on social media, which is a channel of communication.

⑤ *Why do young people tend to waste money*?

I think that's ***down to the fact*** that most of the young people are financially dependent and they don't know the hardship of life and of making money.

⑥ *Why is online shopping so popular these days*?

I believe it's ***due to the fact*** that online shopping is so much more convenient than retail shopping, especially as modern life tend to be more fast-paced and people are too busy to go shopping.

(二)原因短语

1.语言素材

(that's/it's) because of + 名词…
(that's/it's) thanks to + 名词…
(that's/it's) down to + 名词…
(that's/it's) due to + 名词…

2.真题范例

① *Why do so many people live in flats rather than houses these days*?

I guess that's ***due to*** the housing prices. Most people can't afford to buy a house, so they choose flats instead.

② *Why is online shopping so popular these days*?

I think online shopping is popular ***because of*** its convenience and low price.

3.练习

请用理由模块完成以下问题:

① *Do you think more people will live in the countryside in the future*?

Yes, I think so. This is due to the fact that _____

_____.

No, I don't think so, because _____

_____.

② ***Do you think well-developed tourism will have negative effects on local people***?

Absolutely because _____

_____.

No, I don't think so because _____

_____.

③ ***Do you think there should be classes for training young people and children how to relax***?

Yes, I think so, because _____

_____.

No, I don't think so, because _____

_____.

④ ***Is it easier to get promotion in big companies***?

Yes, definitely, because _____

_____.

Definitely not, because _____

_____.

⑤ ***Why do some people prefer slow-paced life***?

I guess that is due to the fact that _____

_____.

参考答案:

① many city dwellers have got tired of the hustle and bustle of the city and they long for the peace and quietness in the countryside;

city life is more convenient and interesting with more public amenities such as public transportations, pubs, museums, to name just a few

② tourism will bring about large number of tourists who tend to put a strain on the natural resources, such as water, land, fossil fuels, to name just a few. On top of that problems like environmental destruction, traffic jams will arise;

tourism will bring about tremendous benefits that can lead to transformative social and economical development in local community, which in turn will help to solve the environmental problems caused by the tourism

③ the young generation today have been used to the sedentary lifestyle and have been obsessed with the digital world, which is certainly not a good way for relaxation;

different people have different tastes or hobbies, which will guide each individual on the choices of relaxation forms

④ big companies have higher platforms that offer them better opportunities for self-growth as well as for promotion;

it is much more competitive in big companies where there are more outstanding talents, making promotion more difficult

⑤ they have been tired of the fast-paced life which has driven them crazy and taken a toll on their physical and mental wellbeing

注意：在回答关于 Why 的问题时，考生应跳过第一步"阐明观点"，直接陈述理由，理由尽可能简单直接，不要拐弯抹角或过于复杂抽象。

二、小结

在理由模块 R 中，常用的方法如表 4-2 所示。

表 4-2 理由模块 R 常用方法

类别	语言素材	范例
原因短语	because of + 名词 …； thanks to + 名词 …； down to + 名词 …； due to + 名词 …	① *Why do so many people live in flats rather than houses these days*? I guess that's *due to* the ever increasing housing prices. Most people can't afford to buy a house, so they choose flats instead. ② *Why is online shopping so popular these days*? I think online shopping is popular *because of* its convenience and low price.
原因从句	because + 从句…； since + 从句…； as + 从句…； due to the fact that + 从句…	① *Why do some people start their own business*? I suppose that's *because* they don't like working for other people, or they want to work in an industry they are more passionate about. ② *Why do some people like to share news on social media*? I think it's *due to the fact* that people like to connect with their friends and family by updating the news on social media, which is a channel of communication. ③ *Why do young people tend to waste money*? I think that's *due to the fact* that most of the young people are financially dependent and they don't know the hardship of life and of making money.

第四节　Part 3 描述模块

在阐述理由之后,接下来可以联系相关的社会现象,对前面提到的原因进行拓展,也可为后面的举例论证做铺垫。很多问题与当下的社会生活息息相关,可以通过描述他人倾向、变化趋势、建议措施及观点罗列四种方法展开。描述模块既可单纯描述倾向,也可以与前面的观点模块(O)、原因模块(R)或后面的举例模块(E)融为一体,通过描述模块说明观点、原因或进行举例。描述模块既可充实答案内容,又可展示语言的多样性。

一、常用方法

(一)他人倾向

1.语言素材

people +观点或行为(一般现在时)

某类人群+ 观点或行为 (一般现在时)

Part 2 往往是描述个人经历,而 Part 3 则是讨论人们在观点、态度、行为等各方面的倾向性。因此,在 Part 3 的回答中,往往以人们或者某类人群为主语,通过对人们倾向性的描述来解释原因。例如:

People need to relax and unwind sometimes.

People enjoy playing sports with each other.

People don't want to spend too much money on food.

Parents encourage their children to participate in sports.

Seniors are very concerned about their health condition.

Many tourists like to buy souvenirs while they travel.

此外,针对某类人群可以用介词短语或定语从句进行修饰,以展示语言多样性并避免词汇的重复。

homeowners = people who own their home

seniors = people over 65 years old

commuters = people who travel to work

parents = people who have children

tourist = people who are visiting places of interest

2.真题范例

① *Why do people like visiting historical places*?

I think it's due to people's intrinsic curiosity (R:陈述理由). ***People are just interested in knowing about what happened in the past and they want to gain a deeper understanding of*** *history by looking into "the window of the past". Certainly visiting the historical places in person makes learning more fun and impressive than learning from books or documentaries* （D：描述他人倾向）. So I think people are driven by their curiosity to explore the past through visiting the historical sites（O：重申观点）.（People + 观点或行为）

② *How will ebooks affect paper books*?

Well，I know a lot of people have said that e-books will replace hard copies eventually，but actually I believe that many people still prefer reading real books（O：阐明观点）because they enjoy the feeling of paper in their hands and of turning the pages（R：陈述理由）. *When I take the bus to work*，*I see a lot of people reading physical novels and magazines too*（*D+E*：以例子描述他人倾向），so although people are consuming stories and most of their entertainment through screens，I don't think ebooks will make paper books obsolete any time soon（O：重申观点）.（People + 观点或行为）

③ *What skills take a long time to learn*?

I think creative or artistic skills take a very long time to master（O：阐明观点）. Probably this is because those skills have to be very professional and *even nearly perfect to draw people's attention and appreciation*（R+D：陈述理由+描述倾向）. *For example*，*musicians usually start learning when they are kids and don't become professionals until they are much older. Likewise*，*artists are still perfecting their craft throughout their entire lives*（D+E：以例子描述某类人群倾向），*so I think those are some skills that take ages*（O：重申观点）.（某类人群+观点或行为）

以上例子中的 musician 和 artist 可以理解为是针对某类人群的倾向进行描述，同时也是以 musician 和 artist 为例，进行举例论证，把描述倾向与举例论证融为一体。

3.练习

请用以上方法完成以下句子：

① Lots of tourists choose to take package tour while travelling, because people _____
_____.

② Parents in my country push their kids study hard and even deprive them of the time for relaxation and entertainment, because people _____
_____.

③ A lot of people spend an awful amount of time each day on their phones, because they
_____.

④ Traffic is really heavy and slow during the Spring Festival, because people _____
_____.

⑤ The housing price in metropolitan cities have been soaring up in recent years, because
_____.

⑥ Many commuters choose to take public transportation today, because people _____
_____.

参考答案：

① enjoy the comfort and convenience provided by the package tour

② believe academic excellence is very important to children's future profession

③ are obsessed with the digital world where they can do everything

④ from all over the country are travelling back home for the family reunion and festival celebration

⑤ urbanization has made the cities more and more densely populated and the demand for housing is increasing accordingly

⑥ enjoy the efficiency and reliability that the public transportation system provides

(二) 变化趋势

讨论人或事物的变化趋势是 Part 3 常考话题，比如：

How has education changed in your country?

How has your hometown changed over the years?

How has people's lifestyle changed in the last decade?

描述变化趋势(D)可以融入 ORDER 的各个环节，灵活运用描述模块，既能展示现在完成时，体现时态多样性，也能以描述模块论述相关背景、原因、举例等答题信息，使回答内容充实，逻辑严谨。

1. 语言素材

(1) 现在完成时表达"变得更加……"：*have/has gotten/become* + … + *a lot/much/slightly/a little* + 形容词比较级(+时间短语)。

① With the ever-worse inflation, everything has become more expensive, like rent, gas, food, housing for example. However, people's income has only gotten a little higher over the last 10 years.

② People have got tired of the hustle and bustle of the city and therefore have flocked to spend holidays in the quiet and soothing countryside.

③ Online learning has become/got much more popular all over the world over the years. With online learning people have more options and flexibility regarding their learning venues, pace and content.

④ Technology has gotten/become much cheaper than ever before and it has become more integrated into people's day to day life.

还可以用形容词连用表达"越来越……"的意思，比如：

① It seems children have gotten less and less interested in reading books.

② I think people have gotten more and more comfortable about putting their personal information online.

③ We have become/got a lot more aware of our impact on the environment and therefore more and more environmental campaigns have been taken up all over the world.

描述变化趋势还可以把现在完成时与最高级连用，表示"已经变得最……"，比如：

① China **has become one of the most prosperous countries.**

② Environmental protection **has become one of the most important challenges** in modern world.

（2）现在完成时表达"变得/习惯于……"：**have/has gotten/become used to doing sth**。

① People have gotten/become used to doing everything on their phone, shopping, entertaining, working and study. They have gotten used to looking at their phone screens from the moment they wake up until they go to bed. They have been hooked on the phone day and night.

② I suppose children have gotten/become used to seeing adults using technology all the time, so naturally they want to use it too.

③ People today have gotten/become used to having small family and to living away from the extended family.

④ People today have gotten/become used to living fast-paced lives with much work stress and less spare time for relaxation and entertainment. As a result, their health condition has been threatened.

（3）现在完成时表达"A 已经使 B 怎么样"：**A has helped/enabled B do sth**；**A has made B +形容词**；**A has given B opportunity/ways to do sth**。

① Modern technology has helped/enabled us to live more comfortably.

② Modern technology has made us lazier in almost every aspect in life.

③ Modern technology has given us new ways to explore the world.

2. 真题范例

① **Do you think people are less willing to help others these days compared to the past**?

Unfortunately, yes, to some extent. People **have become more indifferent** to each other, particular to strangers. I think this is due to the fact that modern life **has become more fast-paced** and competitive. People have become **much busier** that they are less willing to help others. On top of that, I think people **have become less trusting** towards each other because they hear so many shocking and sensational stories in the news about crime and cheating, so they don't reach out to help people they don't know for fear that they might be cheated.

② **Is it important to teach students about environmental protection at school**?

Absolutely, yes. I think **it has become more important than ever before**（D+O：以描述变化趋势表达观点）, because climate change **has become a lot more dangerous**, and our oceans **have become much more contaminated** with plastic and waste（D+E：以描述变化趋势举例说明）, so teachers need to show the future generations the significance of changing our planet for the better.

③ **Are people in your country happier now than they were 30 years ago**?

On the whole, I think so, because China **has become one of the most prosperous countries** in Asia（D+R：以描述变化趋势说明原因）, and our quality of life **has become better and better**. 30 years ago, my parents told me that life was very hard and their living standards were a lot lower than they are now, *so they have become much happier.* On top of that, we have more choices of cars, clothes and food from around the world — like going out for steak or pizza *has become a common activity* for a lot of people of my age. So I think that's why most people are happier nowadays.

④ *Why are social networking sites so popular these days*?

Despite the fact that a lot of people have concerns about their privacy on social media, I actually think we *have gotten used to being connected* with our friends and loved ones 24/7（O：阐明观点）. I think it stems from the fact that people *have gotten used to sharing* pictures and videos to make their friends laugh, and they can keep in touch with their family and loved ones anywhere in the world（R+E：说明原因+举例论证）. On top of that, I think *we've all gotten so busy* lately that social media is sometimes the only way for friends to catch up with each other（R：说明原因）. So l think those are two reasons why social networks are so big nowadays（R：重述观点）.

⑤ *Do you think online shopping will replace retail shopping in the future*?

Well, I know lots of people say online shopping will replace retail shopping in the future, but I don't think that will be the case. Even though people *have become used* to making purchases online, which is more convenient and less expensive as compared to off line shopping. However, that doesn't mean retail stores will be replaced. With the economic development, stores, boutiques, and shopping malls *have sprung up* all over the country, which *have attracted* crowds of shoppers, particularly during weekends or holidays. The shoppers can stroll around the stores, really see, feel or try on the commodities before they make the purchase, which is impossible with online shopping. So I think online and retail shopping will co-exist in the future.

⑥ *Do you think technology always has positive effects*?

Not always, but generally speaking, I think it does bring us a lot of benefits. To start with, technology, such as smartphones, *has made our lives much easier*, because we can basically do anything on our phones, searching for information, doing shopping, streaming movies or music, navigating, etc. Likewise, the Internet *has given people new ways* for friends to stay in touch with each other and make new friends too. However, technology has also resulted in some downsides. People from all walks of life *have been spending* so much more time on the screen than they used to. Consequently, their time for real life social activities and outdoor activities are sacrificed, which *has taken a heavy toll* on people's physical and psychological wellbeing. So these are the pros and cons of technology.

⑦ *Do you think the Internet helps to build relationships*?

I know some people say that Internet relationships are not "real" relationships, but I don't think that is true. I think the Internet can be a great place for people to make friends or find love. The Internet *has given us new platforms and ways to* find people with similar interests to us, so I think Internet relationships can be just as real as face-to-face ones. On top of that, it *has made connecting* with other people from anywhere in the world *much easier than ever before.* Social media also ***helps friends stay in touch*** with each other even if they can't meet each other face-to-face, so I think the Internet has been great for building friendships and relationships.

3. 练习

请用描述变化趋势的几种方法回答以下问题：

① ***Do you think people are leading less healthy life than they used to***?

Yes, definitely. People have become _____, their average daily screen time _____ because they work, study and have entertainment in the digital world, which _____. As a result, their physical activities, particularly their outdoor activities _____. On top of that, the household chores _____ due to the application of the modern technology and facilities.

② ***How have your hometown changed over the years***?

Lots of changes _____ in my hometown over the years. Public transportation system _____ with more subway lines, trains and buses. Economy _____, which means _____ which have housed tons of shopping malls, restaurants, recreation facilities, etc. _____, making it more densely populated. The city has become _____.

③ ***How have people's eating habit changed in recent years***?

Well, generally speaking, people today ***have paid more attention*** to their diet, they ***have been*** more conscious about where their food comes from and how it was produced. However, there are still some people, particular the young generation, who _____ the greasy and unhealthy food full of chemicals and unnatural ingredients.

④ ***How have people's daily routine changed over the years***?

Even though some people's daily routine ***hasn't changed*** much, particularly the elderly people who _____ getting up early and going to bed early, I supposed there are a lot of people today who _____ staying up late and becoming night owls. This is partly due to the fact that people ***have been so much tied up*** with their work and study that they _____ staying up late to accomplish their assignments or tasks before due time.

参考答案：

① more and more obsessed with the digital world; has been increasing sharply; has been a more and more important part of their life; have become more and more limited; have become fewer than ever

② have taken place; has been expanded; has been further boosted; more and more skyscrapers have been set up; More and more people have moved and settled down here; more and more prosperous

③ haven gotten used to

④ have gotten used to; have gotten used to; have gotten used to

（三）建议措施

提出建议措施是 Part 3 讨论题的常见题型之一。考官就某个社会问题，提问考生可能的解决方案和途径。比如：

What can people do to live more healthily?

How can human being protect the environment?

How can we encourage people reduce the screen time?

1.语言素材

(by) doing sth.

can/should/could do sth.

try/start/think about/avoid/stop doing sth.

例句：

People **can try taking public transport** more often.

They can **think about buying** a more eco-friendly car.

By doing this, they can have a clearer mind.

We should reduce air pollution by minimizing the burning of fossil fuels.

Spending high quality time with your neighbors is a very effective way to build a close community.

They could avoid driving their car when they only have to travel short distances.

2.真题范例

① **How can people improve their public speaking skills**?

I think the easiest way to practice is **talking** in front of a mirror. **By doing that**, they **can start** getting used to speaking out loud and **they can know** how they look when they speak. They **could also practice** in less intimidating situations, like with just their friends or family, for example. If there's no pressure on them, **they can start improving** and feeling more comfortable about speaking in public.

② **How can people improve their decision-making skills**?

They can weigh up the pros and cons of an issue before making a decision. **To begin with**, **they can brainstorm and jog down** the pros and cons on a piece of paper. **By doing this**, **they can have** a clearer mind and better comparison before making the final decision. **Apart from that they can think about seeking opinions** from their family and friends who they trust. So those are two tips I think people **can consider trying** while making decisions.

③ **How should parents educate their children before they start school**?

Well, there are lots of things parents should teach their children before they go to school. **First and foremost**, **parents should cultivate** good values in their kids, such as honesty, responsibility, politeness, etc. And the best way to nurture the kids is always to teach in real life, to demonstrate how the principles and morals of life are applied, to be the role models of the kids. *Apart from that*, *I think parents should also* hold appreciation and high expectation for the kids, which will then be transmitted consciously or unconsciously, verbally or non verbally to the kids, who will then be inspired and confident and will exploit their potential to fulfill their dreams.

④ *How can we improve our relationships with neighbors*?

Well, there are tons of things we can do to strengthen the bond with our neighbors. To start with, *we should reach* out to our neighbors whenever they are in need. *By doing that*, we make our neighbors feel like we are family members whom they can turn to for help in times of difficulty. Secondly, *exchanging gifts is another way* to strengthen the relationship. The delicious food we cook or some souvenirs from our trips can be excellent gifts to share with our neighbors. Last but not least, *spending high quality time with our neighbors* is a very effective way to build a close community. We can have all kinds of socials with our neighbors, such as potluck party, festival celebration, eating out or travelling.

⑤ *How should boss reward their employees*?

Well, I guess the most common practice is *raising the salary* or offering some material incentives, *on top of that* there are many other forms to reward the employees for their excellent or desired performance. *A boss can recognize* the contribution of an employee by verbal praise either privately or publically. We all have the experience of being praised by our bosses or parents and we remember our tremendous pleasure and satisfaction we gain from that. That is, the reward can be material or spiritual, both are effective and inspiring to the employees.

3.练习

请用建议措施方法完成以下问题的回答：

① *What should be done to protect the environment*?

Well, lots of strategies _____ to protect our mother nature, to start with, we _____ air pollution by _____ the burning of fossil fuels, that is, using more public transportation, favoring energy-efficient appliances, seeking renewable resources, etc. Secondly, we _____ maintaining the biodiversity by animal protection, particularly saving animals threatened with extinction. Last but not least, _____ human-deduced deforestation is very critical, because forests absorb carbon dioxide and provide habitat for species. Those are the things we can do to maintain a healthy and thriving ecosystem on earth.

② *What can people do to improve the air quality in cities*?

First of all, people _____ public transport more often. They _____ _____ driving their car when they only have to travel short distances. On top of that, they _____ buying a more eco-friendly car or installing solar panels to reduce their carbon footprint. Those are some general ways that come to my mind.

(四) 观点罗列

在 Part 3 中，我们经常需要分要点说明观点或事实，在要点之间需要一些衔接词，以凸显答案的条理性与连贯性。

1. 语言素材

(1) 罗列：to begin with/first of all/first and foremost …; second/secondly …; finally/lastly/last but not least …

(2) 此外：on top of that; besides that; apart from that; in addition; as well as that …

(3) 表达比较：while; whereas; on the other hand; at the same time; however …

2. 真题范例

① *Are there many people in your country who want to become actors*?

Absolutely, firstly because a lot of people think being an actor is a fun and well-paid job. On top of that, these days a lot of people have become obsessed with fame and wealth, so becoming an actor would be a good way to achieve that. Last but not least, celebrities usually lead exciting, glamorous, and luxurious lifestyle, which is appealing to a lot of people.

② *How have people's eating habits changed in your country*?

Firstly, I suppose people have become more conscious about where their food comes from, so organic and free-range produce has gotten much more popular. Besides that, I think globalization has given people the chance to eat more diverse food, since nowadays you can find foreign cuisine from all over the world so easily. Lastly, I guess we've gotten bigger and taller because we've eaten more nutritious meals. So those are some changes that come to my mind.

③ *How do people start a conversation*?

Well, I think there are tons of ways to start a conversation. To begin with, you can start with a greeting, particularly greeting about the weather, which is a popular and pleasant topic. Secondly, you can try giving a compliment, for example, if you want to talk with someone, you may start with showing your appreciation for his clothes or accessories. That is a very smart way. By giving compliments, you instantly gain good impression. I mean who doesn't like compliments, right? At last, you can raise a question, liking asking the way. Those are some tips that can serve as icebreakers.

④ *Why do people lose contact with their friends after graduation*?

Well, I think there are a handful of reasons as to why this is the case. First and foremost, after graduation people get to their own paths with new settings, new social circles. As a result, their time and energy don't allow them to be in contact with all those old friends who are scattered in different areas. Secondly, when people no longer study or work together, the geological distance will automatically make them less close socially or emotionally, which I think, is the natural tendency. Last but not least, after graduation, people will take up different majors, directions or professions, so people just don't have many common things to share with each other.

⑤ *What are the differences between being polite and being friendly*?

Well, I think there are a handful of differences between being polite and being friendly. First and foremost, with regard to being polite, it is a passive action, which means people have to do something in a reluctant way, and they have to pretend to be nice even if when they are facing people they don't like, whereas in terms of being friendly, it is an active action, which means people do things sincerely, without any reluctance. Apart from that, being polite is usually more related with the verbal manner, that is how and what to say to convey politeness, whereas being friendly involves both the behaviors and the language to convey kindness and willingness to help.

二、小结

在描述模块 D 中，常用的方法如表 4-3 所示。

表 4-3　描述模块 D 常用方法

类别	语言素材	范例
他人倾向 （一般 现在时）	people+观点或行为； 某类人群+观点或行为	① *Why do people like visiting historical places*? I think it's due to people's intrinsic curiosity. They are just interested in knowing about what happened in the past and they want to gain a deeper understanding of history by looking into "the window of the past", that is, the museum. Certainly visiting the historical places in person makes learning more fun and impressive than learning from books or documentaries. ② *How will ebooks affect paper books*? Well, I know a lot of people have said that ebooks will replace hard copies eventually, but actually I believe that people still prefer reading real books, because they enjoy the feeling of paper in their hands and turning the pages. ③ People need to relax and unwind sometimes. ④ People enjoy playing sports with each other. ⑤ People don't want to spend too much money on food. ⑥ Parents encourage their children to participate in sports. ⑦ Seniors are very concerned about their health condition. ⑧ Many tourists like to buy souvenirs while they travel.

续表 4-3

类别	语言素材	范例
变化趋势（现在完成时）	have/has got/become a lot/much/slightly/a little+形容词比较级（变得更加……）；have/has got/become used to doing sth.（变得习惯于……）；A has helped B do sth./A has made B + *adj.*/A has given ...（变得可以/能够……）	① *Are people in your country happier now than they were* 30 *years ago*? On the whole, I think so, because China *has become one of the most prosperous countries* in Asia, and our quality of life *has become better and better*. 30 years ago, my parents told me that life was very hard and their living standards were a lot lower than they are now, *so they have become much happier.* On top of that, we have more choice of cars, clothes and food from around the world — like going out for steak or pizza *has become a common activity* for a lot of people of my age. So I think that's why most people are happier nowadays. ② *Why are social networking sites so popular these days*? Despite the fact that a lot of people have concerns about their privacy on social media, I actually think we *have got used to being connected* with our friends and loved ones 24/7. I think it stems from the fact that people *have got used to sharing* pictures and videos to make their friends laugh, and they can keep in touch with their family and loved ones anywhere in the world. On top of that, I think *we've all got so busy* lately that social media is sometimes the only way for friends to catch up with each other. So I think those are two reasons why social networks are so big nowadays. ③ *Do you think the Internet help to build relationships*? I know some people say that Internet relationships are not "real" relationships, but I disagree because I think the Internet can be a great place for people to make friends or find love. The Internet *has given us new platforms and ways to* find people with similar interests to us, so I think Internet relationships can be just as real as face-to-face ones. On top of that, It *has made connecting* with other people from anywhere in the world *much easier than ever before.* Social media also *helps friends stay in touch* with each other even if they can't meet each other face-to-face, so I think the Internet has been great for building friendships and relationships. ④ On-line learning has become more popular all over the world. ⑤ Technology has got much cheaper than ever before. ⑥ Housing prices have become a lot higher whereas people's salaries have only got a little higher over the last 20 years. ⑦ Modern technology has helped us lead a comfortable life. ⑧ Modern technology has enabled us to work more efficiently and live more comfortably. ⑨ Modern technology has made us lazier in almost every aspect.

续表 4-3

类别	语言素材	范例
建议措施	By doing sth; can/may/should do sth. ; can/may/should try/start/stop; think about doing sth.	① *How can people improve their public speaking skills*? I think the easiest way to practice is *talking* in front of a mirror. *By doing that*, they *can start* getting used to speaking out loud and *they can know* how they look when they speak. They *could also practice* in less intimidating situations, like with just their friends or family, for example. If there's no pressure on them, *they can start improving* and feeling more comfortable about speaking in public. ② We can enhance our physical well-being by adopting healthier lifestyle. ③ We should eat well to live well.
观点罗列	to begin with/first of all/first and foremost … (首先); second/secondly/on top of that/besides that/apart from that/in addition/as well as that …(第二/其次); finally / lastly / last but not least (最后); while/whereas/on the other hand/at the same time/however (一方面……另一方面)	① *How do people start a conversation*? Well, I think there are tons of ways to start a conversation. *To begin with*, *you can start with* a greeting, particularly greeting about the weather, which is a popular and pleasant topic. *Secondly*, *you can try giving a compliment*, for example, If you want to talk with someone, you may start with showing your appreciation for his clothes or accessories. That is a very smart way. By giving compliments you instantly gain good impression. I mean who doesn't like compliments, right? *At last*, *you can raise a question*, liking asking the way. Those are some tips that can serve as icebreakers. ② Firstly, I suppose people have become more conscious about where their food comes from. ③ Besides that, I think globalization has given people the chance to eat more diverse food. ④ Lastly, I guess we've gotten bigger and taller because we've eaten more nutritious meals.

第五节　**Part 3 举例模块**

举例是论证观点非常有效的方法。举例不局限于针对具体事例的论证，还包括对当前情境、假设条件以及源自个人知识阅历的举例论证。

一、常用方法

(一) 具体事例

1. 语言素材

like somebody/somewhere, for example …
like when sb. did sth. …

例句：

Like Wu Shengming, *for example*, who rebuilt her career and started a company at late 70s after experiencing all the life tragedies.

Like the parks in my city, *for example*, that draw lots of visitors of all ages.

Like Taobao, *for example*, *which* is the most popular shopping platform in my country.

Like when my nephew Tom bought an iPhone 8 years ago, five of his colleagues followed suit and replaced their old iPhone with iPhone 8.

2. 真题范例

① *What do you think influences people to buy new things*?

Well, it depends. If you are talking about old people, I think generally speaking the occasion that they will buy new things is that the old ones are broken and can no longer function. This is due to the fact that old people are usually very frugal and they don't want to waste money. If you mean younger generation, I think a very important factor to motivate them buy new stuff is related with peer pressure. *Like when my nephew Tom bought* an iPhone 8 years ago, five of his colleagues followed suit and replaced their old iPhone with iPhone 8. So keeping up with the Joneses is one of the traits of young people who are keen on seeking trend and fashion.

② *Do you think monuments to famous people are a waste of money*?

No, definitely not. The monuments aren't a waste of money, instead they are treasures of the local city. *Take the monuments of Chairman Mao in my city as an example.* We have a sculpture of Chairman Mao on the Orange Island as well as in front of Hunan University. Those monuments have meant a lot to us. First and foremost, they have become the land icons in the city that have drawn tourists from all over the country or even the world, which means the boost to the tourism-related business as well as an increase in tax revenues. On top of that, those monuments remind us of our brilliant and shinning heroes in history, who have continued to inspire us and connect us with the historical period in which they lived. Our sense of belonging and of pride are thereby enhanced. Those monuments are just like precious pieces of artefact from history for people today to learn, to appreciate and to be inspired.

③ *What is necessary to become a successful businessman*?

Well, successful businessmen have many basic common qualities, such as honesty, hardworking, self-discipline, etc. One essential element that is indispensable to success is perseverance. *Like Susan*, *for example*, *who rebuilt her career and started a company at her*

70s after experiencing all the life tragedies as bankruptcy, being jailed, divorce, and losing her only child. It was definitely her perseverance and strong-mindedness that led her out of the chaos of life and regained success and fame.

(二) 当前情境

当前情境下的举例模块与描述模块中的趋势变化有所不同但又密切相关。两者都是从当前情境入手,但描述模块重在描述当前的趋势变化,而举例模块重在引证当前情境下在某人或某处发生的某事。两个模块可以结合起来运用。比如:

Especially nowadays more and more young people have been so obsessed with the digital world that they have been used to the sedentary lifestyle and have ended up becoming couch potatoes, which has exerted harmful effect on their physical and mental health(描述趋势变化)。Nowadays it's common to see young people staring onto their screens at parties, over meals, in the living rooms and bedrooms, just anywhere anytime(当前情境下的举例论证)。

1. 语言素材

Especially nowadays it's common to/(you can) see people doing sth. somewhere …

One big trend is that nowadays you can always see people doing sth. somewhere.

You can find people doing sth.

There are a lot of people doing sth. somewhere.

People do (are doing) sth. somewhere.

以人—地—事为线索展开例子论证,说明在某地看到人们做什么,人们在某地做什么或某地有什么等。

例句:

In the grocery stores *you can see shoppers* buying food.

One big trend is that nowadays you can always see commuters looking at screens in the subways.

At parties, for example, *you can/(it's common to) find people* introducing friends from different social groups to each other.

At school, for example, *teachers will lecture* on environmental protection.

At parties, for example, *friends might introduce* other friends from different social groups to each other.

In office, for example, *colleagues might become* friends after working together for a while.

There are so many tourists on the beach that it's always noisy, crowded and dirty.

On social media, for instance, *there are lots of groups and pages helping* people with similar interests connect with each other.

2. 真题范例

① *Do you think online shopping will replace retail shopping in the future*?

Well, I think it depends on what the stores carry. For example, in regards to the stores that carry books or electrical device, they will be eventually pushed out by the on-line ones because those products don't need to be checked on the spot or tried on before being purchased, whereas in terms of stores for clothes or shoes, I think there will always be a need for physical shops. Actually the truth is that with the economic development, *all over the country more and more stores, the clothing stores, shoe stores, have sprung up. You can find people hustling in and out of these stores*, where they can really see, feel or try on the commodities before they make the purchase, which is impossible with online shopping. So some physical stores will extinct while others will continue to prosper in the future depending on the commodities they carry.（此例中描述模块描述了全国有越来越多的实体店这一趋势，而举例模块则说明经常看到人们熙熙攘攘涌向商场这一情境。）

② *Is fast food popular in your country?*

I think it depends on whom you are talking about. In regards to middle-aged or old people, generally they are more health conscious and try to stay away from fast food as it is high in calories but low in nutritious values, whereas in terms of the young people, particularly the millennial generation, *fast food has been very popular with them*（描述模块表示趋势）. *In MacDonald's or KFC you can see the youngsters or parents of children lining up for hamburgers, fries, chicken, etc. In offices, for example, there are lots of young professionals who have gotten used* to ordering fast food as their lunch（当前情境下的举例）. So yes, fast food has been very popular with the young generation.

③ *Where do people in your country buy clothes from?*

Even though people still buy clothes from boutiques or shopping malls, *more and more people have become used to* buying clothes online（描述模块表达趋势）. Like Taobao, for example, has become the most popular shopping platform that people from all over the country buy clothes from. *Like when my friend started* a clothing store online 10 years ago, she had the yearly sale of around 100,000 RMB, but now the yearly sale has reached nearly 1 million（具体事例举例）. So the soar of the online sale of the clothing *demonstrates the trend that nowadays* more and more people are buying clothes on Taobao（当前情境举例）.

④ *Which is more exposed to noise, the city or the countryside?*

Definitely, the noise pollution is more serious in the city than in the country. In regard to the city, as we know city dwellers have to face up to a rich variety of noises on a daily basis. *For example, all over the city people are bothered* by the traffic noise, which goes on and on day and night, very annoying（当前情境举例）. *Apart from that is the noise from factories or construction sites which scatter all over the city. Whereas in terms of the countryside, you can hear* the chirping of the birds, the tinkling of the brooks, that sound of nature is really soothing（当前情境举例）. So in the city there is so much noise resulted from the human activity whereas in the countryside we can enjoy the tranquility of nature.

⑤ *What advantages can tourism bring to a city?*

The industry of tourism definitely brings various benefits to the local city. To start with, it promotes local economic development. *Take Zhangjiajie, a place of interest in my province as an example*（具体事例）. It used to be a poor and remote town, but ever since it became the national forest park decades ago, its economy has been roaring. *Today in Zhangjiajie you can find the town* has expanded into a vigorous and prosperous city with sky scrapers, luxurious cars, big shopping malls, high-end hotels, etc. (当前情境举例). *Especially nowadays you can always see tourists* from all over the world flocking to Zhangjiajie, admiring its fantastic scenery (当前情境举例), which increases the tax revenue for government as well as the income for the local residents. Apart from that, tourism also connects the local people with the outside world through the tourists. *In Zhangjiajie it's common to see* all those happy and interesting conversations between the local people and tourists (当前情境举例). Some peddlers even learned some English to better serve their international customers.

⑥ *How do people in your country make friends these days*?

Generally speaking, I think most people meet new friends through other friends or through work or Internet. *In offices, for example*, colleagues might become friends after working together for a while. *At parties, for example*, friends might introduce other friends from different social groups. *On social media, for instance, there are lots of groups and pages* created to help people with similar interests connect with each other. *On the Internet, for instance, you can find* forums, message boards and communities of people who enjoy playing a certain sport, doing a hobby or learning specific skills.

3. 练习

请用当前情境举例方法，完成以下练习：

① *Do people like to read news on the Internet*?

Yes, definitely! Thanks to smartphones and technology, the Internet has become most people's main source of information. _____ on the laptop or smartphone anywhere anytime. This is due to the fact that reading through Internet is just so convenient and economical. So _____ their fragmented time to read the news through their smartphones, for example, when they are waiting for someone at lunch, while on the metro during their morning commute, or at night before sleep.

② Over the country _____ hustling in and out of these stores.

③ In offices, for example, _____ ordering fast food as their lunch.

④ The soar of the online sale of the clothing demonstrates the trend that _____ _____ buying clothes on Taobao.

参考答案：

① Nowadays you can see people reading news; currently it's common to see people using

② people are

③ there are lots of young professionals who have gotten used to

④ more and more people are

(三) 假设条件

如前所述，条件句包括真实条件句与虚拟条件句。真实条件句是指有可能发生的事实，而虚拟条件句是假设的事实，不可能或不太可能发生。两者都用 if 来引领条件句。

1. 语言素材

If ... sb./sth. will ... （真实条件句）

If ... sb./sth. would ... （虚拟条件句）

例句：

If children can reduce their screen time and go out for sports, such as playing basketball, volleyball, jogging or cycling, to name just a few, *they can certainly be healthier and stronger* physically and mentally.

If the celebrities give some public speeches on the importance of health and share with the public what they do to maintain health, *people will be very likely to follow.*

If someone didn't return money they borrowed from me I would have a few concerns.

2. 真题范例

① *How can people improve their decision-making skills?*

They can weigh up the pros and cons of an issue before making a decision. To begin with, they can brainstorm and jog down the pros and cons on a piece of paper. *If they jog down everything*, they can have a clearer mind and better comparison before making the final decision. Apart from that they can think about seeking opinions from their family and friends who they trust. So those are two tips I think people can consider trying while making decisions.

② *How should parents educate their children before they start school?*

Well, there are lots of things parents should teach their children before they go to school. First and foremost, parents should cultivate good values in their kids, such as honesty, responsibility, politeness, etc. And the best way to nurture the kids is always to teach them in real life. *If the parents can demonstrate* how they faithfully carry out the principles and moral in their day to day life, the kids can pick up from there and regard the parents as their role models. Apart from that, I think parents should also hold appreciation and high expectation for the kids. *If they think positively about the kids* and hold positive expectations for them, they will transmit those expectation consciously or unconsciously, verbally or nonverbally to the kids, who will then be inspired and confident and will exploit their potential to fulfill their dreams as well as the expectations of their parents.

③ *How can we improve our relationships with neighbors?*

Well, there are tons of things we can do to strengthen the bond with our neighbors. To start with, we should reach out to our neighbors whenever they are in need. *If we do that*, we can make our neighbors feel like we are family members whom they can turn to for help in times of difficulty. Secondly, exchanging gifts is another way to strengthen the relationship. *If we can share with our neighbors* the delicious food we cook or bring them some souvenirs from our trips, the bound with our neighbors can be greatly strengthened. Last but not least, spending high quality time with our neighbors is a very effective way to build a close community. We can have all kinds of socials with our neighbors, such as potluck party, festival celebration, eating out or travelling.

④ *How should boss reward their employees*?

Well, I guess the most common practice is by raising the salary or offering some material incentives, on top of that there are many other forms to reward the employees for their excellent or desired performance. A boss can recognize the contribution of an employee by verbal praise either privately or publically. *If the boss gives his employees praise* at the meetings or expresses his appreciation privately, the employees will certainly be overjoyed and very much inspired to work even harder and better.

⑤ *What's the difference between learning face-to-face with teachers and learning by yourself*?

I think there are several differences between the two. First of all, students in a classroom can rely on their teacher for answers and extra information. *If they have a doubt or a query*, *they can raise* their hands and their teachers can give them the answer they need and they can move on. They also have the benefit of working in groups. *If they collaborate on a project*, *students can* help each other and learn from each other. However, *if they study by themselves*, *they have to* be more independent and self-reliant. *If they need to* find out some specific information, they will have to go on the Internet or to a library to get the answers they need.

⑥ *What would you do if someone didn't return money they borrowed from you*?

Whenever I lend people money, I always try to give them a long time to pay it back. However, *if I didn't hear from them* for a couple of weeks or even months, I would start to have a few concerns. At first I would try to approach the situation tactfully and sensitively and ask them if they could pay me back or if they could afford. *If they were honest with me and told me the truth*, *I would* have no problem giving them extra time. However, *if they lied to me or tried to give me less than what I lent*, *I would* get frustrated and that could harm our relationship. Thankfully, I've never been in that position, but those are the steps I would take.

⑦ *What are the causes of traffic jams*?

There are lots of situations that can lead to traffic jams, such as poor road conditions, heavy traffic, bad weather, etc. One of the most important causes, however, is traffic accident (具体事例), *because should an accident*, *particularly a serious accident*, *take place* (虚拟条件), all the vehicles involved shouldn't be cleared away until all the necessary investigation is done. It's very common to see a long line of vehicles queuing up on the highway with an accident at the start of the line (当前情境). Apart from that, weather contributes to lots of traffic jams. As we know *under the terrible weather*, *such as blizzard*, *downpour* (真实条件), traffic accidents and jams are just too common due to the slippery road as well as the low visibility.

3. 练习

请用条件假设方法完成下面练习：

① *Why do people lose contact with their friends after graduation*?

Well, I think there are a handful of reasons as to why this is the case. First and foremost, after graduation people get to their own paths with new settings, new social circles. _____

_____ who scatter in different areas, they won't have enough time or energy to adapt to the new settings and to socialize with new friends. Apart from that, after graduation, people will take up different majors, directions or professions, _____,

they will find they don't have as many common grounds or topics as they used to, as a result, their motivation of contacting their former friends will fade.

② *Is it difficult for adults to talk with children*?

Well, it depends. _____, then they won't have warm and positive relationship with the kids, hence, a smooth and successful communications will be unlikely. On the contrary, _____, respecting the kids and treating them as friends, then the kids will respond accordingly, talks will be easy.

③ *Do young people take their parents' advice when choosing a major*?

Not necessarily. _____, that is, _____ or the inner interest of the kid, then they will be more likely to take. On the contrary, _____

_____, such as their own personal preferences or consideration of job opportunities, then the kids might be more reluctant to take their parents' suggestions. I guess it is important for the kids to follow their heart and exploit their potential while choosing their major.

④ *Do you think it is useful to give money as gifts*?

Yes, definitely! In my culture hongbao, that is, the red envelop with money inside is a very popular gift, particularly for special occasions like new year, birthday or wedding. _____

_____, it is always a struggle to choose the right gift regarding what to buy and whether the gift will be liked, _____, the receiver can pick out what they like with the money or they can save up the money. They will have more flexibility with money than with any other forms of gifts.

⑤ *Will people feel happy when receiving an expensive gift*?

Well, it depends. _____, say, parents, children or spouse, I guess they are happy, because the more expensive, the more precious the gift is. _____

_____, they probably won't be happy, instead, they will feel like they owe too much a favor and they are obligated to return something fancy or even something more expensive.

参考答案：

① If they continue to keep contact with all of their former friends; if they communicate with their former classmates

② If the adults are aggressive and harsh; if the adults are friendly and democratic

③ If the parents' advice is a good one; if it fits in with the potential; if the parents' suggestion is based on other factors

④ If you send a gift; but if you give money

⑤ If they receive an expensive gift from their immediate family members; However, if the costly gift is from friends or someone not that close to them

（四）知识阅历

举例论证还可根据个人的知识阅历展开，说明自己的所见所闻及所了解到的资源信息。

1. 语言素材

I (have) read/heard/saw/noticed/watched/been told …

I've learned from many different resources that …

Someone (has) told me that …

例句：

I read in some newspaper that people spend over 11 hours a day looking at screens.

I saw in a documentary about climate change that said global warming has gotten worse.

My colleague told me that he spends over 2 hours commuting to work every day.

当表示多次听说某事时可用现在完成时表达，表示迄今为止已听说过多次。

I have read from a few different websites that people spend over 11 hours a day looking at screens.

I have seen (in many documentaries) that global warming has gotten worse.

Several friends have told me that they spend over 2 hours commuting to work.

2. 真题范例

① *What can be done to improve the air quality in cities*?

I think the easiest solution would be for people to move around more eco-friendly. Instead of driving private vehicles, they may opt to take public transportation or to ride bicycles. *I read that* the bike path system in my city will be further expanded to encourage the residents cycle to work, which will certainly curb the air-pollution as well as save energy. *I've also heard from different resources that the municipal government* in my city is planning to raise the fuel tax for 30 percent in the hope of reducing the use of private cars. I think, both of the measures are effective to enhance air qualities in cities.

② *Is fast food popular in your country*?

Yes, fast food has become very popular in my country, particular among the millennial generation. *I've learned from different resources* that more than 60 percent of the young people eat fast food on a regular basis, at least 3 times a week. *I also learned from one of my friends* that many of his colleagues have gotten used to ordering fast food as their lunch. So yes, fast food has been very popular with the young generation.

③ *Why do some adults hate to throw away old things, such as clothes*?

I learned from my grandfather that life used to be very hard and they could hardly make ends meet, as a result, they have gotten used to being frugal and hating any kind of waste, like throwing away old stuff. *I also read from different resources that* when people getting older, they become more nostalgic, and keeping those old stuff like clothes is a way to connect themselves with the past.

④ ***Can you explain why many people are interested in the private lives of famous people***?

Well, ***I once read an article about this question*** which said that people like to peek into the personal life of the celebrities to satisfy their curiosity. Because in their mind the celebrities are different from themselves and they would like to explore what those differences are. ***I also learned from one of my friends***, who is a paparazzo, that young people today have gotten used to talking about their favorite singers' personal life, which has become a common topic when they socialize with each other and if you know nothing about those stuff, you are out. Hence, it is trendy to learn about and talk about the personal life of the celebrities among young people.

⑤ ***How can famous people raise the image of a country***?

Well, there are lots of ways that the celebrities can enhance the reputation of their countries. For example, by winning medals in international games. ***I've watched so many times from TV that*** the medal winners of Olympic Games stood on the medals podium with the whole world applauding for them, their respective national flag risen and national anthem played. This certainly enhances the images of their home countries. Apart from that, many celebrities make great contribution to the world by scientific breakthroughs, such as Yuan Longping, the father of hybrid rice. ***I learned from many different resources*** that a large population have been saved from starvation because of his work. I think public figures have more opportunities to be exposed to the world and they are even regarded as the business card of a country. Their fame or contribution can definitely enhance the country reputation.

3. 练习

请用知识阅历模块完成下面练习：

① ***Why is it important for children to learn about traditional products***?

Well, it is definitely important to pass on the knowledge of traditional products to the young generation. _____ that some of our traditional products, particularly those produced in remote countryside, have been threatened with extinction because fewer and fewer young people are learning the skills. Apart from that, the traditional products is part of our culture which gives us a sense of pride and connects us with our history and ancestors, therefore, it's worthwhile to have more people know about them, regardless of their age.

② ***Are balanced meals important to us***?

Yes, a balanced diet is definitely crucial to our health and overall wellbeing. To start with, balanced diet provides our body with the various nutrients we need. Our body needs the appropriate amount of carbohydrate, protein and fat in order to work efficiently. Apart from that, _____ that a balanced diet not only reduces the risks of diseases like obesity and diabetes but also sharpens our mind and increases our work efficiency.

③ *Will people no longer cook at home in the future*?

_____ that said that people in the future will cook more at home due to the fact that people are becoming more and more conscious about their health and home-cooked food is definitely the best option with the higher quality ingredients and more balanced diet. _____ that household chores including cooking will be made even simpler and easier with the application of home robots. So both are the reasons why I think people will cook more rather than less at home in the future.

参考答案：
① I have learned in several different resources
② I learned from different resources
③ I read an article in a magazine; I also heard from several different resources

二、小结

在举例模块 E 中常用的方法如表 4-4 所示。

表 4-4 举例模块 E 常用方法

类别	语言素材	范例
具体事例	(like) somebody/somewhere, for example …; like when sb. did sth. …	① *Like Wu Shengming, for example*, who rebuilt her career and started a company at late 70s after experiencing all the life tragedies. ② *Like the parks in my city, for example*, that draw lots of visitors of all ages … ③ *Like Taobao, for example, which* is the most popular shopping platform in my country. ④ *Like when my nephew Tom bought* an iPhone 8 years ago, five of his colleagues followed suit and replaced their old iPhone with iPhone 8. ⑤ *What is necessary to become a successful businessman*? Well, successful businessmen have many basic common qualities, such as honesty, hardworking, self-discipline, etc. One essential element that is indispensable to success is perseverance. *Like Susan, for example, who rebuilt her career and started a company at her 70s* after experiencing all the life tragedies as bankruptcy, being jailed, divorce, and losing her only child. It was definitely her perseverance and strong-mindedness that led her out of the chaos of life and regained success and fame.

续表4-4

类别	语言素材	范例
当前情境	Especially nowadays it's common to/（you can）see people doing sth. somewhere …; One big trend is that nowadays you can always see people doing sth./people are doing sth. You can find people doing sth./people are doing sth. somewhere; There are a lot of people doing sth. somewhere	① *Nowadays it's common to see young people staring* onto their screens at parties, over meals, in the living rooms and bedrooms, just anywhere anytime. ② *One big trend is that nowadays you can always see commuters* looking at screens in the subways. ③ At school *you can see teachers lecturing* on environmental protection. ④ In the grocery store *you can see shoppers buying food.* ⑤ *On social media, for instance, there are lots of groups and pages* helping people with similar interests connect with each other. ⑥ *Is fast food popular in your country*? I think it depends on whom you are talking about. In regards to middle-aged or old people, generally they are more health conscious and try to stay away from fast food as it is high in calories but low in nutritious values, whereas in terms of the young people, particularly the millennial generation, *fast food has been very popular with them. In MacDonald's or KFC you can see the youngsters or parents of children lining up for hamburgers, fries, chicken, etc. In offices, for example, there are lots of young professionals who have gotten used* to ordering fast food as their lunch. So yes, fast food has been very popular with the young generation.
假设条件	If … sb./sth. will …（真实条件句）; If sb./sth. would …（虚拟条件句）	① *If children can reduce their screen time* and go out for sports, such as playing basketball, volleyball, jogging or cycling, to name just a few, they can certainly be healthier and stronger physically and mentally. ② *If the celebrities give some public speeches* on the importance of health and share with the public what they do to maintain health, people will be very likely to follow. ③ *If someone didn't return money they borrowed from me* I would have a few concerns. ④ *What's the difference between learning face-to-face with teachers and learning by yourself*? I think there are several differences between the two. First of all, students in a classroom can rely on their teacher for answers and extra information. *If they have a doubt or a query, they can raise* their hand and their teacher can give them the answer they need and they can move on. They also have the benefit of working in groups. *If they collaborate on a project, students can* help each other

续表 4-4

类别	语言素材	范例
		and learn from each other. However, *if they study by themselves, they have to* be more independent and self-reliant. *If they need to* find out some specific information, they will have to go on the Internet or to a library to get the answers they need. ⑤ *What would you do if someone didn't return money they borrowed from you*? Whenever I lend people money, I always try to give them a long time to pay it back. However, *if I didn't hear from them for a couple of weeks or even months, I would* start to have a few concerns. At first I would try to approach the situation tactfully and sensitively and ask them if they could pay me back or if they could afford. *If they were honest with me and told me the truth, I would* have no problem giving them extra time. However, *if they lied to me or tried to give me less than what I lent, I would* get frustrated and that could harm our relationship. Thankfully, I've never been in that position, but those are the steps I would take.
知识阅历	I read/heard/saw/noticed/ watched/was told ...; I have read/heard/seen/ watched/noticed ...	① *I read in some newspaper* that people spend over 11 hours a day looking at screens. ② *My colleague told me* that he spends over 2 hours commuting to work every day. ③ *I have read from a few different websites* that people spend over 11 hours a day looking at screens. ④ *I have seen* (*in many documentaries*) that global warming has gotten worse. ⑤ *Several friends have told me* that they spend over 2 hours commuting to work. ⑥ *What can be done to improve the air quality in cities*? I think the easiest solution would be for people to move around more eco-friendly. Instead of driving private vehicles, they may opt to take public transportation or to ride bicycles. *I read that* the bike path system in my city will be further expanded to encourage the residents cycle to work, which will certainly curb the air-pollution as well as save energy. *I've also heard from different resources that the municipal government* in my city is planning to raise the fuel tax for 30 percent in the hope of reducing the use of private cars. I think, both of the measures are effective to enhance air qualities in cities.

第六节　**Part 3** 总结模块

ORDER 答题框架的最后一步是用一句话进行总结，重申观点（restatement）。

一、常用方法

（一）封闭式问题

1.语言素材

So I think …

So I guess …

So I assume …

So I believe …

对封闭式问题的回答，可在总结中重复问题中的助动词，以形成前后呼应，如表 4-5
所示。

表 4-5　封闭式问题的总结

问题	重申观点
Is it important to visit family members?	So I think it is very important to visit family members.
Should governments use celebrities to help people raise health awareness?	So I guess celebrity effect can be employed to influence people's health awareness.
Do men and women play the same kind of sports?	So I guess those are the gender differences regarding the types of sports.
Do young people like to do sports?	On the whole I think the young generation today are not physically active enough.
Is it hard for young people to learn skills?	So I believe learning new skills is not that difficult for young people.
Are elderly people happy being with their families?	So I think the senior people are bound to be happy spending time with their families.

2.真题范例

***Do people trust each other as much as they used to**?*

Overall, I think people have started trusting others much less. I think that's down to the media, because they always share stories about strangers attacking, robbing or hurting people, which, to a large extent, make people become less trusting towards each other. On top of that, there are a lot of Internet scams nowadays, like fake profiles or viruses, which have made people more suspicious towards strangers. ***So I don't think people trust each other as much as they used to due to these reasons.***

(二) 开放式问题

1. 语言素材

So I think …
So I guess …
So I assume …
So I believe …

对开放式问题的总结应与问句中的特殊疑问词相对应, 也可以在总结句中将主题词加上形容词进行修饰, 使句子内容更丰富, 如表 4-6 所示。

表 4-6 开放式问题的总结

问题	重申观点
Why	So I think that's the reason/cause why … So I think those are the leading causes/common reasons/major reasons why …
When	So I think that's the time when … So I think those are the times/situations/moments/occurrences when …
Who	So I think that's the person who/those are people who … So I think those are the types of people/celebrities/business people/individuals/ characters/employers/professionals who …
Where	So I think that's the place where … So I think those are the common places/popular stores/ideal destinations/great nations/ majestic buildings where …
How	So I think that's the way we can … So I think those are the effective ways/measures/ ideas/methods/ways we can …
What (thing, idea, solution, problem …)	So I think that's a thing/an idea/a solution/a problem that … So I think those are the things/ideas/problems/types of activities that … So I think those are useful/common solutions that … So I think those are major/leading reasons that …

2. 真题范例

① ***How do you think government could encourage more people to exercise and participate in sport?***

Well, government can do tons of things to encourage people to lead a more active life. This is due to the fact that government has the authority and resources to exert influence on its citizens. First and foremost, government can enhance people's health awareness by media coverage, such as newspaper or TV. Secondly, government can launch sports events for the public, like marathon or games. Last but not least, government can also build more public facilities such as hiking or walking trails, parks, gyms, pools, etc. or even provide subsidies to low-income families for free membership to gyms. By doing this more people will have access to the sport facilities. *So those are the major things I think government can do promote active and healthy lifestyle in its citizens.*

② *How can we encourage children to exercise*?

There are tons of ways to encourage kids to play sports and games as the kids usually have much energy and curiosity. By saying that I don't mean that if you leave the kids in the gym or on the playground, they will go for exercise. No, they won't. But if the parents accompany them, play with them, and make exercise as a family event and part of the daily routine, kids will certainly love exercise so much that they find it difficult to stop. Apart from that, if the children are registered in some clubs that they like, such as swimming, rafting or basketball clubs, they will be more likely to grow interest in those sports simply because they can gain some skills from professional coaches and once they are good at something , they will love doing it, not to mention that they can make friends and enlarge their social cycle in the clubs. *So those are some effective ways we can motivate kids to exercise.*

二、小结

在结尾模块 R 中，常用的方法如表 4-7。

表 4-7　结尾模块 R 常用方法

类别	语言素材	范例
封闭式/ 开放式	So I guess that is/those are…; So I think that is/those are…; So I don't think…; So I believe …	① So those arethe major things I think government can do to promote active and healthy lifestyle in its citizens. ② So those are some effective ways we can motivate kids to exercise. ③ So I don't think people trust each other as much as they used to due to these reasons.

第七节　**Part 3** 真题实训

一、题目整合

Part 3 的讨论题是雅思口语三个部分中难度最大的。Part 3 的讨论题与 Part 2 主题相关，但不拘泥于 Part 2 的话题，考官可以进行拓展式、发散式提问，问题涉及的范畴非常广。我们把 2022 年 4 月到 2023 年 4 月的 Part 3 的 432 道常见讨论题进行分析归类。在主题类别方面，教育教学、兴趣爱好、人际交往、媒体科技、交通环境、职业发展这几类常见的主题有 306 道题目，占总数的 71%，其他 25 个主题为 126 道题，占 29%。主题类别的构成如表 4-8 所示。

表 4-8　主题类别构成

主题类别	题目数量
教育教学	64
兴趣爱好	55
人际交往	55
媒体科技	42
交通环境	56
职业发展	34
其他主题	126
合计	432

在题型方面，最常见的题型是对比题。在 432 道题目中，涉及对比的题目高达 79 道，占所有题目的 18%。对比包括年龄对比、性别对比、时代对比、城乡对比、优劣对比、实体与网络对比等方面。其中，年龄对比题比重最大，共有 33 道题，涉及老年人和青年人在学习、爱好、科技、社交等多方面的差异。

本节将各类对比真题进行汇总。

(一)年龄对比(共 33 题)

1.学习

① What kind of help do you think old people need?

② From whom can children learn more, parents or grandparents?

③ What are the differences in things children can learn from parents and those from grandparents?

④ What practical skills can young people teach old people?

⑤ What skills can young people teach old people besides technology?

⑥ How can young people teach old people skills?

⑦ What can old people teach young people?

⑧ Is it hard for young people to learn skills? What about old people?

⑨ How do young and old people react differently to new things?

⑩ Is it easier for young people to change?

2. 爱好

① Do you think young people and old people enjoy the same kind of music?

② Do young children like the same stories as older children?

③ Do you think old people and young people can share interests?

④ Are older people as fashionable as young people? Why?

⑤ Do you think only old people have time for leisure?

⑥ Compared with young people, do old people prefer to live in quiet places?

⑦ Why is fashion more important to some people?

⑧ What do young people do to keep fit?

⑨ What do old people do to keep fit?

⑩ Do you think young people and old people have different types of hobbies?

⑪ What leisure facilities can be used by people of all ages?

3. 科技

① Do old people spend much time on social media?

② Do you think old people and young people use the same kind of social media app?

③ What are the differences between old people and young people when they use the Internet?

④ What are the differences between young people and old people when they use cellphones?

4. 社交

① What disagreements do parents and children usually have?

② Is it difficult for adults to talk with children?

③ Who are more likely to make complaints, older people or young people?

④ Do you think people's relationship with friends will change when they get older?

⑤ Who behave better when waiting, children or adults?

⑥ Is it difficult for adults to talk with children?

⑦ Do people of different age groups have different diet habits?

⑧ Do you think younger people should be less paid than older people?

(二) 其他对比 (共 46 题)

1. 性别对比

① Do women have more leisure time than men do?

② Do boys and girls like the same kind of toys?

③ Are women more fashionable than men? Why?

④ Do men and women play the same kind of sports?

2. 时代对比

① What are the differences between the outdoor activities children did in the past and now?

② What are the differences between food production today and that in the past?

③ What are the differences between traditional and modern agriculture?

④ What are some of the differences between the toys kids play with nowadays and those they used to play with in the past?

⑤ Are there any differences regarding celebrities in the past and celebrities now?

⑥ Why do some habits change when people get older?

3. 支持与反对

① What are the advantages and disadvantages of wearing uniform at work and school?

② What are the advantages and disadvantages for people being famous?

③ What are the advantages and disadvantages of cultural diversity?

④ What are the advantages and disadvantages of eating in restaurants?

⑤ What are the advantages and disadvantages when people keep busy?

⑥ What are the advantages and disadvantages coming along with changing jobs?

4. 差异

① What are the differences between actors/actresses who earn much and those who earn little?

② What are the differences between every day meals and celebration meals?

③ Why do people dress casually in daily life and dress formally at work?

④ Who can influence children more, teachers or parents?

⑤ Which one is more important, keeping a good relationship with colleagues or doing well at work?

⑥ Why do some people like to get news on the Internet instead of getting it from TV?

⑦ What's the difference between the Internet and television?

⑧ Which influences young people more when choosing a job, income or interest?

⑨ Why do some people choose to eat out instead of ordering takeout?

⑩ Do you think the support from a friend is different from the support from a family member?

⑪ What are the differences between live concerts and online concerts?

⑫ Do you prefer to read ebooks or paper books?

⑬ What are the differences between shopping online and in stores?

⑭ Do you think online shopping will replace in-store shopping in the future?

⑮ What are the differences between watching movies at home and in the cinema?

⑯ What's the benefit of letting kids watch animal videos than visiting zoos?

⑰ Which one do you prefer, living in a city or only visiting it as a tourist?

⑱ Are there benefits when one person is interested in another person? Why?

⑲ What are the differences between houses or buildings in the city and in the countryside?

⑳ Do you prefer to live in the city or in the countryside?

㉑ What are the differences between the houses that young people and old people like?

㉒ Do you think students can learn better at school or at home?

㉓ Are big companies better than small companies?

㉔ Which one is better when making complaint, by talking or writing?

㉕ Which is more important, a work-related appointment or an appointment with a friend? Why?

㉖ Do you think negative feedback is more important that positive feedback?

㉗ Do you think people are born with time management skills or they can develop them?

㉘ Do most elderly people live in the city or in the countryside?

㉙ What are the differences between being friendly and being polite?

㉚ Which is more important, mental relaxation or physical relaxation?

根据对 Part 3 题库的分析与整合,我们可以掌握 Part 3 题目的大体规律:其一是提问聚焦于几类重要主题,对这几类主题,平时应多积累语言主题模块。其二是对比问题的题型占很大的比例,尤其是老年人与青年人的对比。

二、部分题目解析

本节将以人物关系、运动健康、兴趣爱好三个主题为例,在充分学习每个主题的语言模块基础上,结合框架模块,回答每个主题的相关讨论题。

我们先来复习一下 ORDER 框架模块:

(1) O (opinion):说明观点。

Broadly speaking ...

In regards to ... whereas with ...

There are a lot of people who believe ... but I think ...

(2) R (reason):说明理由。

This is due to the fact that ...

(3) D (describe tendency):描述趋势。

have become/been ...

(4) E (example):举例说明。

It is common to see ...

You can see ...

For example ...

Like when sb. do sth. ...

I have learned from many different resources that ...

(5) R (restatement):重述观点(可略)。

So I think ...

(一) 人物关系

1. 语言模块

(1) 年龄对比。

关于年龄对比题，我们可以先把老年人和青年人的基本特征差异进行比较，比如两者在体能体力、个性观点、优势劣势等方面的差异可解释两者在行为习惯及兴趣爱好方面的差异，从而使对比分析更为透彻具体，且有规可循，以不变(基本差异)应万变(各类表现形式的差异)。因此，老年人与青年人的基本特征差异的语言模块可以广泛运用于各类年龄对比题(表4-9)。

表4-9　年龄对比常用语言模块

特征	青年人 (young/kids/teenagers)	老年人 (old people/senior people/elderly people/people with advanced age)
Physical strength	Physically: energetic, strong, vigorous Intellectually: quick-minded, sharp-minded, retentive memory (好记性)	Physically: low energy, weak Intellectually: failing memory, slow-minded, lose activities with age
Personality	Adventurous with fighting spirit: take challenges Ambitious Dynamic & innovative: try new things, seek trendy & fashion, grasp new skills quickly, flexible and willing to adapt Careless & reckless Impulsive & passionate Immature & inexperienced	Cautious over risks Conservative Stubborn & stabilized: Set/established/stuck in their ways/thinking/lifestyle Reserved & composed Tolerant & understanding Quiet & calm Mature & analytical
Digital world	Digital natives: familiar with the latest trends and technology	Digital immigrants: low digital proficiency
Finance	More lavish, splurge money	Frugal, thrifty, saving for retirement
Time	Dwell in future with dreams and aspirations Broad-outlook	Nostalgic, look back upon the past Narrow-minded
Music	Pop & rock/hip-hop: loud & exciting Reason: Like strong beat, stir up excitement, chase the fashion, energetic & vigorous	Classic/folk/country music Reason: Peaceful and soothing, pleasant to the ears, nostalgic, calm & composed
Activities	Extreme sports and intensive sports: scuba diving, bungee jumping, cycling, hiking, basketball Reason: wind down, blow off steam, seek fun/adventure/excitement, energetic, adventurous, vigorous	Low-impact sports: Taichi, swimming, yoga, walking Reason: Stay healthy, maintain active, stretch out, lose activity with age, less vigorous

续表4-9

特征	青年人（young/kids/teenagers）	老年人（old people/senior people/elderly people/people with advanced age）
Strength	Native in digital world, familiar with devices and gadgets	Rich life experience with wisdom and life lesson to draw from
Weakness	Inexperienced in life, limited life lessons and wisdom	lag behind in technology

（2）家庭关系。

① *Importance of family*：

Family relationship is important for every person at every stage of life. Our mental growth, overall wellbeing and stability all depend largely on our family relationship. A harmonious and affectionate family gives us a feeling of togetherness and of constant support.

② *Feeling of togetherness*：

A family allows us to feel safe, connected, protected, accepted and loved despite our shortcomings.

③ *Feeling of constant support*：

A supportive family sticks with you through thick and thin. When life gets hard, the kind words from your mother, spouse, or siblings calm your soul and give you the strength and courage to move on, to help you manage your stress and get over the tough times.

When life seems challenging, your family plays a role in supporting you, navigating you through ups and downs.

Children brought up in a healthy family will be able to form better bonds outside their home, have better attitudes and richer values.

④ *Spending quality time*：

Even though family members can keep in touch with each other through texting, making video or voice calls, it is far from enough than spending quality time with their family, preparing and sharing meals, sharing day to day life, organizing family events and having fun together, which are the source of life happiness.

⑤ *Change of family*：

Families have become more widely dispersed. People have traveled more, and then have ended up living far from their families. I think this is a shame because it means there is a breakdown of communities. I also think that because families are spread over a wider geographical area, elderly people usually live on their own and they tend to be forgotten to some extent.

2.真题演练

① *What kind of help do you think old people need? / What practical skills can young people teach old people?*

Well, broadly speaking, elderly people need assistance in many ways, particularly in technology. This is due to the fact that they are lagged behind in the application of gadgets. People today have been more and more reliant on technology. We have used technology to do everything from learning, shopping, entertaining to socializing. However it is common to see old people having difficulty integrating into the digital world. You can see many elderly people don't know how to make reservations online or to make cashless payment, which has brought much inconvenience in life.

Options:

I have read from different resources that more than 60 percent of the senior people can't make reservation online or make cashless payment, which brought them great inconvenience in life.

For example when I bought my grandfather a smart phone and taught him to use it, he got tremendous happiness from the modern technology. He can now make video calls through WeChat with family members, watch short videos on Tiktok and even browse the latest news on TouTiao by himself, which brings much convenience and solace in his life. So I think seniors need youngsters' assistance to cross "digital divide".

② *What skills can young people teach old people besides technology*?

Well, broadly speaking, elderly people need assistance in many ways, with technology as the most important domain I think. Apart from technology, a very important skill I think the old can learn from the young is the skill of enjoying life. This is due to the fact that old people tend to be so frugal in life and they save up every penny for their future or for their decedents. I think if the young people take their grandparents out for nice dinners, for holidays, for travelling, they will make their grandparents live more worthwhile and interesting life. Like when I took my grandparents to a trip to Hainan Island last year, they were so happy and they came back with ponds of favorite memory. So I think it's really important for the old people to learn to enjoy life when they can.

③ *What can old people teach young people*?

Broadly speaking, the elderly people can teach the young lots of things about life, this is because old people are just like a library who has accumulated much knowledge and wisdom from their life experience. The modern world has become more and more competitive for the young people who have to deal with all the stress and pressure from their personal and professional life but who are also inexperienced in solving their problems and dealing with challenges. So especially nowadays it's very common to see young people turn to old people for advice or suggestions when they come across some difficulties in their life. Like when I have to make some important decisions in life, such as choosing my major or my girlfriend or setting the goals. I often consult my grandpa whom I trust and admire a lot. I think those are the perspectives young people can learn from old people.

④ *Is it hard for young people to learn skills*? *What about old people*?

Well, generally speaking, it is not very difficult for young people to acquire new skills. This is due to the fact that young people are intellectually quick-minded and they tend to yearn for exploring the world, learning new skills. So the capability and motivation are on their side. The modern world has been developing dramatically at an unprecedented speed. New knowledge and skills have been highly demanded in almost all the professions. It's therefore very common today to see young people engaging themselves to learn new skills in different domains such as skills of driving, of using computer and other gadgets, of socializing, etc.

Well, in regards to elderly people, I don't think it is easy for them to learn new skills. This is simply because they lose their activities physically and intellectually with age and they are pretty set in their thinking and behavior. They have got used to their own way of life and as a result they tend to be not passionate about learning new things. Like when I tried to teach my grandfather to use iPad that I bought him as a new year gift, he simply had no interest in learning and complained it was too hard to learn. Similarly, when I learned to drive, it only took me a couple of months to get the license but it took my father nearly one year to get it and my grandparents simply gave up the attempts of learning to drive. So I believe learning new skills is much easier for the young than for the old.

⑤ *What disagreements do parents and children usually have*?

Well, generally speaking, parents and children tend to disagree in many issues. This is due to the fact that generation gap does exist. The modern world has been developing dramatically in an unprecedented speed, which means the young generation and the old generation have grown up in totally different eras. It's very common to see the parents and their kids argue about everything from the choices of clothing to the lifestyle, their way of spending money, etc. In regards to the kids, they tend to seek fashion and trend, stay up late, be obsessed with the gadgets and welcome challenges and risks, whereas with their parents they tend to lead more frugal and established life and they are more cautious with risks. All those are the perspectives that give rise to disagreements between parents and children.

⑥ *Is it difficult for adults to talk with children*?

Well, actually it depends, because family relationship varies widely from case to case. In regards to those harmonious and loving family, it's common to see the parents and children having friendly talks that cover almost any topics. Children in these families have much trust in their parents, so their conversation is relaxing, smooth and light-hearted, whereas in those families with undesirable relationship, you will find significant conversations nearly impossible. Parents and children simply argue about everything from the lifestyle, the choice of friends and of jobs to the values and life goals. So I don't think there is an identical answer to this question.

⑦ *How do young and old people react differently to new things*?

Well, even though it is true that some people are old in their body, they are young and vibrant at heart welcoming new things, and vice versa. Generally speaking, the old and young hold totally different attitudes towards new things. In regards to young people, they tend to be more dynamic and adventurous and they yearn for exploring the world, learning new stuff. At the universities you can see lots of students flocking to training centers or driving schools to hone their edges by learning new skills, whereas with the elder people, they tend be more set in their opinions, behaviors or lifestyles. As a result, they are not interested in learning new things. Of course, old people are losing their activities physically and intellectually with age, which means it is harder for them to learn new stuff. So I think those are the points how the old and young differ regarding their attitude and behavior toward new stuff.

⑧ *Is it easier for young people to change*?

Well, even though it is true that some people are young in body, they are already old and settled in their thinking and lifestyle, and vice versa. Generally speaking, it is way much easier for the young generation to make changes and to adapt to new surroundings. This is because young people are more open-minded and more flexible. Nowadays it is very common to see young people always on the go, changing jobs, travelling, experiencing a new lifestyle. They have got used to the dynamic and adventurous life, which requires them to make changes constantly to adapt to the new settings. So I think young people are generally more capable and willing to make changes.

⑨ *Who are more likely to make complaints, older people or young people*?

Even though personality varies widely from person to person and age is definitely not the only factor that influences people's tolerance to frustrations, generally speaking, I think young people tend to complain more often than the elderly people. This is due to the fact that young people are usually more reckless and impulsive whereas elderly people are more mature and composed. They have gone through all the life challenges and have learned how to flatten the life roller coasters, so they are generally less likely to make complaints. Like when I took a package tour last summer, it was always the young tourists rather than the old ones to complain about the food, the accommodation and the travel itinerary, etc. So I guess more often than not, it is the young people that tend to make complains more often.

⑩ *Who behave better when waiting, children or adults*?

Even though personality varies widely from person to person and age is definitely not the only factor that influences people's patience. Generally speaking, I guess adults are more patient while waiting. This is due to the fact that adults have learned to be more tolerant, understanding and patient in life, whereas children usually tend to be more impulsive and dynamic. Like when our family took a package tour last spring festival, it was always my nephew who kept urging us to move on. He just didn't have the patience to queue up online or to wait for something. So I think adults are doing better regarding waiting.

⑪ *Is it important to visit family members*?

Definitely it is very significant to visit family members. This is due to the fact that our mental growth, overall wellbeing and stability all depend largely on our family relationship. A harmonious and affectionate family gives us a feeling of togetherness and of constant support. However, in today's world families have become more widely dispersed. People have traveled more and have ended up living far from each other. It is of vital importance to keep connected with each other, to visit each other so as to maintain and nurture the family bond. I learned from many different resources that more than half of the adult children live in different cities or even different countries with their parents. Even though family members can keep in touch with each other through texting, making video or voice calls, it is far from enough than spending quality time together, cooking and having meals together, sharing their day to day life, organizing family events and having fun together, which are the source of life happiness. So I believe it is important to meet family members.

⑫ *Why is family bonding necessary for happiness in life*?

Well, yes, family bonding is essential to our happiness in our day-to-day life. This is due to the fact that our mental growth, overall wellbeing and stability all depend largely on our family relationship. The modern world has become more and more competitive, which means people today have been under more stress and pressure than they used to. Our families give us a feeling of togetherness and of constant support, which helps us to navigate through ups and downs in life. Like when I am in hard times, the kind words from my parents, spouse and siblings calm my soul and give me strength and courage to move on. A supportive and affectionate family is definitely a blessing to us that provides us with happiness, strength in life and more positive attitudes towards life and towards people around us. So I guess those are the reasons why family bonding is essential to happiness in life.

⑬ *Do you think elderly people are happy being with their families*?

Yes, generally speaking, senior citizens are happy spending time with their families, I guess. This is due to the fact that many old people today, particularly those living on their own, are very lonely. As we know in today's world families have become more widely dispersed, spreading over a wider geographical area. It's very common to see elderly people left behind, forgotten or neglected. Even though the senior can keep in touch with their children or grandchildren through texting, making video or voice calls, it is far from enough than spending quality time with their family: preparing and sharing meals, sharing day to day life, organizing family events and having fun together, which are the source of life happiness. Spending time with their family will definitely make the elderly people feel connected, protected and loved, thereby their emotional and physical needs can be met and their life satisfaction and happiness be enhanced. So I think the senior people are bound to be happy spending time with their families.

⑭ *Do you think the support from a friend is different from the support from a family member*?

Well, there are a lot of people who believe that good friends are just like family members and that support from a friend is the same as that from a family member, but I don't think that is the case. In regards to friends, more often than not their support is limited to the companionship, encouragement or comfort, which are definitely necessary and important to us, however, friends have their own family to take care of and they are not obliged or expected to offer too much concrete help or to offer financial support, whereas with the family, the members are expected to stay together through thick and thin and to spare no effort to help out each other, to provide support in various aspect, emotionally, physically or financially. Like when I am in need of financial support, I tend to turn to my family rather than my friends for help. As we say, blood is thicker than water. I think family support is more essential than support from friends.

⑮ *What are the values of family in your country*?

Well, generally speaking, we have some distinctive family values in my country that are different from those in most of the western countries. This is due to the fact that our society is a collectivist one rather than an individualist one. Even though in the modern society families have become more widely dispersed, spreading over a wider geographical area, we have attached much importance to family integrity and family bond. We have held deeply our family values such as respecting the old, sacrificing individual benefits for the wellbeing of the family, fulfilling family responsibilities, etc. So it's common to see elder siblings giving up their schooling to support the family in times of difficulty. To sum up, keeping the family close and making every member feel safe, connected, protected, accepted and loved are very important values in my culture.

(二)运动健康

1.语言模块

(1)途径与手段。

First and foremost/…, secondly, … last but not least …

To begin with …, apart from that …

By doing this …

If … sb./sth. will/can …

So *if children can reduce their screen time* and go out for sports, such as playing basketball, volleyball, jogging or cycling, to name just a few, *they can certainly be healthier and stronger* physically and mentally.

If the celebrities give some public speeches on the importance of health and share with the public what they do to maintain health, *people will be very likely to follow.*

(2)趋势与现状。

have been/done … common to see …

learned from many resources that …

This is due to the fact that more and more young people *have been so obsessed* with the digital world that they *have been used to* the sedentary lifestyle and *have ended up* becoming couch potatoes, which has exerted harmful effect on their physical and mental health. Nowadays it's *common to see* young people staring onto their screens at parties, over meals, in the livingrooms and bedrooms, just anywhere anytime.

In my country there *have been* more and more outdoor sports facilities in the city as well as in the country, such as hiking trails, cycling paths, parks, etc. So throughout the year, particularly in spring and summer, it's ***common to see*** people walking, jogging, cycling or hiking in the park, by the rivers or on the mountains.

In my country there ***have been*** more and more table tennis courts in gyms, residential communities, public squares and playgrounds, etc. It's ***common to see*** people playing table tennis both indoors and outdoors. That is the sport that fits everybody, young or old, men or women.

I ***learned from many different resources*** that a great majority of old people have strong health awareness which results in strong motivation of leading an active life by doing some low-impact exercises, such as walking, doing Taiji, which help them to stretch out and maintain health.

I ***learned from many different resources*** that table tennis is a very good cardio exercise that not only increases heart rates, burns calories, builds muscles but also improves body coordination.

I ***learned from many different resources*** that more than half of the young people today spend at least 20 hours on screen weekly, which takes a toll on their overall health.

（3）运动种类。

Extreme sports, like scuba diving, bungee jumping or skydiving, demonstrate the personalities of being adventurous, ambitious and perseverant as well as the motive for trying new things.

The cardio exercises, such as cycling, jogging, walking, dancing, swimming or hiking, to name just a few, help us improve heart rate, build our muscle and burn extra calories.

It's common to see young people participating in a wide range of activities, from the ***high-intensity sports*** like playing basketball, volleyball or mountain climbing to the ***low-intensity sports*** like walking, jogging and dancing.

（4）结尾总结。

So I think those are the reasons why ...

So in my opinion those are the most popular outdoor activities in my country.

So those are two things I think government can do to promote active and healthy lifestyle in its citizens.

I think those are the two tips parents can consider doing to help their children stay healthy.

2. 真题演练

① ***What outdoor activities are popular in China?***

Well, we have tons of popular outdoor activities in China. This is due to the fact that many people, like myself, tend to be nature enthusiasts. In my country there have been more and more outdoor sports facilities in the city as well as in the country, such as hiking trails, cycling paths, parks, etc. So throughout the year, particularly in spring and summer, it's common to see people walking, jogging, cycling or hiking in the park, by the rivers or on the mountains. So those are the most popular activities because they are very convenient, flexible and enjoyable. You don't need many gadgets and you can do it by yourself or with your friends. People can fully enjoy the charm of nature, breathing the fresh air, basking in the sunshine while admiring the picturesque scenery. So in my opinion those are the most popular outdoor activities in my country.

② *Should young people try as many new activities as possible*?

Yes, definitely. I think young people should be encouraged to take up as many new activities as possible. This is due to the fact that more and more young people have been so obsessed with the digital world that they have been used to the sedentary lifestyle and have ended up becoming couch potatoes, which has exerted harmful effect on their physical and mental health. Nowadays it's common to see young people staring onto their screens at parties, over meals, in the living rooms and bedrooms, just anywhere anytime. If they take up some activities, such as sports, games, entertainments, or adventures that are new to them, they will not only gain new skills but also become more confident socially and more energetic physically. So those are the reasons why I recommend young people take up new activities.

③ *Are those people who like dangerous activities more likely to be successful*?

Yes, I believe generally speaking the people who take up extreme sports like scuba diving, bungee jumping or skydiving are more likely to achieve success in other areas. This is due to the fact that lots of qualities required in those dangerous activities are also essential elements to success. I mean they are just transferable. For example, those sports like scuba diving, bungee jumping or skydiving demonstrate the personalities of being adventurous, ambitious and perseverant as well as the motive for trying new things. For example, when my cousin who has taken lots of dangerous activities over the years went for a very competitive interview last year, he beated all the other candidates and got the offer. He was told later on that the interviewer was very impressed by his adventurous and innovative spirits as well as his perseverance and strong will that demonstrated in his maneuver of the various extreme sports. So I think those are the reasons why the people who engage in extreme sports tend to have more chances to gain success in other perspectives.

④ *What do young people do to keep fit*?

Well, there are tons of activities for young people to maintain health. This is due to the fact that young people are physically strong, energetic and vigorous and they can do whatever exercise that interests them. It's common to see young people participating in a wide range of activities, from the high-intensity sports like playing basketball, volleyball or mountain climbing to the low-intensity sports like walking, jogging and dancing. So those are the activities I think young people can do to stay in good shape and good health.

⑤ *Do young people like to do sports*?

Well, generally speaking young people today haven't enjoyed sports very much. This is due to the fact that more and more young people have been so obsessed with the digital world that they have been used to the sedentary lifestyle and have ended up becoming couch potatoes, which has exerted harmful effect on their physical and mental health. Nowadays it's common to see young people staring onto their screens at parties, over meals, in the livingrooms and bedrooms, just anywhere anytime. I learned from many different resources that more than half of the young people today spend at least 20 hours on screen weekly, which certainly take away much of their exercise time. That said, there are certainly some young people who are very active in doing sports and are very athletic, but on the whole I think the young generation today are not physically active enough.

⑥ *What do old people do to keep fit*?

Generally speaking, old people tend to take up some low-impact activities to stay healthy. This is due to the fact that they are not as energetic and vigorous as they used to. In my country there have been more and more sports facilities in the city as well as in the country, such as hiking and walking trails, parks, gyms, pools etc, which have offered people lots of options for exercise. Nowadays it's common to see old people walking or doing Taichi in the parks or doing yoga in gyms or swimming in pools. I learned from many different resources that a great majority of old people have strong health awareness, which results in strong motivation of leading an active life by doing those low-impact exercises, which help them to stretch out and maintain health.

⑦ *What are the best ways to keep fit*?

There are tons of great ways to stay healthy and the best ways I believe are the cardio exercise, such as cycling, jogging, walking, dancing, swimming or hiking, to name just a few. This is due to the fact that those exercises help us improve heart rate, build our muscle and burn extra calories. In my country there have been more and more sports facilities in the city as well as in the country, such as hiking and walking trails, parks, gyms, pools etc, which have offered lots of options for exercise to the whole population, young or old, male or female. Nowadays it's common to see people cycling, dancing or doing yoga in the gyms or walking, doing Taichi in the parks or by the rivers. I learned from many different resources that people today have increased sense of health awareness which makes those exercises more popular. I assume those are the favorite exercises that help people maintain health.

⑧ *What is the most popular sport in your country*? / *What is the most popular form of exercise in your country*?

The most popular sport in my country is definitely table tennis. This is due to the fact that we enjoy a very good world reputation on table tennis. We always get the most gold medals in table tennis in the international games, particularly in Olympic Games, which is a great promotion to the popularity of this sport. In my country there have been more and more table tennis courts in gyms, residential communities, public squares and playgrounds, etc. It's common to see people playing table tennis both indoors and outdoors. That is the sport that fits everybody, young or old, men or women. I learned from many different resources that table tennis is a very good cardio exercise that not only increases heart rates, burns calories, builds muscles but also improves body coordination. So these are good reasons why table tennis is our favorite sport.

⑨ *What are the benefits of children doing sports*?

Well, participation of sports brings the children physical, mental and social benefits. Doing sports is extremely important for the kids today. This is because children today have been so obsessed with the digital world that they have been used to the sedentary lifestyle and have ended up becoming couch potatoes, which has exerted harmful effect on their physical and mental health. So if children can reduce their screen time and go out for sports, such as playing basketball, volleyball, jogging or cycling, to name just a few, they can certainly be healthier and stronger physically and mentally. Mentally they will be happier and smarter, and socially they can socialize with their friends, cultivate their communication skills, sportsmanship and team spirits. So those are the benefits that kids can gain through doing sports.

⑩ *Do men and women play the same kind of sports*?

Generally speaking, men and women tend to do different sports. In regards to women, they tend to do some low or media-impact activities, such as walking, dancing, jogging, doing yoga, etc. This is due to the fact that women are usually not as strong as men but they are more flexible than men. Whereas with men, they tend to take up media or high-impact activities, such as playing football, basketball, running, etc. This is due to the fact that men are energetic and vigorous physically and they are aggressive and adventurous with fighting spirits in nature. That said, there are sports that fit for both men and women, such as swimming and dancing. So I guess those are the gender differences regarding the types of sports.

⑪ *Do you think it is useful for governments to use celebrities to help people raise health awareness*?

Even though there are people who believe that celebrities can do little to enhance people's health awareness, I take a different view. I think celebrities can make a great difference on people's health awareness if they take some effective strategies. This is due to the existence of celebrity effect, or the influence from the public figures. In today's world, as we know, celebrities have attracted more and more zealous fans, particularly among the millennial generation. It is common to see the fans following their idols in every way, opinions, behaviors, lifestyles, etc. If the celebrities give some public speeches on the importance of health and share with the public what they do to maintain health, then people, especially their fans, will be very likely to follow. So I guess, celebrity effect can be employed to influence people's health awareness.

⑫ *How do you think government could encourage more people to exercise and participate in sport*?

Well, I think there are tons of things government can do to encourage people take active life-style. This is due to the fact that government has the resources and authority to influence the day to day life of the public. *First and foremost*, government can enhance people's health awareness by media coverage, such as newspaper or TV. *Secondly*, government can also launch sports events for the public, like Marathon or games. *Last but not least*, government can also build more public facilities such as hiking or walking trails, parks, gyms, pools, etc., or even provide subsidies to low-income families for free membership to gyms. ***By doing this*** more people will have access to the sports equipments. So those are two things I think government can do to promote active and healthy lifestyle in its citizens.

⑬ ***How can parents help their children to keep fit***?

Well, I think there are tons of things parents can do to teach their kids how to maintain health. This is due to the fact that parents are the children's first teachers as well as their role models. ***To begin with***, parents can integrate sports and games into their family day to day life, for example, to organize family events like hiking, cycling, playing balls, swimming, etc. ***By doing this***, ***on emotional perspective***, the kids can have high quality time with their parents and strengthen the family bond, ***on physical perspective***, they will be more energetic, healthier and more passionate in doing sports. ***Apart from that***, parents can cook well-balanced nutritious homemade dishes to ensure that the kids eat healthy. I think those are the two tips parents can consider doing to help their children stay healthy.

(三) 兴趣爱好

1. 语言模块

(1) 趋势与现状。

have been/done ... It's common to see ...

learned from many resources that ...

Our world today has been more and more competitive, which means people have been under more stress and pressure than they used to.

With the development of economy and technology, people today have enjoyed more and more free time and disposable income. So it's very common to see people doing things they like, travelling around the globe, hiking, cycling, having picnics, watching movies, listening to music, to name just a few.

The technology has saved people much time for doing household chores. The washing machines, vacuum cleaners, microwave ovens, etc. have made life easier and more convenient.

(2) 条件句。

If ... sb./sth. will/can ...

If they have enough leisure time participating all kinds of sports and entertainments, they will be happier, healthier and more productive.

(3) 分层讨论。

On the physical level, hobbies help people burn extra calories, build their muscles and make them stay healthy and energetic.

On the emotional level, hobbies help people relieve stress, enhance their mood and feel happy and content.

On the social level, hobbies help people strengthen the bond with their friends and family by doing activities together and having fun together.

On the intellectual perspective, watching movies brings us knowledge and inspiration.

On the emotional perspective, movies help us stay focused and entertained.

On the social perspective, we can build the bond with our family and friends. So those are just a few out of the many benefits of watching movies.

(4)分类讨论。

It depends, if you mean ... then I guess ... This is due to the fact that ...

but if you are talking about ... then I think ... Generally speaking ...

I think people's music preferences *change with age. In regards to ... whereas with ... .*

It's common to see women splashing out on trendy clothes, accessories and make-up, *whereas* men have little patience shopping and selecting for their clothes.

(5)列举事实:

First and foremost ...A second reason is related with ...

To begin with ..., apart from that ...

First and foremost, women tend to enjoy chasing trend and fashion whereas men tend to be more intrigued in technology, like gadgets or devices. *A second reason I think is related with* our social values. The society attaches much value or importance to the beauty of women rather than that of men and to the career success of men rather than that of women.

2. 真题演练

① *Is leisure time important to everyone?*

Yes, definitely leisure time is of vital importance to each of us. This is due to the fact that a person who doesn't have sufficient leisure time cannot work efficiently or maintain health. Our world today has been more and more competitive, which means people have been under more stress and pressure than they used to. If they can have enough leisure time participating all kinds of sports and entertainments, such as hiking, cycling, playing balls, travelling, having parties etc, they will be happier, healthier and more productive. As we say, all work and no play makes Jack a dull boy. So I believe having leisure time is important for the overall well-being of each individual.

② *What are the benefits of hobbies?*

Hobbies bring us tons of benefits. On the physical level, the hobbies related with physical activities, such as hiking, swimming, playing balls etc, help people burn extra calories, build their muscles and make them stay healthy and energetic. On the emotional level, hobbies help people relieve stress, enhance their mood and feel happy and content. On the social level, hobbies help people strengthen the bond with their friends and family by doing activities together and having fun together. So hobbies are really important to the overall wellbeing of each individual.

Option：

Hobbies bring us tons of benefits, physically, emotionally and socially. This is due to the fact that hobbies involve us in activities that are beneficial to our mind and body. With the development of economy and technology, people today have enjoyed more and more free time and disposable income. So it's very common to see people doing things they like, travelling around the globe, hiking, cycling, having picnics, watching movies, listening to music, to name just a few. Those activities not only enhance people's mood but also help them strengthen the tie with friends and family. If people take up sports and games, they can also burn calories, build muscles and stay energetic and healthy. So hobbies are really important to the overall wellbeing of each individual.

③ *What are the benefits of watching movies*?

Well, watching movies brings us lots of benefits, emotionally, intellectually and socially. On the intellectual perspective, watching movies brings us knowledge and inspiration. By watching movies we learn about the society, about the world, about the stories of people, and we can connect them with our own lives and draw lessons from the movies. On the emotional perspective, movies are just so captivating and intriguing with its gripping plot, professional acting and the audio-visual effect. Movies help us stay focused and entertained. On the social perspective, watching movies is also a very good social activity, through which we can build the bond with our family and friends. So those are just a few out of the many benefits of watching movies.

④ *What leisure facilities can be used by people of all ages*?

Well, there are not many leisure facilities that fit people of all ages and I guess swimming pool is one of the few facilities that fits everybody, young or old, men or women. This is due to the fact that the aquatic exercise is low-injury activity as the water supports up to 90 percent of the body's weight. It's common to see the newborn babies swimming under the assistance of the nurses or professional nannies. We can also see the swimming pools attracting people of all ages, from the toddlers to the senior citizens. Swimming is great for everybody. It is whole body exercise as well as no sweat exercise. It burns lots of calories. It definitely enhances our physical and mental health and promotes our overall well-being.

⑤ *Do you think it can be a disadvantage to have too much free time*?

Even though there are people who would like to lead an easy life with much free time, I believe too much spare time is not good for our life, because people tend to get lazy and end up turning into idlers if they have too much spare time. It is very common to hear the retired people complaining that they find their life boring and that they feel lonely with all the time totally to themselves with no work commitments. Consequently, they lose their sense of belonging and of achievement and they tend to just idle away their time, which is not good for their overall wellbeing. So I guess, it is definitely detrimental to us if we have too much spare time.

⑥ *Do you think young people and old people have different types of hobbies*?

Yes, generally speaking, the elderly people and the young generation have different tastes in their hobbies. In regards to young people, they like to participate the high-intensity activities such as playing balls, skating, running, or even some extreme sports like scuba diving and bungee jumping. They also enjoy going to the bars, surfing online, playing video games, etc. This is due to the fact that they are strong, energetic and vigorous and they are also adventurous and curious who would like to explore new things and seek trend and fashion, whereas with the elderly people, who are weak in body and conservative in personality, they tend to stick to the low-intensive activities, such as doing Taichi, playing mahjong, listening to music, watching movies, etc. So I assume those are the age differences regarding the choice of entertainments.

⑦ *Do you think young people and old people enjoy the same kind of music?*

No, I don't think so. I think people's music preferences change with age. In regards to young people, they tend to be really into the loud and exciting music, such as hip-hop, rock and roll. This is due to the fact that they are energetic and vigorous. They like the strong beat and they like to chase the fashion, whereas with elder people, usually they are fond of peace and soothing music such as the classic music, folk music or country music because they are calm and quiet and they like to recall the good old days in the past. So I guess those are the age differences regarding the music preferences.

⑧ *Are older people as fashionable as young people? Why?*

Definitely not. I think young people are much more trendy than the elderly people. This is due to the fact that young people enjoy chasing trend and fashion whereas elderly people tend to be conserved and established in their thinking, behavior and lifestyle. As a result, it is common to see the young generation, particularly the millennial generation, splashing out on trendy clothes, accessories and modern lifestyle, whereas with the elder people, they tend to stick to the traditional clothes and are more reluctant to spend money on clothes. Tracing fashion is probably the last thing they would do. I assume those are the reasons why old people are not as fashionable as the young people.

⑨ *Are women more fashionable than men? Why?*

Well, I believe generally speaking, women are trendier than men, even though there are always some exceptions. It's common to see women, particularly the young women, shopping all day long, splashing out on trendy clothes, accessories and make-up, whereas men have little patience shopping and selecting for their clothes. As we know women's wardrobes are always crammed with all kinds of trendy clothes, shoes, accessories. Comparatively speaking, men's wardrobes have much less stuff. As for the reasons, I think, first and foremost, women tend to enjoy chasing trend and fashion whereas men tend to be more intrigued in technology, like gadgets or devices. A second reason I think is related with our social values. The society attaches much value or importance to the beauty of women rather than that of men and to the career success of men rather than that of women. So that is my opinion on the gender difference regarding fashion.

⑩ *Do you think old people and young people can share interests?*

Well, it depends. For lots of entertainments and sports, there are age limits. For example, the high-intensity sports like playing balls, skating, running, or even some extreme sports like scuba diving and bungee jumping are just for the young people, definitely not for the old. However, there are some hobbies that can be enjoyed by both the young and the old, such as swimming, playing mahjong, travelling, walking, to name just a few. It is common to see people of all ages playing mahjong or swimming or travelling together. For example, when my family arrange for some family events, we like to have picnic, play mahjong or watch movies, all those are activities that fit people of all ages, young or old, male or female. So I assume the young and the old can share some if not all of their hobbies.

⑪ *Do young children like the same stories as older children*?

No, I don't think so. Generally speaking, people's preference on stories changes with age. This is due to the fact that old kids and young kids have different personalities, concerns, and behaviors. In regards to young kids, they tend to be captivated by fairy tales, stories about animals. This is due to the fact that their world is kind of limited and they certainly cannot comprehend a bigger or more complicated world, whereas with the older children, they are more interested in the stories related with their own life, stories about the school, their studies, or peer relationship, because those are the things they care about. So yes, I think kids of different ages have different choices on their favorite stories.

⑫ *Do you think only old people have time for leisure activities*?

Well, even though there are people who believe that only the retired senior citizens have time for leisure activities, I personally don't think so. It is true that the modern world has been more and more competitive, leaving the working population with more stress and less spare time, but that doesn't mean that they don't have spare time at all, because the technology has saved people much time for doing household chores. The washing machines, vacuum cleaners, microwave ovens, etc. have made life easier and more convenient. So it's common to see working people enjoying all kinds of leisure activities after work, such as hiking, swimming, working out in the gyms, travelling, etc. People know that all work and no play makes Jack a dull boy. I think the working class actually do have time for leisure activities, with which they can work more efficiently and live more healthily and happily.

⑬ *Do women have more leisure time than men do*?

Well, even though there are people who believe that women have more spare time than men, I personally don't think that is the case. I think women are more occupied than men. This is due to the fact that women usually are more tied up with their family chores and responsibilities despite their work commitment. More often than not, we can see the little kids usually more attached to their mothers rather than to their fathers, which means women usually spend more time caring for kids. I learned from many different resources that about 80 percent of men confessed that they didn't do as much housework as their spouses. So I believe women actually have a tighter schedule than men.

⑭ *Why is fashion more important to some people*?

Well, there are several reasons why some people attach more importance to fashion. First and foremost, I think social expectation plays an important role. Another reason I think is related with people's profession. Some professions are more demanding on fashion, such as the actors and actresses, celebrities and public figures, they tend to be more concerned about their appearance and enjoy seeking trend and fashion, which will help them gain advantages on their career paths. So those are the two reasons regarding people's differences in fashion.

附　录

附录1　主题情境常用习语

1. Health

(1) ***Good health***：

- My mother is ***back on her feet*** (healthy again) after being sick for two weeks.
- She turns 87 this year and she's still (*as*) ***fit as a fiddle*** (in very good health).

(2) ***Bad health***：

- My grandfather was ***as pale as a ghost*** (extremely pale) when he entered the hospital.
- The sales manager was ***at death's door*** (very near death) after his heart attack.
- I'm ***going under the knife*** (undergo surgery) next month to try to solve my knee problems. Hope it helps!
- My uncle is very sick and ***has one foot in the grave*** (near death).
- My boss has been ***under the weather*** (not feeling well) all week and has not come to work during that time.
- He has a fever and ***aches all over*** (one's whole body is sore).
- I ***have a runny nose*** (can't stop sniffing) now and a bit of a cough but I am feeling a lot better.

2. Time

(1) ***Time***：

- The restaurant is open ***around the clock*** (at all times).
- It's hard to predict how this law will really impact people's lives—***only time will tell*** (the outcome will only be known in the future).
- When I said I would move to New York, she offered me the job ***on the spot*** (immediately).
- New Year's Eve is ***just around the corner*** (occurring soon). Have you made party plans

yet?

- I had a beautiful family, a nice home, and lots of money. And then, ***in the blink of an eye*** (instantaneously), it was all gone.

- This is especially used in hypothetical situations. If Joe asked me, I'd marry him ***in a heart beat*** (immediately).

- The new Honda is expected to ***sell like hotcakes*** (sold very quickly) after it's released.

- When he said he wanted to go to the zoo on his birthday it was ***no sooner said than done*** (right away; immediately).

- I can't believe your kid is about to graduate high school. ***How time flies*** (time seems to move very quickly).

- When they telephoned me with the offer of a job abroad, I decided ***on the spur of the moment*** (suddenly; spontaneously) to accept.

- My attitude to money is ***easy come, easy go*** (something that has been obtained very easily and quickly may be lost or wasted in the same way).

- Don't rush me. ***Haste makes waste*** (rushing through a task often creates problems or extra work).

- ***For the time being*** (now, and for a short time in the future), our plans remain unchanged until something convinces us otherwise.

(2) ***On time***：

- You got here ***in the nick of time*** (just in time)—we're just about to start.

- Remember, ***never put off until tomorrow what you can do today*** (do not delay to do something if you can finish it today)!

- She was working in haste to ***meet the deadline*** (finish tasks on time).

(3) ***Frequency & time***：

- ***Never in a million years*** (absolutely never) did I think that I would actually win the lottery!

- ***Once in a blue moon*** (very rarely) you see the Aurora here, but it's not like farther north.

- I don't want to live in the city, but I enjoy visiting ***once in a while*** (occasionally).

- ***Nine times out of ten*** (almost always) your first choice turns out to be the right one.

- If you have problems, call me ***twenty-four seven*** (at any time); it doesn't matter if I'm sleeping.

- Our holiday party is such a bore. ***Year in, year out*** (annually without change) the owner makes the same dumb jokes.

- The presentation will begin at 8 ***on the nose*** (precisely). Don't miss it.

- ***Take your time*** (don't hurry) on the exam. You don't get a bonus for finishing quickly.

- Every time before the final exams, I have no choice but to stay up late for ***days in a row*** (several days) to study.

3. Possibility

- It'll be **a cold day in July** (never happen) when our team wins the championship.
- Sure, I'll go out with Cynthia again **when pigs fly** (never).

4. Hit (开始/击中)

- We better **hit the road** (leave) before traffic get even worse.
- OK, I'll come to the party Friday. But Saturday it'll be time to **hit the books** (study).
- I have to get up at 5 tomorrow morning. It's time to **hit the hay** (go to bed).
- We went to Mark's Midtown for lunch. I had a grilled chicken sandwich, and it really **hit the spot** (give total or desired satisfaction, as food or drink).

5. Quantity

(1) **Many**:

- I have **a million and one** (many) ideas.
- **Every man and his dog** (many people) wanted to interview me after I won the race.
- Having a concert in our friend's cafe was such a good idea! We were **packed in like sardines** (extremely crowded; too many people in limited space), but everyone had a great time.

(2) **Few**:

- The flooding is bad, but this is only **the tip of the iceberg** (only a tiny part can be seen or understood).

6. Weather

- We had to postpone our baseball game because **the heavens opened** (**up**) (a downpour of rain begins) as soon as we got on the field.
- It's been **raining cats and dogs** (rain heavily) all day. I'm afraid the roof is going to leak.
- Let's go out and **soak up some sun** (enjoy the sun).

7. Appearance

- **She's no spring chicken** (young), but she's still very good looking.
- Her cheeks were **as red as a cherry** (very red).
- When Samantha was in her teens she looked ordinary, but in her early 20s she turned into a real **knockout** (an extremely beautiful woman).
- Let me just **put my face on** (apply cosmetics), and I'll meet you at the restaurant in 15 minutes.
- Sure, she seems nice, but **don't judge the book by its cover** (appearances can be deceiving).

- John is pretty **well-built** (well-proportioned; fitted). I think it's because that he works out at the gym on a quite regular basis.
- No matter where she goes, she has to be **well-turned out** (very well dressed, usually in expensive clothing).

8. Secret

- We had planned this to be a surprise party for you, but Jason **spilled the beans** (reveal a secret).
- I would tell you what has happened if you promised not to **let the cat out of the bag** (disclosure of confidentiality).
- OK, I'll tell you the secret about Cynthia, but **zip your lip about it** (be quiet).

9. Comment (about someone)

(1) *Positive*:

- Our principal was a little lady, but she was one **tough cookie** (a very determined person).
- My **eagle-eyed** (sharp vision) sister spotted the car in the parking lot before anyone else did.
- My new girlfriend is very intelligent that she's beautiful is just **icing on the cake** (a bonus).
- I see that the new girl in school has **caught your eye** (attract one's interest, especially due to being visually appealing or attractive).
- Well, a delayed flight isn't an ideal situation, but we'll just have to **grin and bear it** (accept something bad, because you believe you cannot change it).
- My granddad is **a glass half full kind of person** (optimistic) and he only looks on the bright side of things.
- I'm not much of an **outdoorsy** (fond of outdoor activities) type but as a child, I did do my share of camping, fishing and hiking.
- My friend asked me to go and see this film with her because it was **getting rave reviews** (gain highly positive comments).

(2) *Negative*:

- Don't trust Jack around your expensive glassware — he's **all thumbs** (clumsy).
- Sophia acted like she was my friend. But then she **stabbed me in the back** (betray) and went out with my boyfriend.
- Sam is **rotten to the core** (entirely evil). He steals, he lies, he's violent. I'm glad he's in prison.
- James is a **bad egg** (a dishonest person). Don't trust him.
- Tell me where the money is, and don't give me any fishy stories (an explanation that seems highly suspicious).

- *A bad/rotten apple spoils the* (*whole*) *barrel/bunch* (a bad apple can cause other apples begin to rot as well. Hint: one bad person can ruin the whole group).

- Jeremy is really *a bad apple*. After five minutes with my usually well-behaved kids, they're all acting out.

- That's a worthless investment. He's *throwing his money down the drain* (waste money).

- Jeff *smokes like a chimney* (smoke a lot). I worry about his health.

- Don't bother Joseph when he's *in his cups* (drunk) — he's very irritable.

- When we got married, we were both *poor as a church mouse* (very poor) and we had to live with my husband's parents.

- Lisa wants to date a man who loves to travel and explore, not a *couch potato* (a lazy person, who spends most of his time sitting, watching TV).

- You can try talking to Caylee, but she seems too *stiff-necked* (stubborn; excessively formal) to do anything other than what she believes to be the best method.

- You'll never win the case with him as your lawyer—he's just out of law school and still *wet behind the ears* (inexperienced, often because one is young)!

- You know, Jack, you may be my friend, but you can be a real *pain in the neck* (an especially irritating person or situation) sometimes!

- Carla thought the handsome stranger was gentle and kind, but Susan suspected he was *a wolf in sheep's clothing* (a person or thing that appears harmless but is actually dangerous).

- Don't be such a *poor loser* (a person who cannot afford to lose).

- We really get along with each other and we've never *had a falling out* (argue).

- I decide to take up sports because I have been too *sedentary* (sit down a lot and not exercise).

- I used to speak English fluently but I'm *a bit rusty* (not skillful as it used to be) now.

10. Routines

- I wouldn't want *a nine-to-five job* (a job with standard working hours from 9 a. m. to 5 p. m.).

11. Social life

- Doug had a party, but many people did not know each other, so he had us play a game to *break the ice* (make the atmosphere lively).

- Those two *fight like cat and dog* (continually arguing with each other), so please don't put them together on the project.

- Glen is *a lone wolf* (not social) and seldom joins in the activities of the neighborhood.

- Only the *top banana* (boss, leader) can make a decision of that magnitude.

- Talk to Jon. He's the *big fish* (important person) in the organization. He can help you get things done.

- Anelka's outspoken views have regularly **landed him in hot water** (get people angry at him for doing something wrong).

- She **got into hot water** (get angry) for being late.

- In the workplace, you should **know which way the wind is blowing** (understand the situation, usually negative).

- These twins are **like two peas in a pod** (always together and similar).

- I'll be out of town this weekend, but I'll be **in touch** (in contact) when I get back Sunday night.

- I'm not really part of your group. If I come to the party, I'll just be a **fifth wheel** (a superfluous person).

- I tried to hide how sad I felt while I was in front of my parents, but they **read me like an open book** (analyze and understand one very easily and intuitively).

- I **read you loud and clear** (understand exactly what one means), Let's pull together on this.

- She didn't send him a present for his birthday, only a card, but **it's the thought that counts** (one's good intentions are more important than one's actions).

- I know my parents are unhappy that I didn't come home for Christmas, but **you can't please everyone** (it is not possible to satisfy everyone).

- It really doesn't matter to me how you arrange the furniture here, so just **suit yourself** (do exactly what you like)!

- I get that you like doing things your own way, but **it wouldn't hurt to** (it would be a good idea to) have a helping hand now and then.

- I'm **dying to** (eager and excited to do something) see you.

- **Stay out of this** (don't get involved in this) — it's none of your concern.

- Would you please stop **beating around the bush** (speak vaguely so as to avoid talking directly about an unpleasant or sensitive topic)? Are you leaving the company or not?

- Like anyone would be, I am **flattered** (exaggerate one's good points) by your fascination with me.

- **Don't get me wrong** (don't misinterpret what I'm saying as criticism), I appreciate everything your mother has done for us.

- All right, **you're the boss** (you're in charge), we'll do it your way.

- I'm sorry I missed your game. How about **I make it up to you** (to do something that corrects a bad situation) with some ice cream?

- You're not the only one with a lot to do. **We're all in the same boat** (in the same situation; having the same problem).

- We all need to be **on the same page** (thinking in the same manner; having the same general outlook or position) before we try to present this complex idea to the boss.

- If I were **in her shoes** (be in another person's situation), I'd probably want an explanation.

- Todd and Jean decided to **go fifty-fifty** (to divide the cost of something in half with someone) on dinner.

- We should thank the people who are **behind the scenes** (without receiving credit or fame ; out of public view) of our success.

- She's always been there for me **through thick and thin** (through good and bad times) , so I can't turn my back on her now.

- They maintain the closest relations with the masses and **share their weal and woe** (through thick and thin).

- I don't like her, and I think **the feeling is mutual** (shared feeling).

- You do so much for the company that I don't see how anyone could **fill your shoes** (replace you).

- Your boss seems to **think nothing of you** (have little or no regard or concern for someone or something) , judging by the way she speaks about you behind your back.

- **Think nothing of it**. I was delighted to do it.

- Let's **give** our special guest **a big hand** (to give one a loud or enthusiastic round of applause) !

- That explanation **does not hold water** (not able to be proved ; not correct or true).

- I think everyone should travel the world. **Variety is the spice of life** (new and exciting experiences make life more interesting) , after all!

- I know you love Harvard, but **don't put all your eggs in one basket** (don't focus all of your attention on one thing or in one area) — make sure to apply to several other schools too.

- Don't be stupid! You want to hurt him just because he hurt you! **Two wrongs don't make a right** (it is wrong or useless to harm somebody because they have harmed you) , you know.

- We may not get along very well with Mitch, but we have to **give credit where credit is due** (acknowledge someone's contribution or ability) — he worked hard on that project.

- When it comes to this job, you have to **take the bad with the good** (accept the bad aspects of something as well as the good ones). It's hard, but it's worth it.

- None of my family members are fighting with each other right now, so please **don't rock the boat** (don't say or do something that could upset a stable situation) by bringing up politics or any other controversial topics.

- To be honest, you're better off **leaving well alone** (not try to change something or get involved in something) at this point. She's so angry that anything you say will just make things worse.

- He knew when to **leave well alone** and when to interfere.

- **Bumper-to-bumper traffic** (heavy traffic) is not uncommon in my hometown.

- I **am** always **stuck in traffic** (be in a traffic jam) for over an hour.

- Tom **flunked two exams** (not pass the exam) because he paid little attention on study.

- On weekends, I often **while away the time** (kill time) reading news.

- It's not uncommon that people choose to eat a lot of fruits every day in order to **shed pounds** (lose weight).

- I want to **live on the outskirts of the city** (live in the suburb) where it's not as densely populated as the city center.

- This film is full of **twists and turns** (all the dramatic turns of event) and I believe this is what makes the film so impressive.

12. Feeling

(1) *Happy*：

- I always have so much fun when Katie's around — she's totally **a barrel of laughs** (funny, usually with sarcastic tone)!

- I was **full of the joys of spring** (very happy and cheerful) when I found out that I'd gotten an A on my hardest exam.

- The kids really **had a ball** (have a very enjoyable time) at the birthday party — they won't stop talking about it!

- We **had a whale of a time** (enjoy very much) on holiday.

- When my mom bought me a computer, I was **on cloud nine** (very happy).

- I have been **feeling on top of the world** (feel very happy) since I quit my job.

- It's too bad you didn't get the job, but **keep your chin up/pull yourself together** (cheer up) — another one will come along.

- Tom was **happy as a clam** (extremely happy) after winning the competition.

- My favorite actor is Stephen Chow, who never fails to **crack me up** (make me laugh a lot).

(2) *Unhappy*：

- You've been **down in the dumps** (depressed) all week. Let's go to the football game — that'll cheer you up.

- Poor Jane really **cried her eyes** (cry hard for a long time) out during the funeral service.

- I **feel** sort of **under the weather** (slightly ill, sick or depressed) today.

- We're **fed up with** (be irritated by or tired of) our car, but we just can't afford a new one right now.

- I thought the subject would be interesting, but the professor's boring lectures really **turned me off** (cause someone to dislike or lose interest in something).

- I know that the accident really **turned Janet off** to driving on the highway.

- I know you really wanted that job, but you weren't hired, so it's no use **crying over spilled milk** (*to be unhappy about what cannot be undone*) now.

(3) *Angry*：

- My parents are going to **hit the roof** (very angry) if they find out we had a party here!

- When I saw the look on Sarah's face, I just know she'd **blow up** (explode).

- I think he'll **blow his top** (lose his temper) when you give him the news.

- Mom will *freak out/lose it* (lose control of anger or sadness) when she found out we broke her vase!

- My parents are going to *go mental* (extremely angry) if they find out we had a party here!

- Nothing personal, but your voice is really *getting on my nerves* (irritate, grate on, or exasperate one).

- My grandma never *loses her temper* (suddenly become angry).

(4) *Crazy*:

- The noise caused all the neighbors to *go nuts* (become crazy).

- Sure, you can invest a little money, but don't *get carried away* (be overly enthusiastic) — people lose lots of money on the stock market.

- The loud beeping noise is *driving me up the wall* (annoy or irritate).

(5) *Safe*:

- He got home from the party *all in one piece* (unharmed, uninjured, fully intact).

- No matter what happens in coming months, your position in this company is *safe as houses* (extremely secure or well protected).

(6) *Comfortable*:

- Please come in and *make yourself at home* (make yourself comfortable).

- Life isn't always going to be *a bed of roses* (easy and comfortable situation). You have to learn to deal with adversity.

- You didn't think your new job in construction was going to be *a bed of roses*, did you?

(7) *Nervous*:

- I almost didn't go on stage and perform tonight because I *had butterflies in my stomach* (nervous).

- The noise was *giving her a headache* (make somebody feel stressful).

- News enables me to abr ... abre ... sorry, I'm a little *tongue-tied* (unable to say anything because of shyness or nervousness). I mean, it enables me to *keep abreast of* (keep informed of) current affairs.

(8) *Relaxed*:

- Come on, Jim, this is a party! *Let your hair down* (relax and enjoy) and go a little wild!

- I'm just going to *take it easy* (relax) this weekend, maybe go to a movie or a play.

- I have to *get this off my chest* (say something that you have wanted to say for a long time, resulting in relief). I'm tired of your rudeness to me!

- Jogging is great. It helps me *wind down/unwind* (relax) after a stressful day at work.

(9) *Desperate*:

- It is said that her son died in the battle, but there has been no official announcement; that's *the last straw* (an unbearable final attack) she clutches at.

（10）*Embarrassed*：

● Fred **had egg on his face** (embarrassed) after claiming he could climb the tree but then having to give up.

● When Carla transferred to a new school, she felt like **a fish out of water** (a person who feels uncomfortable or embarrassed in unfamiliar surroundings) because she didn't know anyone there.

（11）*Skeptical*：

● James will tell you all about his adventures in Africa, but **take it with a grain of salt** (be skeptical).

（12）*Uncertain*：

● The salary increase is still **up in the air** (not yet decided) — the boss favors it, but she hasn't gotten approval from her superiors.

● Kevin says he was completely **in the dark** (unaware) about the CEO's plans to sell the company.

● You **don't have a clue** (have no idea) about how to talk to people, do you?

（13）*Moved*：

● Your words deeply **touched my heart** (affect someone emotionally).

（14）*Focused*：

● Your kids will **be engrossed in** (be deeply absorbed) designing their own sand or water cascade.

（15）*Uninterested*：

● Thank you for the invitation, but long-distance cycling just **isn't** really **my cup of tea** (not something one prefers, or cares about).

（16）*Curious*：

● I know **curiosity killed the cat** (being curious can get you into trouble), but I can't stop the investigation until I know where the donations are really going.

● I think you'll offend her by asking such personal questions. **Curiosity killed the cat**, after all.

（17）*Envious*：

● I've been unemployed for a year, and you got a new job in a matter of weeks. Geez, **some people have all the luck** (an expression of mild envy).

13. Love

● I think I'm **falling in love** (start feeling love) with my best friend. What should I do?

● John is **fallen head over heels** (love someone deeply) in love with Mary.

● I didn't know Chris and Sue **were an item** (having a romantic relationship). They didn't even look at each other at dinner.

● I thought Luke and Andrea had **broke up/split up** (end the romantic relationship) — is it true that they're an item again?

- I bought a ring, and I'm ready to ***pop the question*** (propose marriage) to Sophia.
- — When are you and Jenny going to ***tie the knot*** (get married)?

  — This year, but we haven't set a date yet.
- At first my marriage was all ***puppies and rainbows*** (perfect), but then reality set in.

14. Difficulty level

(1) *Easy*:

- I stayed up all night studying for that exam, and then it turned out to ***be a breeze*** (very easy)!
- I've already done the difficult parts — finishing the presentation tonight will be a ***piece of cake*** (easy task).
- Passing this quiz will be like ***shooting fish in a barrel*** (very easy). I've studied a lot.
- After learning to drive a stick shift, driving with an automatic transmission is ***child's play*** (a very easy task).
- Just watch. Getting her to go out with me will be ***like taking candy from a baby*** (very easy).

(2) *Difficult*:

- The problem of how to motivate employees can be ***a tough nut to crack*** (a difficult problem) sometimes.
- Who will ***bell the cat*** (agree to undertake a risky and nearly impossible task) and take on the job of reducing corruption in this country?
- We're trying to sell the house, but its undesirable location has proved to be a real ***stumbling block*** (a challenge that prevents the progress).
- Bringing up a family when you're unemployed is ***no picnic*** (difficult).

15. Use faculty

(1) *Think*:

- You shouldn't buy a new car until you've paid off the debt from your student loan. ***Use your head*** (think)!
- We were going to go to Italy, but we ***had second thoughts*** (reconsider something) and came here instead.
- I ***can't imagine why*** (don't know why) she would say that.
- If you deceive your boss now, what do you think will happen if he finds out about it? I mean, ***look before you leap*** (think carefully before you do something)!
- ***Off the top of my head*** (without thinking), I think all teachers should have a good sense of humor.

(2) **Listen**：

- The team was **all eyes and ears** (attentive) as the coach explained the challenges ahead.
- **Lend an ear** (listen), and I'll tell you what people said at the meeting yesterday.
- I **heard through/on the grapevine** (hear or learn of something through an informal means of communication, especially gossip) that she was looking for work.
- Hey, whenever you're at City Hall, **keep your ears open** (remain alert in order to listen for something) for the next big story.

(3) **Agree**：

- I don't **see eye to eye** (agree) with Frances on the workflow, but she's the boss.
- It really pleased me that the boss gave me a **thumbs-up** (approval) on my presentation.
- Who do you **root for** (support) in the Super Bowl?

(4) **See**：

- I often go to bookstores and **flick through books** (look through) to see if anything interests me.

(5) **Remember**：

- I had the answer **on the tip of my tongue** (almost able to be recalled), but couldn't think of it in time.
- Okay, give me a couple of minutes. It will **come to me** (recall something).
- I'm sorry I didn't call you back sooner, it totally **slipped my mind** (forget about something).
- Ever since I moved, none of my old friends have gotten in touch with me. It's **out of sight, out of mind** (it is easy to forget about someone or something when you have not seen them for a long time) with them, evidently.

16. Opportunity

- This is our time. Let's **seize the day** (take the opportunity at the moment without worrying about the future)! We may never get a chance to do this again.
- When I was 29 I was a millionaire. You come from nothing and suddenly **the world is your oyster** (one can do anything and go anywhere they like).
- Think of all the opportunities before you. **The world is your oyster.**
- It's too late for you to ask her to marry you — she's involved with someone else now. **That ship has sailed** (that opportunity has passed).
- I know you're upset about losing the game, sweetie, but **tomorrow is another day** (tomorrow will bring new chances).
- I'm pretty disappointed that I didn't get the job, but I'm trying to remind myself that **there are other good fish in the sea** (there are many other excellent people, things, opportunities, or possibilities in the world).
- They say **every dog has its day** (everyone will, at some time in their life, be successful

or lucky), and mine is on Wednesday, when I will be interviewed for a television programme!

- We should ***make hay while the sun shines*** (take the advantage of a good situation) and finish writing the book at a stretch.

- I have made a mess of my life. I'll ***turn over a new leaf*** (begin again, fresh; reform and begin again) and hope to do better.

- We should get to the book sale as soon as they open; ***it's first come, first served*** (the first people will be the first to receive something).

- They accept all children have problems and ***that's life*** (such negative sides are part of the life).

17. Body parts

(1) *Hand & arm*:

- I like to keep my vocabulary ***at hand*** (nearby).
- Are there enough people ***on hand*** (available) to hold a meeting?
- Employee absenteeism has gotten ***out of hand*** (out of control).
- She'll give you the name of a place to stay — she ***knows*** the area ***like the back of her hand*** (very well).
- Could you ***lend me a hand*** (help) with this piano?
- The money my aunt gave me will ***come in handy*** (be useful when needed) to pay for my music lessons.
- Share holders ***pointed the finger at*** (blame) the board of directors for the losses, and voted most of them out.
- The exam's at two. Will you ***keep your fingers crossed*** (wish for good luck) for me?
- Apparently, all the food tastes delicious there. The only problem is that it ***costs an arm and a leg*** (expensive)!

(2) *Shoulder*:

- You ***give someone the cold shoulder*** (frosty; ignore someone) when you refuse to speak to them.

(3) *Head*:

- Come on, let me help you brainstorm some ideas — ***two heads are better than one*** (two people working together have a better chance of solving a problem than one person working alone)!
- He ***has his head in the clouds*** (not be realistic, have fantasies) while the rest of us are trying to figure out how to fix this!

(4) *Eye*:

- I really ***look up to*** (respect) my dad. He's the most hard-working person I know.

18. Good situation

- It's unsurprising how quickly Sarah has ***moved up in the world*** (advance oneself and become successful) — her tenacity and determination are matched only by her intelligence and talent.

- She has been working at Miramax for over a month now, and **so far so good** (all is going well so far).

- Don't worry; this project will **come out in the wash** (have a positive resolution, like a clothing stain that is washed away).

- Our team **gained the upper hand** (gain advantage or control over someone or something) in the second half of the match.

- We'll **let you off the hook** (free from danger or blame) this time, but if you make any more mistakes like that, you'll lose your job.

- Publishing this novel is really **a dream come true** (a wish or a dream that has become a reality). I never thought I'd see the day it happened.

- This steak is just **what the doctor ordered** (exactly what was needed).

- We **go away back** (be in good relationship). It was 7 years ago that we first met.

- Luck and I **are thick as thieves** (be in good relationship).

- That city **has a friendly vibe** (friendly atmosphere). People there seem to be very nice and hospitable.

19. Bad situation

- I was already late for work and, **to add insult to injury**, I spilled coffee all over myself.

- He is even worse than my ex-boyfriend. I'm **out of the frying pan and into the fire** (things are going from bad to worse).

- It was an interesting year — Danny lost his job; I was off sick for three months and Josh broke his leg. **It never rains but it pours** (misfortunes follow each other and arrive all at the same time), as they say!

- They were already struggling financially, but after Samantha lost her job, **things went from bad to worse** (become more unpleasant, or difficult).

- These blood test results are a good sign, but you're **not out of the woods yet** (Despite improvement, not yet completely free from difficulties or danger, especially financially or physically).

- Go to the bank and ask for the loan again. This time don't **come away empty-handed** (return without gaining anything).

- I'm not thrilled to spend my Saturday cleaning, but **it can't be helped** (no other choices)—the house is a mess!

- Don't worry, **the first step is always the hardest** (starting is the most difficult part of any task)—it'll get easier after that.

- That skier just missed the tree — **what a close call** (narrow escape, near miss).

- The project failed, we're **back to square one** (start again from the beginning).

- What the country was experiencing was not peace, but just ***the calm before another storm*** (a period of unnatural calm before an attack).
- When we reach ***the end of the road*** (the final step of something) on this project, we'll get paid.
- She was nearly ninety when she came to ***the end of the road*** (euphemism: death).

20. Importance

- We're wasting our time on ***small potatoes*** (unimportant things). Let's get to the big news that made us have this meeting.
- I can't help you with your presentation right now. I ***have bigger fish to fry*** (have more important things to do).
- I'm never flying through that airport again! ***Not for all the tea in China*** (Not for anything)!
- I wouldn't work overseas ***for all the tea in China*** if it meant being away from my family.
- When you're in a foreign country, you'll find that a reliable translator is ***worth his weight in gold*** (extremely helpful).
- Wow, this new car of yours ***is really something*** (particularly noteworthy, remarkable, or impressive)!
- It's not such a big problem! You're ***making a mountain out of a molehill*** (talk or complain about an unimportant problem as if it is important and serious)!
- Don't worry about that. ***It's not the end of the world*** (it would not be the worst thing).
- It would be great if I got this teaching position, but I guess ***it isn't the end of the world*** if they pass me over.
- I know ***there's no place like home*** (home is the best place), but you really ought to go out and explore the world!

21. Being busy

- I just have ***a lot/enough on my plate*** (a lot to do) right now while I'm finishing up my degree and doing this huge project for work.
- Ann is exhausted again. She's always ***biting off more than she can chew*** (take on more responsibility than one can handle).
- There's no way I can take a vacation right now, ***I'm up to my ears*** (extremely busy with something) in work at the moment!

22. Waste

- I think we are ***going on a wild goose chase*** (do something pointless). This library doesn't have the books we need.
- I know you want to buy a new TV with your bonus, but you should really ***save*** that money

for a rainy day (save money or things for a time in the future when you might need them).

23. Trend

(1) *In fashion*:

- But before we all ***jump on the bandwagon*** (follow a trend), we need to ask ourselves what we really want to accomplish with social media.

- Yoga pants are ***all the rage*** (very much in fashion) in North America right now, but in two years probably nobody will be wearing them.

- My elder sister ***is*** pretty ***fashion-forward*** (in pursuit of fashion). She buys anything that is trendy.

(2) *Out of date*:

- Such crude methods are ***old hat*** (out of date).

24. Work & employment

- You don't have to do this totally ***by the book*** (follow instructions exactly).

- You all look tired. Let's ***call it a day*** (stop working).

- Nothing that you're saying is ***on point*** (focused on the essence of a particular topic)! You're just wasting time with mindless rambling.

- Sal is known to ***drive a hard bargain*** (work hard to negotiate prices or agreements in one's own favor), so I doubt you'll get that car for the price you want.

- Jane, you ***drive a hard bargain***, but I'll sign the contract.

- I'll be ***burning the midnight oil*** (working late) tonight, but I guarantee I'll finish the paper before class tomorrow at 9.

- There is nothing more rewarding to me than ***getting my hands dirty*** (do hard work, often manual labor) in my garden.

- I really appreciate you guys ***getting your hands dirty*** and helping us move.

- What an awful week this has been. All I can say at this point is ***thank God it's Friday*** (a common expression used to celebrate the end of the working week).

- It will take me a couple of weeks to ***learn the ropes*** (learn the basic details of how to do or perform a job, task, or activity) but after that I should be fine.

- I've been ***out of work*** (unemployed) since December. Hope I find a new job soon!

- ***Do you have any openings*** (a job that is available) for a full-time job?

- I can ***wrap up*** (complete work on something) this little project in a week.

25. Money

- To start with, they are crucial to the finances of ***cash-strapped*** (not enough money to pay for things necessary) universities.

- I'm ***flat broke*** (having no money at all) once again and don't know how I'm going to pay my rent.

- My husband may not be the world's most glamorous guy, but he **brings home the bacon** (earn money for the family).

- My mom always tries to buy me all of these fancy gifts, but I try to remind her that **the best things in life are free** (often the things that have the most value or quality cost nothing).

- Don't be gloomy because you're broke. **The best things in life are free.**

- Yesterday I took my children to the zoo. We didn't spend a penny, but we had a wonderful time. **The best things in life are free.**

- I can't believe you would spend your entire allowance on a silly video game. **Money doesn't grow on trees** (It's not easy to get money).

- That coat must have **cost you a pretty penny** (very expensive)!

- I think you should be very careful about accepting his help. Remember, **there's no such thing as a free lunch** (nothing is ever really given away for free).

26. Mistake

- You're **barking up the wrong tree** (make the wrong choice, ask the wrong person) if you ask her to help you, because she never helps anyone.

- If you think I'll help you cheat, you're definitely **barking up the wrong tree**!

- **I'm sorry to rain on your parade** (spoil someone's plans), but the park is closed tomorrow, so we can't have our picnic there.

27. Innovation

- I've been trying to **think outside the box** (think innovatively) about what I want this term paper to be about. I know the professor hates unoriginal ideas.

- **Cutting-edge** (innovative) musical styles often originate in Britain.

28. Opinion

- I don't want the long version—just tell me what your thesis is **in a nutshell** (in summary; concisely).

- He never made a will, **to the best of my knowledge** (as far as I know).

- I'm in no rush. Any time is fine **as far as I'm concerned** (from my point of view).

- **In my book** (according to my opinion or values), it's worse to run away from a fight than to start one.

- I am going to **lay it on the line** (speak frankly and directly) and you had better listen to me.

- Our soldiers **lay their lives on the line** (put something at risk in the pursuit of something else) every day to defend your freedom.

29. Efforts

- The road to becoming a doctor is long, hard, and exhausting, not to mention expensive! But *no pain*, *no gain* (suffering is needed to make progress).

- Samantha is *working on* (put forth the effort toward something, usually used in the continuous tense) her Ph. D. at the moment.

- I've been *working on* a new play that deals directly with the trauma from my childhood.

- No wonder Mary is ill. She has been *burning the candle at both ends* (work very hard and stay up very late at night) for a long time.

- When it comes to exercise, *every little bit counts* (however small your improvements might seem, they add up and become important).

- My mom is pretty warm-hearted, who always *bends/leans over backwards to* (spare no efforts to do) help those in need.

30. Practice

- *You never know until you try* (It is not possible for you to know whether you can do something until you try). I bet you'd really like them!

- You've been complaining about being out of work for too long. It's time to *take the bull by the horns* (confront a problem head-on and deal with it openly) and go find a job.

31. Virtue

(1) *Persistent*:

- You're doing a great job so far, James! *Keep it up* (continue doing something)!

- Even though I knew I wouldn't win, I *hung in* (persist or persevere in a challenging situation) the race and finished in third place.

- No matter how many things go wrong, *never say die* (never surrender or give up).

(2) *Patient*:

- I've got to wait another two weeks to find out how I did on the exam. Oh well, I suppose *patience is a virtue* (it is good to be patient).

(3) *Honest*:

- Secrets like that will always find their way to the surface, so *honesty is* definitely *the best policy* (telling the truth is the best strategy).

- I think you should just explain what happened, rather than trying to cover your tracks. *Honesty is the best policy.*

(4) *Careful*:

- *Just to be safe* (as a precaution; in order to avoid potential problems), you should take some extra water with you.

- Don't speak too soon (do not draw a conclusion so fast). We are not out of this yet.

32. Others

- I picked up some groceries **on the fly** (do it quickly, without thinking about it or planning it in advance).

- These people can make decisions **on the fly** and don't have to phone home to their boss.

- Children will be admitted to the concert, but sorry, no **babes in arms** (a baby being carried).

- Don't mention George's name to Roger. They had a falling out two years ago. **Let sleeping dogs lie** (stop discussing an issue), if you know what I mean.

- We **left no stone unturned** (look for something in every possible place) looking for that earring, but we still couldn't find it.

- You're **playing with fire** (very risky) if you keep driving that car — the floor under the seat is almost completely rusted out.

- Finding myself in a country with so much delicious food, all thoughts of dieting **went out the window** (be forgotten, disregarded, or lost).

- I'm going to take a (**quick**) **cat nap** (short sleep during the day) before my next shift starts, or else I'll be feeling sluggish for the entire evening.

- She was going to take that job offer in California, but after thinking about how much she would miss her friends and family in Delaware, she had **a change of heart** (a change in one's opinion or feelings on a matter).

- Do I think you need a new car? **Far from it** (not at all). The old one is fine.

- — Does this hat look strange?

  — Far from it. It looks good on you.

33. Proverb

- No egg remains intact in an overturned nest. 覆巢之下，焉有完卵。
- Birds of a feather flock together. 一丘之貉。
- Comparing apples to oranges. 牛头不对马嘴。
- Every cloud has a silver lining. 守得云开见月明。
- It is always darkest before the dawn. 黎明前总是黑暗的。
- Get a taste of your own medicine. 自食苦果。
- Saving for a rainy day. 未雨绸缪。
- Slow and steady wins the race. 稳扎稳打，无往不胜。
- There are other fish in the sea. 天涯何处无芳草。
- You can't have your cake and eat it too. 鱼和熊掌不可兼得。
- You can't judge a book by its cover. 人不可貌相。
- Haste makes waste. 欲速则不达。
- Once bitten, twice shy. 一朝被蛇咬，十年怕井绳。
- First in, best dressed. 先到先得。

附录 2　雅思口语题库

➢ Topic Pool——Part 1

Study

1. Do you work or are you a student?

2. What subject are you studying?

3. Why did you choose that subject?

4. What would you like to do in the future?

5. What are the most popular subjects in China?

6. Do you think it's important to choose a subject you like?

7. Are you looking forward to working?

8. Do you like your subject? (Why? / Why not?)

9. Do you prefer to study in the mornings or in the afternoons?

10. Is your subject interesting to you?

11. Is there any kind of technology you can use in study?

Work

1. What work do you do?

2. Why did you choose to do that type of job?

3. Do you like your job?

4. Do you miss being a student?

5. Is it very interesting?

6. Is there any kind of technology you use at work?

7. Can you manage your time well when you work?

8. Who helps you most at work?

Hometown

1. Has your hometown changed much these years?

2. Is that a big city or a small place?

3. How long have you been living here?

4. For you, what benefits are there living in a big city?

5. Is there anything you dislike about it?

6. What do you like most about your hometown?

7. Where in your country do you live?

8. Where is your hometown?

9. Do you like your hometown? /Do you like living there?

10. Please describe your hometown a little.

11. Do you think you will continue living there for a long time?

Accommodation

1. Are the transport facilities in your city very good?

2. Which room does your family spend most of the time in?

3. Do you live in a house or a flat?

4. Do you plan to live here for a long time?

5. Do you live alone or with your family?

6. How long have you lived there?

7. What do you usually do in your house/flat/room?

8. Which is your favourite room in your home?

9. What's the difference between where you are living now and where you lived in the past?

10. What can you see when you look out of the window of your room?

11. Would you be willing to live in the countryside in the future?

12. What kind of house or flat do you want to live in the future?

13. What kind of accommodation do you live in?

14. Can you describe the place where you live?

15. How long have you lived there?

16. Do you prefer living in a house or a flat?

17. Who do you live with?

18. What part of your home do you like the most?

19. Please describe the room you live in.

The area you live in

1. Do you like the area that you live in now?

2. How has your area changed in recent years?

3. Do you know any famous people in your area?

4. Where do you like to go in your area?

Talents

1. Do you have a talent, or something you are good at?

2. Do you think your talent can be useful for your future work?

3. Do you think people in your family have the same talent?

Feel bored

1. Do you often feel bored?

2. What kinds of things would make you feel bored?

3. What would you do if you feel bored?

Meeting places

1. Where do you usually meet your friends?

2. Do you think there are some places suitable for meeting others?

3. Have the meeting places changed now compared with the past?

Collect things

1. Do you collect anything?

2. Are there any things you keep from childhood?

3. Where do you usually keep things you collect?

Computers

1. In what conditions would you use a computer?

2. When was the first time you used a computer?

3. What will your life be like without computers?

4. In what conditions would it be difficult for you to use a computer?

Watch

1. Do you wear a watch?

2. Have you ever got a watch as a gift?

3. Why do some people wear expensive watches?

Old buildings

1. Have you ever seen some old buildings in your city?

2. Do you think we should keep old buildings in cities?

3. Do you prefer living in an old building or a modern house?

Sitting down

1. Where is your favorite place to sit?

2. Do you always sit down for a long time?

3. Do you feel sleepy after you sit down for a while?

Reading

1. When do you read books?

2. How often do you buy books?

3. Have you ever read a novel that has been adapted into a film?

4. Which one do you prefer, reading books or watching movies?

Advertisements

1. What kinds of advertisements do you watch?

2. Where can you see advertisements?

3. Have you ever bought something because of its advertisement?

4. Do you watch advertisements from the beginning to the end?

Evening time

1. Do you like morning or evening?

2. What do you usually do in the evening?

3. Are there any differences between what you do in the evening now and what you did in the past?

Weather

1. Do you prefer hot or cold weather?

2. Has the weather in your country changed much in the past few years?

3. What is the weather usually like in your country?

4. Do you prefer dry or wet weather?

5. Do you get in the habit of checking the weather forecast? When/ How often?

Websites

1. What kinds of websites do you usually use?

2. What is your favorite website?

3. Are there any changes about the websites you usually use?

4. What kinds of websites are popular in your country?

Taking photos

1. Do you like to take photographs?

2. Do you ever take photos of yourself?

3. What is your favorite family photo?

4. Do you want to improve your picture taking skills?

Cinema

1. Did you usually go to the cinema when you were a child?

2. Do you often go to the cinema with your friends?

3. Do you still like the same kind of movie which you liked when you were a child?

Art

1. Do you like art?

2. Did you learn drawing when you were a kid?

3. Have you ever visited an art gallery?

4. Is there any art work on the wall in your room?

5. Do you like visiting art gallery?

6. Do you want to be an artist?

7. Do you like modern art or traditional art?

Sports

1. Do you like watching sports programs on TV?

2. Do you watch live sports games?

3. Who do you like to watch sports games with?

4. What kinds of games do you expect to watch in the future?

5. What kind of sport did you do when you were young?

6. What's the most common sport in your country?

7. Do you like outdoor activities?

Mobile phone

1. Do you remember your first mobile phone?

2. Do you often use your mobile phone for texting or making phone calls?

3. How has your mobile phone changed your life?

4. Will you buy a new mobile phone in the future?

Street market

1. What do street markets sell?

2. Do you prefer to go shopping in the shopping mall or the street market?

3. When was the last time you went to a street market?

4. Are there many street markets in China?

Emails

1. Do you often send emails?

2. Is sending emails popular in China?

3. Do you think sending emails will be more or less popular in the future?

Lost and found

1. What will you do if you find something lost by others?

2. Have you ever lost anything?

3. Will you post on social media if you lose your items?

Time management

1. Do you make plans every day?

2. Is it easy to manage time?

3. Do you think it's useful to plan your time?

4. Do you like being busy?

Memory

1. Why do some people have good memory while others just don't?

2. Why do more people rely on cellphones to memorize things?

3. Are you good at memorizing things?

4. Have you ever forgotten something that was important?

Mirrors

1. Do you like looking at yourself in the mirror?

2. Have you ever bought mirrors?

3. Do you usually take a mirror with you?

4. Would you use mirrors to decorate your room?

Dreams

1. Do you often remember your dreams?

2. Are you interested in others' dreams?

3. Do you want to make your dreams come true?

Science

1. When did you start to learn science?

2. Is there any technology that you think is helpful in daily life?

3. Do you think science classes are important?

4. What is your favorite subject of science?

Pets and animals

1. Did you have any pets when you were a child?

2. Do you like to see animals in the zoo?

3. What's your favorite animal?

4. What is the most popular animal in China?

Shoes

1. Do you like shoes or are you interested in shoes?

2. Do you ever buy shoes online?

3. Do you prefer comfortable shoes or good-looking fashionable shoes?

4. What kind of shoes do you like the most?

Weekends

1. What do you usually do on weekends? Do you study or work?

2. Would you say weekends are important to us?

3. Do you often go to the cinema on weekends?

4. What do you plan to do for next weekend?

5. Do you like weekends?

6. What did you do last weekend?

Daily routine

1. What is your daily routine?

2. Have you ever changed your routine?

3. Which part of your daily routine do you like best?

Colours

1. What's your favourite colour?

2. Do you prefer dark colours or bright colours?

3. Do any colours have a special meaning in your culture?

4. What colours are the walls of the rooms in your home?

Getting lost

1. Have you ever lost your way?

2. How can you find your way when you are lost?

3. Have you ever helped someone who got lost?

4. Would you use a map when you get lost?

Concentration

1. Is it difficult for you to stay focused on something?

2. What do you do to help you concentrate?

3. What may distract you when you are trying to stay focused?

4. When do you need to be focused?

Public parks or gardens

1. What do you usually do when you go to a park or garden?

2. How have parks changed today compared to the time when you were a child?

3. Would you prefer to go to a personal garden or public garden?

New places

1. Have you been to a new place recently?

2. What's the difference between this place and other places of the same kind?

3. Do you feel nervous when you travel to new places?

Primary school

1. What did you like to do the most when you were in primary school?

2. How did you go to your primary school?

3. How do you like your primary school?

4. What did you do in your leisure time when you are at primary school?

Car trip

1. Do you like to travel by car?

2. Where is the farthest place you travelled to by car?

3. Do you like to sit in the front or back when travelling by car?

Snacks

1. What snacks did you eat when you were young?

2. Do you often eat snacks now?

3. Do you think eating snacks is healthy?

4. What snacks do you like to eat?

5. Did you often eat snacks when you were young?

Birthday

1. What do you usually do on your birthday?

2. What did you do on your birthday when you were young?

3. Do you think it is important for you to celebrate your birthday?

4. Whose birthday do you think is the most important to celebrate in China?

Social media

1. Do you like social media?

2. Do you think your friends spend too much time on social media?

3. Do you want to work in a social media company?

4. What's the most popular social media in China? Why?

Names

1. Does your name have a special meaning?

2. How do people choose names for their children?

3. Does anyone in your family have the same name with you?

4. Are there any differences between how Chinese name their children now and in the past?

Weather

1. Do you prefer hot or cold weather?

2. Do you prefer dry or wet weather?

3. What is the weather like in your hometown?

4. Do you have the habit of checking the weather forecast?

Singing

1. Do you like singing?

2. Have you ever learnt how to sing?

3. If you sing, who would you sing in front of?

4. Do you think singing can bring happiness to people?

Public transport

1. What kind of public transport do you usually take?

2. Did you take public transport when you were a kid?

3. Do most people prefer public transport?

4. When do you usually take public transport?

Cooking

1. Do you like cooking?

2. Would you like to learn how to cook?

3. Who normally does the cooking in your family?

Geography

1. Have you ever studied geography at school?

2. Do you like geography?

3. Do you want to travel to a country because of its geographical conditions?

4. Are you good at reading a map?

Puzzles

1. Did you like doing puzzles when you were a kid?

2. When do you do puzzles, during trips or when you feel bored?

3. Do you like doing word puzzles or number puzzles?

4. Do you think it is good for old people to do puzzles?

Writing

1. Do you write a lot?

2. What do you like to write?

3. Do you prefer typing or handwriting when you are writing something?

4. Do you think the things you write would change?

Technology

1. What technological products do you often use, computers or mobile phones?

2. What electronic devices have you bought lately?

3. Are there any technological devices you want to buy?

4. What benefits does technology bring to us?

Jewelry

1. Do you often wear jewelry?

2. What type of jewelry do you like? /What kind of jewelry do you think looks good?

3. Why do you think some people wear a piece of jewelry for a long time?

4. Have you ever received jewelry as a gift?

5. Do you usually buy jewelry?

Outer space and stars

1. Have you ever learnt about outer space and stars?

2. Are you interested in films concerning outer space and stars?

3. Do you like science fiction movies? Why?

4. Do you want to go into outer space in the future?

5. Do you want to learn more about outer space?

Staying up

1. Do you often stay up late?

2. Did you stay up late when you were a kid?

3. What do you do when you stay up late?

4. What does it feel like the next morning if you stay up late?

Music

1. What music do you like?

2. What music do you dislike?

3. Do you often listen to one type of music? /Do you enjoy the same type of music?

4. What music do your friends like?

5. What's the most popular type of music where you live?

6. Which singer or musician would you like to see in person?

Happy

1. Is there anything that makes you feel happy lately?

2. What made you happy when you were little?

3. What do you think will make you feel happy in the future?

4. When do you feel happy at work? Why?

5. Do you feel happy when buying new things?

6. Do you think people are happy when buying new things?

Library

1. Do you often go to library?

2. Did you go to library when you were a kid?

3. Do Chinese kids often go to library?

Keys

1. Do you always bring a lot of keys with you?

2. Have you ever lost your keys?

T-Shirt

1. Do you like wearing T-shirts?

2. How often do you wear T-shirt?

3. Do you like T-shirts with pictures or prints?

4. Do you think older people who wear T-shirts are fashionable?

5. Would you buy T-shirt as souvenirs on vacation?

Small business

1. Do you know many small businesses?

2. Do you prefer buying things in big companies or small businesses?

Chocolate

1. Do you like eating chocolate? Why or why not?

2. How often do you eat chocolate?

3. Did you often eat chocolate when you were a kid?

4. Why do you think chocolate is popular around the world?

5. What's your favorite flavor?

6. Do you think it's good to use chocolate as gifts to others?

Schools

1. Where do you go to school?

2. Do you go to a good school?

3. Do you like your teachers?

4. Do you like your current learning atmosphere?

5. What are the differences between your school and other schools?

6. Is there anything you want to change about your school?

Noise

1. Which do you think makes louder noise, in cities or in the countryside?

2. What noise do we have in cities?

3. What kind of noise do cars make?

Fast food

1. What do you have for breakfast?

2. Do you eat fast food?

3. What are the different kinds of fast food in China?

Housework and cooking

1. Do you do some cooking/help your family cook at home now?

2. Did you do some house cleaning when you were young?

3. Do you have breakfast at home every day?

4. Do you want to learn how to cook well?

Morning time

1. Do you like getting up early in the morning?

2. What do you usually do in the morning?

3. What did you do in the morning when you were little? Why?

4. Are there any differences between what you do in the morning now and what you did in the past?

➤ Topic Pool——Part 2

People

1. Describe a person you have met who you want to work/study with.

You should say:

Who this person is

How you met this person

How long you have known him/her

And explain why you want to work/study with him/her

2. Describe an interesting old person you met.

You should say:

Who this person is

When/Where you met this person

What he/she did

Why you think he/she is interesting

3. Describe a character from a film.

You should say:

What character it is

Who acted the character

When you saw the film

And explain whether you like this character

4. Describe a person you met at a party who you enjoyed talking with.

You should say:

What party it was

Who this person is

What you talked about

And explain why you enjoyed talking with him/her

5. Describe a person who inspired you to do something interesting.

You should say:

Who he/she is

How you knew him/her

What interesting thing you did

And explain how he/she inspired you to do it

6. Describe a person you know who is from a different culture.

You should say:

Who he/she is

Where he/she is from

How you knew him/her

And explain how you feel about this person

7. Describe a person who is fashionable.

You should say:

Who he/she is

What he/she does

What kind of clothes he/she wears

And explain why you think this person is fashionable

8. Describe a person you know who loves to grow vegetables/fruits.

You should say:

Who this person is

What he/she grows

Where he/she grows those vegetable/fruits

And explain how you feel about this person

9. Describe your favorite childhood friend.

You should say:

Who he/she is

Where you met each other

What you often did together

And explain what made you like him/her

10. Describe an interesting neighbor.

You should say:

Who this person is

How you know this person

What he or she does

And explain why you think this person is interesting

11. Describe a family member you want to work with in the future.

You should say:

Who he/she is

What he/she does

What kind of work you would like to do with him/her

And explain how you feel about him/her

12. Describe a popular/well-known person in your country.

You should say:

Who he/she is

What he/she has done

Why he/she is popular

And explain how you feel about him/her

13. Describe a person you enjoyed talking with.

You should say：

Who he/she is

When you talked

What you talked about

And explain why you enjoyed talking with this person

14. Describe a person you follow on social media.

You should say：

Who he/she is

How you knew him/her

What he/she posts on social media

And explain why you follow him/her on social media

15. Describe a person who makes contribution to the society.

You should say：

Who this person is

How you knew him/her

What type of work he/she does

And explain why you think he/she contributes to the society

16. Describe a person you only met once and want to know more about.

You should say：

Who he/she is

When you met him/her

Why you want to know more about him/her

And explain how you feel about him/her

17. Describe someone you really like to spend time with.

You should say：

Who he/she is

How you knew him/her

What you usually do together

And explain why you like to spend time with him/her

18. Describe a person who impressed you most in your primary school.

You should say：

Who he/she is

How you knew him/her

Why he/she impressed you most

And explain how you feel about him/her

Object

1. Describe a website you often visit.

You should say：

What it is about

How you found out about it

How often you visit it

And explain why you often visit it

2. Describe a piece of technology you own that you feel is difficult to use.

You should say：

When you got it

What you got it for

How often you use it

And explain how you feel about it

3. Describe an unusual meal you had.

You should say：

When you had it

Where you had it

Whom you had it with

And explain why it was unusual

4. Describe a gift you got.

You should say：

What it is

How you got it

What you did

And explain how you felt about it

5. Describe a photo you took and you are proud of.

You should say：

When you took it

Where you took it

What is in this photo

And explain why you are proud of it

6. Describe an object that you think is beautiful.

You should say：

What it is

Where you saw it

What it looks like

And explain why you think it is beautiful

7. Describe a traditional product in your country.

You should say：

What it is

When you tried this product for the first time

What it is made of

And explain how important this product is

8. Describe an invention that changed the world.

You should say:

What the invention was

What it can do

How popular it is

Why it is an important invention

9. Describe something you received for free.

You should say:

What it was

Who you received it from

Why you received it for free

And explain how you felt about it

10. Describe a toy you got in your childhood.

You should say:

What it was

When you got it

How you got it

And explain how you felt about it

11. Describe a piece of clothing that someone gave to you.

You should say:

What it is

Who gave it to you

When you got it

And explain why this person gave you this piece of clothing

12. Describe a gift you would like to buy for your friend.

You should say:

What gift you would like to buy

Whom you would like to give it to

Why you want to buy this gift for him/her

And explain why you would like to choose that gift

13. Describe something you cannot live without (not a computer/phone).

You should say:

What it is

What you do with it

How it helps you in your life

And explain why you cannot live without it

14. Describe a piece of equipment in your home that you broke and then fixed.

You should say:

What it is

How you broke it

How you fixed it

And explain how you felt about it

15. Describe an item on which you spent more than expected.

You should say：

What it is

How much you spent on it

Why you bought it

And explain why you think you spent more than expected

16. Describe a daily routine that you enjoyed.

You should say：

What it is

Where and when you do it

Whom you do it with

And explain why you enjoy it

17. Describe an activity you enjoyed in your free time when you were young.

You should say：

What it was

Where you did it

Whom you did it with

And explain why you enjoyed it

18. Describe something you did that made you feel proud of.

You should say：

What it was

How you did it

What difficult you had

How you dealt with the difficulty

And explain why you felt proud of it

19. Describe something that you did with someone/a group of people.

You should say：

What it was

Whom you did it with

How long it took you to do this

And explain why you did it together

20. Describe an advertisement you don't like.

You should say：

What type of advertisement it is

Where and when you first saw it

What product or service it advertises

And explain why you don't like it

21. Describe a historical period/moment you would like to learn more about.

You should say：

What you are interested in

When it happened

What you know about it

And why you would like to learn more

22. Describe something you would like to learn in the future.

You should say：

What it is

How you would like to learn it

Where you would like to learn it

Why you would like to learn it

And explain whether it's difficult to learn it

23. Describe a piece of good news that you heard about someone you know well.

You should say：

What it was

When you heard it

How you knew it

And explain how you felt about it

24. Describe a movie you watched recently and would like to watch again.

You should say：

What it was about

Where you watched it

Why you like it

And explain why you would like to watch it again

25. Describe a program you like to watch.

You should say：

What it is

What it is about

Whom you watch it with

And explain why you like to watch it

26. Describe an important thing you learned (not at school or university).

You should say：

What it is

When you learned it

How you learned it

And explain why it was important

27. Describe a story or a novel that you have read and you found interesting.

You should say：

When you read it

What the story or novel was about

Who wrote it

And explain why you found it interesting

28. Describe something you do to keep fit and healthy.

You should say:

What it is

When you do it

Whom you do it with

And explain why you think this method is important

29. Describe something that surprised you and made you happy.

You should say:

What it is

How you found out about it

What you did

And explain whether it made you happy

30. Describe something that helps you to focus on study/work.

You should say:

What it is

How often you do it

When you start doing it

And explain how it helps you concentrate

31. Describe a song or piece of music you like.

You should say:

What the song or music is

What kind of song or music it is

Where you first heard it

And explain why you like it

32. Describe a story someone told you and you remember.

You should say:

What the story was about

Who told you this story

Why you remember it

And explain how you feel about it

33. Describe an ambition that you haven't achieved.

You should say:

What it is

Why you haven't achieved it

What you have already done

And explain how you felt about it

34. Describe a rule that you would like to change.

You should say：

What it is

Why you want to change it

How others feel about the rule

And explain whether you have followed the rule

35. Describe something that helped you learn a foreign language.

You should say：

What it was

What language you learnt

Why you chose to learn that language

And explain how this thing helped you

36. Describe a difficult skill you have learned from an old person.

You should say：

What it is

Why the skill was learned from this old person

How you learned it

And explain how you felt after you learned the skill

37. Describe a habit that your friend has and you want to develop.

You should say：

Who your friend is

What habit he/she has

When you noticed this habit

And explain why you want to develop this habit

38. Describe a skill that was difficult for you to learn.

You should say：

What the skill was

When you learned it

How you learned it

And explain how you felt about learning it

Place

1. Describe another city you would like to stay for a short time.

You should say：

Where the city is

Whom you will go there with

What you will do there

And explain why you will stay there just for a short time

2. Describe a new development in the area where you live (e. g. shopping mall, park ...).

You should say：

What the development is

When/Where you noticed it

How long it took to complete it

And explain how you feel about it

3. Describe a noisy place you have been to.

You should say：

Where it is

When you went there

What you did there

And explain why you feel it's a noisy place

4. Describe your favourite place in your house where you can relax.

You should say：

Where it is

What it is like

What you enjoy doing there

And explain why you feel relaxed at this place

5. Describe a place you visited where the air was polluted.

You should say：

Where the place is

When you visited

Why the air was not good

And explain how you felt about the place

6. Describe a place in your country that you would like to recommend to visitors/travelers.

You should say：

What it is

Where it is

What people can do there

And explain why you would like to recommend it to visitors/travelers

7. Describe a popular place for doing sports (e. g. stadium).

You should say：

Where it is

When you went there

What you did there

And explain how you feel about this place

8. Describe the home of someone you know well and you often visit.

You should say：

Whose home it is

How often you go there

What it is like

And explain how you feel about the home

9. Describe a quiet place where you like to spend your time.

You should say：

Where it is

How often you go there

What you do there

And explain how you feel about this place

10. Describe an important river/lake in your country.

You should say：

Where it is

How big/long it is

What it looks like

And explain why it is important

11. Describe a place in the countryside that you visited.

You should say：

Where it is

When you visited this place

What you did there

And explain how you feel about this place

12. Describe a city that you think is interesting.

You should say：

Where it is

What the city is famous for

Why it is interesting

And explain how you feel about it

13. Describe an apartment or a house that you would like to have.

You should say：

What it is like

Where it would be

Why you would like to have such place

And explain how you feel about the place

14. Describe a place you visited on vacation.

You should say：

Where it is

When you went there

What you did there

And explain why you went there.

Event

1. Describe a time when you missed or were late for an important meeting/event.

You should say：

When it happened

What happened

Why you missed/were late for it

And explain how you felt about this experience

2. Describe a time when you taught a friend/relative something.

You should say：

Who you taught

What/how you taught

What the result was

And explain how you felt about the experience

3. Describe your first day at school that you remember.

You should say：

Where the school was

How you went there

What happened that day

And how you felt on that day

4. Describe a time when you made a complaint and were satisfied with the result.

You should say：

When it happened

Whom you complained to

What you complained about

And explain why you were satisfied with the result

5. Describe a problem you had while shopping online or in a store.

You should say：

When it happened

What you bought

What problems you had while shopping online

And explain how you felt about it

6. Describe a time when you made a decision to wait for something.

You should say：

When it happened

What you waited for

Why you made the decision

And explain how you felt about the decision

7. Describe a time when you received money on your birthday.

You should say：

When it happened

Who gave you the money

Why he/she gave you the money

And explain how you felt about it

8. Describe a time when you had an argument with a friend.

You should say:

When it happened

Why you argued

How you resolved this argument

And explain how you felt about this experience

9. Describe an outdoor activity you did in a new place recently.

You should say:

What the activity is

Who invited you to participate in it

Whether you asked for help during the activity

And explain what change you had in the activity

10. Describe a time when you forgot an appointment.

You should say:

What the appointment was for

Whom you made it with

Why you forgot it

And explain how you felt about the experience

11. Describe a time when you shared something with others.

You should say:

What you shared

Whom you shared it with

Why you shared it

And explain how you felt about sharing it

12. Describe a time when you needed to search for some information.

You should say:

What information it was

When you searched for it

How you searched for it

And explain why you needed to search the information

13. Describe a time when you saw a lot of plastic waste (e. g. in a park, on the beach, etc.).

You should say:

Where you saw the plastic waste

When you saw the plastic waste

What you did

And explain how you felt about this experience

14. Describe a time when you enjoyed an impressive English lesson.

You should say:

When and where you had the lesson

Who gave the lesson

What the lesson was about

And explain why you enjoyed the lesson

15. Describe a time when you used your cellphone to do something important.

You should say：

When it happened

What happened

How important the cellphone was

And explain how you felt about it

16. Describe a time when someone gave you positive advice on your work.

You should say：

When it happened

Who the person is

How the advice affected you

And explain how you felt about it

17. Describe an occasion when you lost something in a public place.

You should say：

What you lost

When and where you lost it

What you did to find it

And explain how you feel about this experience

18. Describe a contest/competition you would like to participate in.

You should say：

What the contest is about

Where the contest will take place

When it will be held

And explain why you would like to participate in it

19. Describe an important event you celebrated.

You should say：

What the event was

When it happened

Who attended the event

And explain how you feel about the event

20. Describe a positive change you made in your life.

You should say：

What the change was

When it happened

How it happened

And explain why it was a positive change

21. Describe a special day out that didn't cost you much.

You should say:

When the day was

Where you went

How much you spent

And explain how you feel about that day

22. Describe a time when you helped a child.

You should say:

When it happened

Who you helped

How you helped him/her

And explain how you felt about it

23. Describe a time when you were caught in a traffic jam.

You should say:

When it happened

Where it happened

How you passed the time while waiting

And explain how you felt when you were in that traffic jam

24. Describe a time when you were very busy.

You should say:

When it happened

Where you were

What you did

And explain why you were very busy

25. Describe a recent change in life that helps you save a lot of time.

You should say:

What it is

What you have done

How it helps you save time

And explain how you feel about this change

26. Describe an occasion when you had a special cake.

You should say:

When this happened

Where this happened

Who gave you the cake

And explain why it was a special cake

27. Describe a time you visited a new place.

You should say:

Where it is

When you went there

Why you went there

And explain how you feel about the place

28. Describe a happy event you organized.

You should say：

What the event was

When you had it

Who helped you to organize it

And explain how you feel about it

29. Describe a long walk you have been on.

You should say：

When this happened

Where you walked

Who you were with

And explain how you felt about this long walk

30. Describe a time when someone said something positive about your work.

You should say：

What the advice is

What your work is

Why it is a positive advice

And explain how you feel about it

31. Describe an interesting conversation you had with someone.

You should say：

When it was

Whom you had it with

What you talked about

And explain why you think it was interesting

32. Describe a time when you waited for something special to happen.

You should say：

What you waited for

Where you waited

Why it was special

And explain how you felt while you were waiting

33. Describe a bicycle/motorcycle/car trip you would like to go on.

You should say：

Who you would like to go with

Where you would like to go

When you would like to go

And explain why you would like to go by bicycle/motorcycle/car

34. Describe a good service you received.

You should say：

What the service was

When you received it

Whom you were with

And explain how you felt about it

35. Describe a time when you were friendly to someone you didn't like.

You should say：

When and where it happened

Who he/she was

Why you didn't like this person

And explain why you were friendly to him/her on that occasion

36. Describe a time when you got up early.

You should say：

When it was

What you did

Why you got up early

And explain how you felt about it

37. Describe an activity you usually do that wastes your time.

You should say：

What it is

When you usually do it

Why you do it

And explain why you think it wastes your time

38. Describe a time when you felt proud of a family member.

You should say：

When it happened

Who the person is

What the person did

And explain why you felt proud of him/her

39. Describe a time when you gave a piece of advice to another person.

You should say：

Who you gave it to

Why this person needed your advice

What advice you gave

And explain how you felt about the result

➤ Topic Pool——Part 3

People

1. Describe a person you have met who you want to work/study with.

① *Why should children be kind to their classmates?*

② *Can children choose their desk-mate?*

③ *What matters most about a colleague's personality?*

④ *Are good colleagues important at work?*

⑤ *What kind of people are popular at work?*

⑥ *Are knowledgeable people popular at work?*

2. Describe an interesting old person you met.

① *Do you think old people and young people can share interests?*

② *What can old people teach young people?*

③ *Are there benefits when one person is interested in another person? Why?*

④ *Do you think many people today are too self-centered?*

3. Describe a character from a film.

① *Is it interesting to be an actor/actress?*

② *What can children learn from acting?*

③ *Why do children like special costumes?*

④ *What are the differences between actors/actresses who earn much and those who earn little?*

4. Describe a person you met at a party who you enjoyed talking with.

① *On what occasions would people get to know new people?*

② *Where would people get to know new people?*

③ *How do people start a conversation?*

④ *Is it difficult for Chinese people to communicate with people from other countries?*

⑤ *Why are some people unwilling to have conversations with others?*

⑥ *Is it difficult for adults to talk with children?*

5. Describe a person who inspired you to do something interesting.

① *What qualities make someone a role model?*

② *Why should children learn from role models?*

③ *Who can influence children more, teachers or parents?*

④ *What kind of international news inspires people?*

⑤ *Besides parents and teachers, who else can motivate children?*

⑥ *Can online teaching motivate students to learn? How?*

6. Describe a person you know who is from a different culture.

① *How can we get to know people from different cultures better?*

② *What are the advantages and disadvantages of cultural diversity?*

③ *How can traditional culture and other cultures coexist?*

④ *Which Chinese traditions are disappearing?*

7. Describe a person who is fashionable.

① *Are older people as fashionable as young people? Why?*

② *Are women more fashionable than men? Why?*

③ *Why is fashion more important to some people?*

④ *Do you think online shopping will replace in-store shopping in the future? Why?*

8. Describe a person you know who loves to grow vegetables/fruits.

① *What do you think of the job, being a farmer?*

② *Are there many people growing their own vegetables now?*

③ *Do you think it's good to let kids learn how to plant?*

④ *What are the differences between traditional and modern agriculture?*

9. Describe your favorite childhood friend.

① *Why do people lose contact with their friends after graduation?*

② *How does modern technology influence friendship?*

③ *Do you think people's relationship with friends will change when they get older?*

10. Describe an interesting neighbor.

① *Do you have a good relationship with your neighbours?*

② *How can we improve our relationships with neighbours?*

③ *Do you think neighbours are important?*

④ *Do you think people's relationships with their neighbours today is the same as it was in the past?*

11. Describe a family member you want to work with in the future.

① *What kinds of family businesses are common in China?*

② *Why do people want to do family business?*

③ *What are the benefits of working with family members?*

④ *Is it easier to get promotion in big companies?*

12. Describe a popular/well-known person in your country.

① *What kinds of people are popular at work?*

② *Are bosses more popular than employees at work?*

③ *Which one is important, keeping a good relationship with colleagues or doing well at work?*

④ *What benefits can children get if they become popular at school?*

13. Describe a person you enjoyed talking with.

① *What do young people talk about when they meet up?*

② *Do you think it is necessary to be honest when talking with friends?*

③ *On what occasions do we need to talk with strangers?*

14. Describe a person you follow on social media.

① *Do you think old people and young people use the same kind of social media app?*

② *Do old people spend much time on social media?*

③ *What can people do on social media?*

④ *Are television and newspaper still useful?*

15. Describe a person who makes contribution to the society.

① *What kinds of jobs are well-paid?*

② *What are the changes in working conditions?*

③ *Do you think younger people should be less paid than older people?*

16. Describe a person you only met once and want to know more about.

① *Is it important to have the same hobbies and interests when making friends?*

② *What qualities make true friends?*

③ *On what occasions do people like to make friends?*

17. Describe someone you really like to spend time with.

① *What kinds of people are easy to get along with?*

② *How do leaders get along with their subordinates?*

③ *Do people have extra time for themselves nowadays?*

18. Describe a person who impressed you most in your primary school.

① *Why do people always miss their childhood?*

② *Are kids happier than adults?*

③ *Why do people still remember many of their friends from primary school?*

④ *What kinds of primary school teachers will impress students?*

Object

1. Describe a website you often visit.

① *What are the most popular and least popular apps in China?*

② *What's the difference between the Internet and television?*

③ *Why do some people like to get news on the Internet instead of getting it from TV?*

④ *Is the library still necessary? Why?*

⑤ *What kinds of people would still go to the library to read and study?*

⑥ *What are the differences between old people and young people when they use the Internet?*

2. Describe a piece of technology you own that you feel is difficult to use.

① *What technology do people currently use?*

② *Why do big companies introduce new products frequently?*

③ *Why are people so keen on buying iPhones even though they haven't changed much from one iPhone to the next?*

④ *Why do technology companies keep upgrading their products?*

⑤ *What changes has the development of technology brought about in our lives?*

⑥ *Does the development of technology affect the way we study? Why?*

3. Describe an unusual meal you had.

① *What are the advantages and disadvantages of eating in restaurants?*

② *What fast food are there in your country?*

③ *Do people eat fast food at home?*

④ *Why do some people choose to eat out instead of ordering takeout?*

⑤ *Do people in your county socialize in restaurants?*

⑥ *Do people in your country value food culture?*

4. Describe a gift you got.

① *Do people like expensive gifts?*

② *Why do people send gifts?*

③ *What kinds of gifts do young people like to receive as rewards?*

5. Describe a photo you took and you are proud of.

① *Why do some people like to record important things by photos?*

② *What can people learn from historical photographs?*

③ *Is taking photo the best way to remember something?*

④ *Which is better, taking photos or keeping a diary?*

6. Describe an object that you think is beautiful.

① *Do you think there are more beautiful things now than in the past? Why?*

② *What beautiful scenic spots are there in your country?*

③ *Where do you think people usually come into contact with beautiful things?*

④ *Why do you think people create beautiful things?*

7. Describe a traditional product in your country.

① *Do young people admire traditional products?*

② *Why is it important for children to learn about traditional products?*

③ *Does the government have responsibility to protect traditional products?*

④ *Do you think traditional products have better quality that modern products?*

8. Describe an invention that changed the world.

① *What kinds of equipment are important in schools?*

② *Which invention do you think is the most useful at home?*

③ *Do you think there will be no teachers in school in the future?*

9. Describe something you received for free.

① *Do you think people should pay for higher education by themselves?*

② *What free gifts do companies usually give to their customers?*

③ *Why do customers like to receive free gifts from companies?*

10. Describe a toy you got in your childhood.

① *Do boys and girls like the same kind of toys?*

② *Why do you think some parents buy lots of toys for their kids instead of spending more time with them?*

③ *What are some of the differences between the toys kids play with nowadays and those they used to play with in the past?*

④ *Are there any kinds of electronic games or computer games that can have educational benefits for young children?*

⑤ *What do parents usually buy for their children to make them happy?*

11. Describe a piece of clothing that someone gave to you.

① *Why do people dress casually in daily life and dress formally at work?*

② *What are the advantages and disadvantages of wearing uniform at work and school?*

③ *Why do people from different countries wear different clothes?*

12. Describe a gift you would like to buy for your friend.

① *When do people send gifts to others?*

② *Do people give gifts or red packets on traditional festivals?*

③ *Is it hard to choose a gift?*

④ *Will people feel happy when receiving an expensive gift?*

13. Describe something you cannot live without (not a computer/phone).

① *Why are children attracted to electronic devices?*

② *Why do some adults hate to throw away old things, such as clothes?*

③ *What do you think influences people to buy new things?*

14. Describe a piece of equipment in your home that you broke and then fixed.

① *Are IT-related jobs valued more by society?*

② *Is the quality of products worse than before?*

③ *What kinds of things do people like to repair by themselves?*

15. Describe an item on which you spent more than expected.

① *Do you often pay more than you expected?*

② *What do you think young people spend most of their money on?*

③ *Do you think it is important to save money?*

16. Describe a daily routine that you enjoyed.

① *Should children have learning routines?*

② *What are the advantages of children having a routine at school?*

③ *Does having a routine make kids feel more secure at school?*

④ *How do people's routine differ on weekdays and weekends?*

⑤ *What daily routines do people have at home?*

⑥ *What are the differences between people's daily routines and in the last 15 years?*

17. Describe an activity you enjoyed in your free time when you were young.

① *Is it important to have a break during work or study?*

② *What sports do young people like to do now?*

③ *Are there more activities for young people now than 20 years ago?*

④ *What activities do children and adults do nowadays?*

⑤ *Do adults and children have enough time for leisure activities nowadays?*

18. Describe something you did that made you feel proud of.

① *Which one is more important, personal goals or work goals?*

② *Have your life goals changed since your childhood?*

③ *Does everyone set goals for themselves?*

④ *What kinds of rewards are important at wok?*

⑤ *Do you think material rewards are more important than other rewards at work?*

⑥ *What makes people feel proud of themselves?*

19. Describe an advertisement you don't like.

① *What are the most advertised products in your country?*

② *Which one is more important, newspaper advertising or online advertising?*

③ *What are the benefits of advertising?*

④ *What do you think of celebrity endorsements in advertising?*

⑤ *Does advertising encourage us to buy things we don't need?*

⑥ *What role does social media play in advertising?*

20. Describe something that you did with someone/a group of people.

① *What do young people learn from being with others in class?*

② *Is it important for school children to like their classmates?*

③ *What makes someone a good colleague?*

④ *Is it the most important to have good colleagues in a job?*

21. Describe a historical period/moment you would like to learn more about.

① *Should everyone know history?*

② *In what ways can children learn history?*

③ *What are the differences between learning history books and from videos?*

④ *Is it difficult to protect and preserve historic buildings?*

⑤ *Who should be responsible for protecting historic buildings?*

⑥ *Who should pay for the preservation of historical buildings?*

22. Describe something you would like to learn in the future.

① *What's the most popular thing to learn nowadays?*

② *At what age should children start making their own decisions? Why?*

③ *Which influences young people more when choosing a course, income or interest?*

④ *Do young people take their parents' advice when choosing a major?*

⑤ *Besides parents, who else would people take advice from?*

⑥ *Why do some people prefer to study alone?*

23. Describe a piece of good news that you heard about someone you know well.

① *Is it good to share something on social media?*

② *Should the media only publish good news?*

③ *How does social media help people access information?*

④ *What kind of good news do people often share in the community?*

⑤ *Do most people like to share good news with others?*

⑥ *Do people like to hear good news from their friends?*

24. Describe a movie you watched recently and would like to watch again.

① *What are the differences between watching movies at home and in the cinema?*

② *Are actors or actresses important to movies?*

③ *Why are there fewer people going to the cinema to watch movies?*

④ *Where do people normally watch movies?*

25. Describe a program you like to watch.

① *What programs do people like to watch in your country?*

② *Do people in your country like to watch foreign TV programs?*

③ *Do teachers play videos in class in your country?*

④ *What's the benefit of letting kids watch animal videos than visiting zoos?*

26. Describe an important thing you learned (not at school or university).

① *What can children learn from parents? What about grandparents?*

② *Do you think some children are well-behaved because they are influenced by their parents?*

③ *Is it necessary for adults to learn new things?*

④ *How can people learn new things?*

27. Describe a story or a novel that you have read and you found interesting.

① *How does technology help people tell stories?*

② *Why are mystery novels so popular these days?*

③ *What kinds of stories do children like?*

④ *Do you prefer to read e-books or paper books?*

28. Describe something you do to keep fit and healthy.

① *How do old people keep fit?*

② *How can parents help their children to keep fit?*

③ *Do you think it is useful for governments to use celebrities to help people raise health awareness?*

29. Describe something that surprised you and made you happy.

① *Is it good for people to be happy?*

② *How do people express happiness in your culture?*

③ *Do you think happiness has any effect on people?*

30. Describe something that helps you to focus on study/work.

① *Why do children nowadays find it hard to concentrate on study?*

② *What kinds of distractions are common in your life?*

③ *Why do children need to learn to focus?*

④ *What kinds of jobs require higher concentration?*

31. Describe a song or piece of music you like.

① *Do you think young people and old people enjoy the same kind of music?*

② *Why are many music competitions popular in China?*

③ *What are the differences between live concerts and online concerts?*

32. Describe a story someone told you and you remember.

① *Do young children like the same stories as older children?*

② *How has technology changed the way of storytelling?*

③ *Why do children like stories?*

33. Describe an ambition that you haven't achieved.

① *What ambitions do children usually have?*

② *Why are some people very ambitious at work?*

③ *Why do some people not have any dreams?*

34. Describe a rule that you would like to change.

① *What kind of rules do schools in China have?*

② *What rules should children follow at home?*

③ *Why do you think children should be taught to obey rules?*

④ *Do people often violate rules or laws in China?*

⑤*Do you think people sometimes should break laws?*

⑥ *What kind of penalty is appropriate for small crimes?*

35. Describe something that helped you learn a foreign language.

① *What difficulties do people face when learning a language?*

② *Do you think language learning is important?*

③ *Is studying abroad a good way to learn a foreign language?*

36. Describe a difficult skill you have learned from an old person.

① *What can children learn from parents? What about grandparents?*

② *From whom can children learn more, parents or grandparents?*

③ *What kind of help do you think old people need?*

37. Describe a habit that your friend has and you want to develop.

① *What habits should children have?*

② *What should parents do to teach their children good habits?*

③*What influences do children with bad habits have on other children?*

④*Why do some habits change when people get older?*

38. Describe a skill that was difficult for you to learn.

① *What skills do young people need to master?*

② *Is it hard for young people to learn skills? What about old people?*

③ *Is a good teacher important for students to learn?*

④ *Do you think students can learn better at school or at home?*

Place

1. Describe another city you would like to stay for a short time.

① *Why do people sometimes go to other cities or other countries to travel?*

② *Why are historical cities popular?*

③ *Do most people like planned traveling?*

④ *Why is the noise pollution worse in tourism cities than in other cities?*

2. Describe a new development in the area where you live (e. g. shopping mall, park …).

① *What transportation do you use the most?*

② *Is public transportation popular in China?*

③ *What can be improved in public transport services?*

④ *What leisure facilities can be used by people of all ages?*

⑤ *Do you think young people in your country like to go to the cinema?*

⑥ *How is the subway system developing in your country?*

3. Describe a noisy place you have been to.

① *Do you think it is good for children to make noise?*

② *Should children not be allowed to make noise under any circumstances?*

③ *What kinds of noises are there in our life?*

④ *Which area is exposed to noise more, the city or the countryside?*

⑤ *How would people usually respond to noises in your country?*

⑥ *How can people consider others' feelings when chatting in public?*

4. Describe your favorite place in your house where you can relax.

① *Why is it difficult for some people to relax?*

② *What are the benefits of doing exercise?*

③ *Do people in your country exercise after work?*

④ *What is the place where people spend most of their time in their home?*

⑤ *Do you think there should be classes for training young people and children how to relax?*

⑥ *Which is more important, mental relaxation or physical relaxation?*

5. Describe a place you visited where the air was polluted.

① *Is there more pollution now than in the past?*

② *In what ways can air pollution be reduced effectively?*

③ *Do you think the city is cleaner or dirtier than the countryside? Why?*

④ *What can factories and power plants do to reduce pollutants?*

⑤ *Do you think many companies have been forced to reduce pollutants?*

⑥ *Do you think the wind has any effect on pollution? How?*

6. Describe a place in your country that you would like to recommend to visitors/travelers.

① *Is it important to take photos while traveling?*

② *Can you trust other people's travel journals on the Internet?*

③ *What factors affect how people feel about travel?*

④ *Will you go to a foreign country to travel because of the distinct landscapes?*

7. Describe a popular place for doing sports (e. g. stadium).

① *What are the benefits of children doing sports?*

② *Do young people like to do sports?*

③ *Is it necessary to build sports venues?*

④ *What do you think of companies donating sports venues for poor children?*

8. Describe the home of someone you know well and you often visit.

① *What are the differences between houses or buildings in the city and in the countryside?*

② *Do you prefer to live in the city or in the countryside?*

③ *What are the safety risks in residential buildings in cities?*

④ *Is it expensive to decorate a house or an apartment in the place where you live?*

9. Describe a quiet place where you like to spend your time.

① *Is it hard to find quiet places in cities?*

② *Why is it quieter in the countryside?*

③ *Compared with young people, do old people prefer to live in quiet places?*

10. Describe an important river/lake in your country.

① *How can rivers/lakes benefit local people?*

② *How do rivers/lakes affect local tourism?*

③ *Are rivers/lakes useful for transport?*

11. Describe a place in the countryside that you visited.

① *Is there anything special about the countryside in China?*

② *What do people usually do when going to the countryside?*

③ *Do you think more people will live in the countryside in the future?*

12. Describe a city that you think is interesting.

① *What advantages can tourism bring to a city?*

② *Why do some young people like to live in cities?*

③ *Do most elderly people live in the city or in the countryside?*

④ *Do you think well-developed tourism will have negative effects on local people?*

13. Describe an apartment or a home that you would like to have.

① *Is it expensive to buy an apartment in China?*

② *Do people usually rent or buy an apartment in China? Why?*

③ *What are the differences between the houses that young people and old people like?*

④ *What kinds of factors will influence people to buy an apartment?*

14. Describe a place you visited on vacation.

① *What are some popular attractions that people like to visit in your country?*

② *Do old people and young people choose different places to go for vacation?*

③ *Do old people and young people have different considerations regarding their travel plans?*

Event

1. Describe a time when you missed or were late for an important meeting/event.

① *Are you a punctual person?*

② *Do you think it is important to be on time?*

③ *Do you always avoid being late?*

④ *Why are people often late for meetings or appointments?*

⑤ *Are people in your country often late for meeting?*

⑥ *Do you think people are born with time management skills or they can develop them?*

2. Describe a time when you taught a friend/relative something.

① *What practical skills can young people teach old people?*

② *What skills can young people teach old people besides technology?*

③ *How can young people teach old people skills?*

④ *How can we know what to do when we want to learn something new?*

⑤ *Do you think "showing" is a better way than "telling" in education?*

⑥ *Do people in your country like to watch videos to learn something?*

3. Describe your first day at school that you remember.

① *What should parents prepare when their kids go to school on the first day?*

② *How do children socialize with each other?*

③ *Is socialization important for children?*

④ *What are the reasons for job change?*

⑤ *Are big companies better than small companies?*

⑥ *What are the advantages and disadvantages coming along with changing jobs?*

4. Describe a time when you made a complaint and were satisfied with the result.

① *What do people often make complaints about in your country?*

② *Which one is better when making complaint, by talking or writing?*

③ *Who are more likely to make complaints, older people or young people?*

④ *Why it is important for companies to respond well to customers' complaints?*

5. Describe a problem you had while shopping online or in a store.

① *What kind of service do you think is good?*

② *What would you do if you bought something disappointing from the Internet?*

③ *Do you think online shopping will replace in-store shopping in the future?*

④ *What are the differences between shopping online and in stores?*

6. Describe a time when you made a decision to wait for something.

① *Why do some people prefer slow-paced life?*

② *Is it necessary for people to learn to be patient?*

③ *Are people less patient now than in the past?*

④ *Do people in your country like to take public transportation?*

7. Describe a time when you received money on your birthday.

① *Why do people rarely use cash now?*

② *Do you think it is useful to give money as gifts?*

8. Describe a time when you had an argument with a friend.

① *What do you do if you disagree with someone?*

② *How do we stop an argument from escalating into a fight?*

③ *What disagreements do parents and children usually have?*

④ *Who do you think should teach children to respect their teacher?*

9. Describe an outdoor activity you did in a new place recently.

① *What outdoor activities are popular in China?*

② *What are the differences between after-class activities done by young and older children?*

③ *Should young people try as many new activities as possible?*

④ *Are those people who like dangerous activities more likely to be successful?*

⑤ *Do you think it's better for people to change jobs when there are new chances?*

10. Describe a time when you forgot an appointment.

① *How do people who are busy every day remember things they need to do?*

② *Do you think people should remember family history?*

③ *If someone doesn't really like whom they are going to meet, they may deliberately miss their appointment. Is that true? Why?*

④ *Which is more important, a work-related appointment or an appointment with a friend? Why?*

11. Describe a time when you shared something with others.

① *What are the consequences if children don't know how to share?*

② *How do people feel about sharing accommodation with others on campus?*

③ *How can parents and teachers teach young children to share?*

12. Describe a time when you needed to search for some information.

① *How can people search for information now?*

② *With the development of the Internet, are libraries still important?*

③ *Does the development of the Internet have any influence on disadvantaged people?*

④ *What information can people get from television?*

13. Describe a time when you saw a lot of plastic waste (e.g. in a park, on the beach, etc.)

① *Do you think we should use plastic products?*

② *How can we reduce our use of plastic products?*

③ *What kinds of plastic waste are often seen in your country?*

④ *Why do people like to use plastic products?*

14. Describe a time when you enjoyed an impressive English lesson.

① *Is it interesting to be a foreign language teacher?*

② *What makes a good foreign language teacher?*

③ *Do you think language learning is important?*

④ *Do you think grammar is important when learning a foreign language?*

15. Describe a time when you used your cellphone to do something important.

① *What do you usually do with a cellphone?*

② *What are the differences between young people and old people when they use cellphones?*

③ *Do you think there should be a law to stop people from making phone calls in public places?*

16. Describe a time when someone gave you positive advice on your work.

① *Is it important to give children positive feedback?*

② *What would happen if parents overly encourage their children?*

③ *Do you think negative feedback is more important that positive feedback?*

17. Describe an occasion when you lost something in a public place.

① *What kinds of things do people usually lose?*

② *What do people often do when they lose personal belongings?*

③ *What kinds of people often lose things?*

18. Describe a contest/competition you would like to participate in.

① *What are the contests commonly seen on TV?*

② *Why are competition shows popular?*

③ *Do you think it is necessary to encourage people to compete with others in companies?*

19. Describe an important event you celebrated.

① *What kinds of events do people usually celebrate?*

② *Do people often celebrate events with a large group of people or just few people?*

③ *Do people often celebrate festivals with families?*

20. Describe a positive change you made in your life.

① *Is it easier for young people to change?*

② *What are the disadvantages when people keep making changes in life?*

21. Describe a special day out that didn't cost you much.

① *How do people spend their leisure time in China?*

② *How does technology affect the way people spend their leisure time?*

③ *Do you think only old people have time for leisure?*

22. Describe a time when you helped a child.

① *Do you often help kids? How?*

② *Why is it necessary to do volunteer services?*

③ *Who benefit more from the volunteer services, the volunteers or the people they help?*

23. Describe a time when you were caught in a traffic jam.

① *When do traffic jams usually happen?*

② *What are the causes of traffic jams?*

③ *Do you think the problem of traffic congestion will be eased in the future or will it become worse?*

④ *What would you suggest as possible solutions to the problem of congested traffic?*

24. Describe a time when you were very busy.

① *What are the advantages and disadvantages when people keep busy?*

② *What kind of stressful things do people experience at work?*

25. Describe a recent change in life that helps you save a lot of time.

① *Do you think technology helps people to save time?*

② *Do you think parents and schools should be responsible for teaching children to save time?*

③ *Do you think it will be easier for people who can manage time well to become successful?*

26. Describe an occasion when you had a special cake.

① *What's the difference between special food in China and foreign countries?*

② *Do Chinese people usually cook special food in traditional festivals?*

③ *Do Chinese families like to eat together during traditional holidays?*

④ *Why do people spend more on special food on special occasions?*

27. Describe a time you visited a new place.

① *Which one do you prefer, living in a city or only visiting it as a tourist?*

② *How do children react when they go to a new school for the first time?*

③ *How do young and old people react differently to new things?*

④ *Why do some people want to go to college that are far away from home?*

28. Describe a happy event you organized.

① *How can parents help children to become organized?*

② *On what occasions do people need to be organized?*

③ *Do people need others' help when organizing things?*

29. Describe a long walk you have been on.

① *Do women have more leisure time than men do?*

② *Is leisure time important to everyone?*

③ *What are the differences between the outdoor activities children did in the past and now?*

30. Describe a time when someone said something positive about your work.

① *Is it important to give children positive feedback?*

② *What would happen if parents overly encourage their children?*

③ *Do you think parents should reward their children if they achieve something?*

31. Describe an interesting conversation you had with someone.

① *When do children normally begin to form their own views?*

② *What do young people usually talk about?*

③ *In what industries do you think communication is a necessary skill?*

32. Describe a time when you waited for something special to happen.

① *On what occasions do people usually need to wait?*

② *Who behave better when waiting, children or adults?*

③ *Do you think waiting is harder now?*

33. Describe a bicycle/motorcycle/car trip you would like to go.

① *Which form of vehicle is the most popular in your country? Bikes, cars or motorcycles?*

② *Do you think air pollution comes mostly from mobile vehicles?*

③ *Do you think people need to change the way of transportation fundamentally to protect the environment?*

④ *How are the transportation systems in urban areas and rural areas different?*

34. Describe a good service you received.

① *What do you think of the relationship between companies and customers?*

② *As a customer, what kinds of services would you expect to receive from a company?*

③ *Why should companies react quickly when customers have difficulties?*

④ *What kinds of jobs involve coping with the public?*

35. Describe a time when you were friendly to someone you didn't like.

① *Why do people sometimes have to be friendly with the person they don't like?*

② *What are the differences between being friendly and being polite?*

③ *What do you think of people who are always straightforward?*

④ *What kinds of people are usually friendly?*

36. Describe a time when you got up early.

① *Do you know anyone who likes to get up early?*

② *Why do people get up early?*

③ *What kinds of occasions need people to arrive early?*

④ *Why do some people like to stay up late?*

37. Describe an activity you usually do that wastes your time.

① *How do you balance life and work?*

② *Will you continue doing something when you aware that it's a waste of time?*

③ *What kinds of things make people feel pressured?*

④ *Why do some people refuse to abide by rules?*

38. Describe a time when you felt proud of a family member.

① *When would parents feel proud of their children?*

② *Should parents reward children? Why and how?*

③ *Is it good to reward children too often?*

④ *On what occasions would adults be proud of themselves?*

39. Describe a time when you gave a piece of advice to another person.

① *Is it good to ask advice from strangers online?*

② *What are the problems if you ask too many people for advice?*

③ *What are the personalities of people whose job is to give advice to others?*